THE
DELL BOOK
OF
LOGIC
PROBLEMS #6

THE
DELL BOOK
OF
LOGIC
PROBLEMS #6

Editor-in-Chief • Erica L. Rothstein
Senior Editors • Gail Accardi
Stacey E. Feinman
Abby Meher Taylor
Theresa Turner

A DELL TRADE PAPERBACK

A DELL TRADE PAPERBACK

Published by
Dell Publishing
a division of
Bantam Doubleday Dell Publishing Group, Inc.
1540 Broadway
New York, New York 10036

ISBN: 0-440-50738-3

Printed in the United States of America
Published simultaneously in Canada

September 1996

10 9 8 7 6 5 4 3 2 1

SEM

A WORD ABOUT THIS BOOK

Fun! Need we say more? To those of you who are familiar with Logic Problems from solving those in the Dell Puzzle Magazines and/or in the previous five books in this series, perhaps not — you know what you're getting into. As for the rest of you . . .

First of all, never fear; everything you need to solve these puzzles (except a pencil or pen and your own enthusiasm) is right here. There are no initiation rites, no secret handshakes, no instruction manuals or software packages. Solving these Logic Problems may show you what you've been missing; but when it comes to the problems in this book, you haven't missed a thing.

You might begin by reading through the section titled How to Solve Logic Problems, beginning on page 13. These instructions guide you through a few sample Logic Problems to show you how to go about applying your own common sense to solving. That's all Logic Problems are, really — just exercises in common sense. If you've ever taken care of a home, a family, a career, etc., you've solved Logic Problems more complicated than any in this book. But these problems are for fun only, and intended to be solved at a leisurely pace. You will never find a time limit on a Logic Problem; they're not that kind of puzzle. You may feel your mind rushing to sort out all the bits of information, and that flying feeling of exhilaration as the points come together. If that turns to frustration, try taking a break; on your return you may see something that you didn't before.

Once you've seen how to begin solving, you're on your own, and as ready as any Logic Problem veteran to tackle these puzzles. It is true, practice does make closer to perfect when it comes to this kind of solving. But there are 75 brand-new problems in this book — that's plenty to practice on. And each one starts again from square one, proceeding somewhat differently from all the others before it; so each one is a new solving experience. They range in difficulty from easy to challenger, and are grouped by level so you'll know at the outset how tough the problem is going to be.

To all, welcome. To longtime solvers, thank you for your support; it is because of you that this book exists.

The Editors
Dell Book of Logic Problems #6

A LETTER FROM THE EDITOR

I have been editing puzzles for 25 of the 65 years the Dell Puzzle Magazines have been published.

One might think that kind of longevity would bring with it some special insight; it does and it doesn't. Granted, when someone hands me a puzzle to solve I no longer feel that flash of panic I did back then as low man on the totem pole, "Omigod, they expect me to know how to **do** this?!?!?" Indeed, it is rare now that a puzzle comes along that hasn't been seen before in one form or another. I am now comfortable knowing that I do not have to be able to solve everything that crosses my desk. But there is still, and always, the fresh challenge inherent in every unsolved puzzle — "Can I crack it and how much fun will it be?" The thrill of the hunt, so to speak.

Every puzzle is different. Each one depends upon the ingenuity of its constructor and is as idiosyncratic as the person who devised it. Hard as it may be for the novice solver to believe, when you solve enough puzzles, you begin to recognize the work of individuals. There's something in the way each constructor's mind works that leaves its imprint on a puzzle and you eventually get to the point where you really look forward to pitting your skills against those of the constructor. You recognize their names and greet a new offering as you would an old friend (or nemesis).

This is especially true of Logic Problems. A Randall Whipkey puzzle is distinctly different from a Susan Zivich or a Mary Marks Cezus. David Champlin's style is clearly distinguishable from Robert Nelson's and not just because the premises of any two puzzles are different. Each has an approach to structure as individual as his fingerprints. They're among the best constructors in the world and we're thrilled to include their puzzles in this book. Solvers evidently enjoy their efforts as well, since this is the sixth edition of The Dell Book of Logic Problems. We've been fielding questions about its on-sale date for months.

I'm very proud of this book. It is the collaborative effort of all the constructors who made the puzzles, the editors who tested, fixed, and retested them, and the proofreaders who painstakingly went over each word and comma to make sure that the logic stands up to the scrutiny of the toughest audience there is. Do, please, enjoy every minute you crack heads with all these experts! I certainly did.

Erica L. Rothstein
Editor-in-Chief
Dell Puzzle Magazines

CONTENTS

MEDIUM LOGIC PROBLEMS

HARD LOGIC PROBLEMS

CHALLENGER LOGIC PROBLEMS

Solutions begin on page 135.

HOW TO SOLVE LOGIC PROBLEMS

For those of you who are new to Logic Problems: On the following pages you will find some insights into the thought processes that go into solving these puzzles, as well as detailed instructions on the use of charts as solving aids. We suggest you scan these instructions to familiarize yourself with the techniques presented here. Whenever you feel that you're ready to try your hand at solving, turn to the first puzzle (which you will find on page 25) and dig right in. If, even after you have studied these instructions, you should find yourself stuck while solving, turn to the solution for that puzzle and try to follow the reasoning given there. The solutions are not just a listing of "who did what," but rather a step-by-step elimination of possibilities, which you should find invaluable on your journey along the road to mastery of Logic Problems.

The 75 Logic Problems in this book are just that — problems based on logic, to which you need bring no specialized knowledge or extensive vocabulary. Instead, all you will need is your common sense, some reasoning power, and a basic grasp of how to use the charts or other solving aids provided. The problems themselves are all classic deduction problems, in which you are usually asked to figure out how two or more sets of facts relate to each other — what first name belongs with which last name, for example. All of the facts you will need to solve each puzzle are always given.

The puzzles are mostly arranged in increasing order of difficulty — the first few are rather easy to solve, then the puzzles get more difficult as you continue through the book. The final puzzles are especially challenging. If you are new to Logic Problems, we suggest that you start with the first puzzles, progressing through the book as you get more expert at solving. Of the three examples which follow, the first is, of course, the most basic, but the skills utilized there will help you tackle even the most challenging challenger. Example #2 will help you hone those skills and gives valuable hints about the use of a more complicated chart as a solving aid. The third member of the group will introduce those puzzles for which the normal solving chart is not applicable. You will notice that in each of these examples, as in all the Logic Problems in this book, the last part of the introduction will tell you what facts you are to establish in solving that puzzle. Now, if you are ready to begin, read through the introduction and the clues given with Example #1.

EXAMPLE #1

A young woman attending a party was introduced to four men in rather rapid succession and, as usual at such gatherings, their respective types of work were mentioned rather early in the conversation. Unfortunately, she was afflicted with a somewhat faulty memory. Half an hour later, she could remember only that she had met a Mr. Brown, a Mr. White, a Mr. Black, and a Mr. Green. She recalled that among them were a photographer, a grocer, a banker, and a singer, but she could not recall which was which. Her hostess, a fun-loving friend, refused to refresh her memory, but offered four clues. Happily, the young woman's logic was better than her memory, and she quickly paired each man with his profession. Can you? Here are the clues:

1. Mr. White approached the banker for a loan.

2. Mr. Brown had met the photographer when he hired him to take pictures of his wedding.

3. The singer and Mr. White are friends, but have never had business dealings.

4. Neither Mr. Black nor the singer had ever met Mr. Green before that evening.

	Black	Brown	Green	White
banker				
grocer				
photo.				
singer				

You know from the last part of the introduction what it is you are to determine—you are to match each man's last name with his profession. The chart has been set up to help you keep track of the information as you discover it. We suggest that you use an X in a box to indicate a definite impossibility and a • (dot) in a box to show an established fact.

Your first step is to enter X's into the chart for all of the obvious possibilities that you can see from information given in the clues. It is apparent from clue 1 that Mr. White is not the banker, so an X would be entered into the White/banker box. Clue 2 makes it clear that Mr. Brown is not the photographer, so another X in the Brown/photographer box can be entered. Clue 3 tells you that Mr. White is not the singer. And from clue 4 you can see that neither Mr. Black nor Mr. Green is the singer. Each of these impossibilities should also be indicated by X's in the chart. Once you have done so, your chart will look like this:

	Black	Brown	Green	White
banker				X
grocer				
photo.		X		
singer	X		X	X

Remembering that each X indicates that something is *not* a fact, note the row of boxes at the bottom—corresponding to which of the men is the singer. There are four possibilities, and you have X's for three of them. Therefore, Mr. Brown, the only one left, has to be the singer. Put a dot (•) in the singer/Brown box. Also, remember that if Mr. Brown is the singer, he is not the photographer (which we knew, we have an X); and he cannot be the grocer or the banker either. Thus, you would put X's in those boxes too. Your chart would now look like this:

	Black	Brown	Green	White
banker		X		X
grocer		X		
photo.		X		
singer	X	•	X	X

Now you seem to have a "hopeless" situation! You have used all the clues, and you have matched one man with his profession — but the additional X's entered in the chart do not enable you to make another match, since the possibilities have not been narrowed down sufficiently. What to do next?

Your next step is to reread the clues, at the same time considering the new information you have acquired: You know that Mr. Brown is the singer and that he has done business with the photographer (clue 2). But the singer has never done business with Mr. White (clue 3) or with Mr. Green (clue 4). And that means that neither Mr. White nor Mr. Green can possibly be the photographer. You can now place X's in those boxes in the chart. After you have done so, here is what you will have:

	Black	Brown	Green	White
banker		X		X
grocer		X		•
photo.	•	X	X	X
singer	X	•	X	X

And you see that you do have more answers! The photographer must be Mr. Black, since there are X's in the boxes for the other names. Mr. White, also, must be the grocer, since there is an X in the other three boxes under his name. Once you have placed a dot to indicate that Mr. Black is the photographer and a dot to show that Mr. White is the grocer (always remembering to place X's in the other boxes in the row and column that contain the dot) your chart will look like this:

	Black	Brown	Green	White
banker	X	X		X
grocer	X	X	X	•
photo.	•	X	X	X
singer	X	•	X	X

You can see that you are left with one empty box, and this box corresponds to the remaining piece of information you have not yet determined — what Mr. Green's profession is and who the banker is. Obviously, the only possibility is that Mr. Green is the banker. And the Logic Problem is solved!

Most of the Logic Problems in this book will ask you to determine how more than two sets of facts are related to each other. You'll see, however, that the way of solving a more involved Logic Problem is just the same as Example #1 — *if* you have a grasp of how to make the best use of the solving chart. The next example of a Logic Problem is presented in order to explain how to use a bigger chart. As before, read through the problem quickly, noting that the introduction tells you what facts you are to determine.

EXAMPLE #2

Andy, Chris, Noel, Randy, and Steve — one of whose last name is Morse — were recently hired as refreshment vendors at Memorial Stadium; each boy sells only one kind of fare. From the clues below, try to determine each boy's full name and the type of refreshment he sells.

1. Randy, whose last name is not Wiley, does not sell popcorn.
2. The Davis boy does not sell soda or candy.
3. The five boys are Noel, Randy, the Smith boy, the Coble boy, and the boy who sells ice cream.
4. Andy's last name is not Wiley or Coble. Neither Andy nor Coble is the boy who sells candy.
5. Neither the peanut vendor nor the ice cream vendor is named Steve or Davis.

	Coble	Davis	Morse	Smith	Wiley	candy	ice.	pean.	pop.	soda
Andy										
Chris										
Noel										
Randy										
Steve										
candy					
ice.					
pean.					
pop.					
soda					

Note that the chart given is composed of three sets of boxes — one set corresponding to the first and last names; a second set (to the right) corresponding to first names and refreshment; and a third set, below the first set, corresponding to the refreshment and last names. Notice, too, that these sets are separated from each other by heavier lines so that it is easier to find the particular box you are looking for.

As in Example #1, your first step is to enter into the boxes of the chart the impossibilities. Keep in mind that you have many more boxes to be concerned with here. Remember, ROW indicates the boxes that go horizontally (the Andy row, for example) and the word COLUMN indicates the boxes that go vertically (the Coble column, for instance).

Clue 1 tells you that Randy's last name is not Wiley, and Randy does not sell popcorn. Thus, enter an X into the Randy/Wiley box and another X in the Randy/popcorn box in the Randy row. Clue 2 says that the Davis boy sells neither soda nor candy. Find Davis and go down that column to the Davis/soda box and put an X in it; then find the Davis/candy box in that same column and place an X in that box.

Clue 3 tells you a few things: It gives you all five of the boys, either by his first name (two of them), his last name (another two of them), or by what refreshment he sells (the remaining boy). You then know something about all five — one boy's first name is Noel, another's is Randy; a third boy has the last name Smith, a fourth has the last name Coble; and the fifth sells ice cream. All of these are different people. So, in the chart you have a lot of X's that can be entered. Noel's last name is neither Smith nor Coble, so enter X's in the Noel/Smith, Noel/Coble boxes; nor can Noel be the ice cream seller, so put an X in the Noel/ice cream box. Randy is neither Smith nor Coble, and Randy does not sell ice cream, so put the X's in the Randy/Smith, Randy/Coble, and Randy/ice cream boxes. And neither Smith nor Coble sells ice cream, so enter an X in those two boxes.

Clue 4 tells you that Andy's last name is neither Wiley nor Coble. It also says that Andy does not sell candy and neither does the Coble boy. By now you probably know where to put the X's — in the Andy/Wiley box, the Andy/Coble box, the Andy/candy box, and in the box in the Coble column corresponding to candy. From clue 5 you learn that neither Steve nor Davis is the boy who sells either peanuts or ice cream. (One important point here — read clue 5 again, and note that this clue does *not* tell you whether or not Steve's last name is Davis; it tells you only that neither the peanut seller nor the ice cream vendor has the first name Steve or the last name Davis.) Your chart should now look like this:

16

	Coble	Davis	Morse	Smith	Wiley	candy	ice.	pean.	pop.	soda
Andy	X				X	X				
Chris										
Noel	X			X		X				
Randy	X			X	X	X			X	
Steve						X	X			
candy	X	X								
ice.	X	X		X						
pean.		X								
pop.										
soda		X								

From this point on, we suggest that you fill in the above chart yourself as you read how the facts are established. If you look at the Davis column, you will see that you have X's in four of the refreshment boxes; the Davis boy is the one who sells popcorn. Put a dot in the Davis/popcorn box. Now, since it is Davis who sells popcorn, none of the other boys does, so you will put X's in all of the other boxes in that popcorn row.

Your next step will be to look up at the other set of refreshment boxes and see what first names already have an X in the popcorn column. Note that Randy has an X in the popcorn column (from clue 1). Thus, if you know that Randy does not sell popcorn, you now know that his last name is not Davis, since Davis is the popcorn seller. You can then put an X in the Randy/Davis box. Afar you've done this, you'll see that you now have four X's for Randy's last name. Randy has to be Morse, the only name left, so enter a dot in the Randy/Morse box. Don't forget, too, to enter X's in the boxes of the Morse column that correspond to the first names of the other boys.

Now that you know Randy is Morse, you are ready to look at what you've already discovered about Randy and transfer that information to the Morse column — remember that since Randy is Morse, anything that you know about Randy is also true of Morse, as they're the same person. You'll see that an X for Randy was entered from clue 3: Randy does not sell ice cream. Then Morse cannot be the ice cream seller either, so put an X in the Morse column to show that Morse doesn't sell ice cream.

Once the Morse/ice cream X is in place, note what you have established about the Wiley boy: His is the only last name left who can sell ice cream. Put the dot in the Wiley/ice cream box and enter X's in the Wiley column for all the other refreshments. Your next step? As before, you are ready to determine what this new dot will tell you, so you will go up to the other set of refreshment boxes and see what you have established about the ice cream vendor. He's not Noel or Steve—they have two X's already entered in the chart. Now that you have established the Wiley boy as the ice cream seller, you know that his first name can't be either Noel or Steve because neither of those boys sells ice cream. Once you've put X's in the Noel/Wiley box and the Steve/Wiley box, you'll see that you know who Wiley is. Remember that clue 4 had already told you that Andy's last name is not Wiley, so you have an X in the Andy/Wiley box. With the new X's, do you see that Wiley's first name has to be Chris? And since Chris is Wiley, and Wiley sells ice cream, so, of course, does Chris. Thus, you can put a dot in the Chris/ice cream box. And don't forget to put X's in the Chris row for the other refreshments and also in the ice cream column for the other first names.

Notice that once Chris Wiley is entered in the chart, there are now four X's in the Coble column, and Steve is the one who has to be the Coble boy. Put in the dot and then X's in the Steve row, and your chart looks like this:

	Coble	Davis	Morse	Smith	Wiley	candy	ice.	pean.	pop.	soda
Andy	X		X		X	X	X			
Chris	X	X	X	X	•	X	•	X	X	X
Noel	X		X	X	X		X			
Randy	X	X	•	X	X		X		X	
Steve	•	X	X	X	X		X	X		
candy	X	X			X					
ice.	X	X	X	X	•					
pean.		X			X					
pop.	X	•	X	X	X					
soda		X			X					

See that there are four X's in the Smith/first name column, so Smith's first name must be Andy. And Noel's last name is Davis, because he's the only one left. Remember — look down the Davis row and see that we already know Davis sells popcorn. So, Noel, whose last name is Davis, sells popcorn. And, of course, there should be X's in all the other boxes of the Noel row and the popcorn column.

Now that you have completely established two sets of facts — which first name goes with which last name — you can use the two sets of refreshment boxes almost as one. That is, since you know each boy's first name and last name, anything you have determined about a first name will hold true for that boy's last name; and, naturally, the reverse is true: whatever you know about a boy's last name must also be true of that boy's first name.

For example, you know that Coble is Steve, so look down the Coble column and note that you have already put X's in the candy, ice cream, and popcorn boxes. Go up to the Steve row and enter any X's that you know about Coble. After putting an X in the Steve/candy box, you'll see that you've determined that Steve sells soda. As always, don't forget to enter X's where appropriate once you've entered a dot to indicate a determined fact. These X's are what will narrow down the remaining possibilities.

Things are really moving fast now! Once you've entered the appropriate X's in the Steve row and the soda column, you will quickly see that there are four X's in the candy column — so, Randy (Morse) is the candy vendor. By elimination, Andy (Smith) sells peanuts and this Logic Problem is completely solved.

Many of the Logic Problems in this book will have charts that are set up much like the one in Example #2. They may be bigger, and the puzzle may involve matching more sets of facts, but the method of solving the Logic Problem using the chart will be exactly the same. Just remember:

Always read the whole problem through quickly. What you are to determine is usually stated in the last part of the introduction.

When using solving charts, use an X to indicate a definite impossibility and a • (dot) to indicate an established fact.

Once you have placed a dot to indicate an established fact, remember to put X's in the rest of the boxes in the row and the column that contains the dot.

Every time you establish a fact, it is a good idea to go back and reread the clues, keeping in mind the newly found information. Often, you will find that rereading the clues will help you if you seem to be "stuck." You may discover that you *do* know more facts than you thought you did.

Don't forget, when you establish a fact in one part of a solving chart, check to see if the new information is applicable to any other section of the solving chart — see if some X's or dots can be transferred from one section to another.

Just one other note before we get to Example #3, and this note applies to both the most inexperienced novice and the most experienced expert. If ever you find yourself stymied while solving a problem, don't get discouraged and give up — turn to the solution. Read the step-by-step elimination until you get to a fact that you have not established and see if you can follow the reasoning given. By going back and forth between the clue numbers cited in the solution and the clues themselves, you should be able to "get over the hump" and still have the satisfaction of completing the rest of the puzzle by yourself. Sometimes reading the solution of one puzzle will give you important clues (if you'll pardon the pun) to the thought processes involved with many other puzzles. And now to the last of our trio of examples.

Sometimes a Logic Problem has been created in such a way that the type of chart you learned about in Example #2 is not helpful in solving the problem. The puzzle itself is fine, but another kind of chart — a fill-in type — will better help you match up the facts and arrive at the correct solution. Example #3 is a puzzle using this type of solving chart.

EXAMPLE #3

It was her first visit home in ten years, and Louise wondered how she would manage to see her old friends and still take in the things she wanted to in the seven days she had to spend there. Her worry was needless, however, for when she got off the plane Sunday morning, there were her friends — Anna, Cora, Gert, Jane, Liz, and Mary — waiting to greet her with her seven-day visit all planned. The women knew that Louise wanted to revisit the restaurant where they always used to have lunch together, so Louise's vacation began that Sunday afternoon with a party. After that, each of the women had an entire day to spend with Louise, accompanying her to one of the following things: a ball game, concert, the theater, museum, zoo, and one day reserved for just shopping. From the clues below, find out who took Louise where and on what day.

1. Anna and the museum visitor and the woman whose day followed the zoo visitor were blondes; Gert and the concertgoer and the woman who spent Monday with Louise were brunettes. *(Note: All six women are mentioned in this clue.)*

2. Cora's day with Louise was not the visit that occurred the day immediately following Mary's day.

3. The six women visited with Louise in the following order: Jane was with Louise the day after the zoo visitor and four days before the museumgoer; Gert was with Louise the day after the theatergoer and the day before Mary.

4. Anna and the woman who took Louise shopping have the same color hair.

	Monday	Tuesday	Wednesday	Thursday	Friday	Saturday
friend						
activity						

As before (and always) read the entire puzzle through quickly. Note that here you are to determine which day, from Monday to Saturday, each woman spent with Louise and also what they did that day. The solving chart, often called a fill-in chart, is the best kind to use for this puzzle. You won't be entering X's and dots here; instead, you will be writing the facts into the chart as you determine them and also find out where they belong.

From clue 1 you can eliminate both Anna and Gert as the woman who took Louise to the museum and the concert. And neither of these activities took place on a Monday, nor did Anna or Gert spend Monday with Louise. You have discovered some things, but none of them can yet be entered into the chart. Most solvers find it useful to note these facts elsewhere, perhaps in the margin or on a piece of scratch paper, in their own particular kind of shorthand. Then when enough facts have been determined to begin writing them into the chart, you will already have them listed.

Do you see that clue 2 tells you Mary did not see Louise on Saturday? It's because the clue states that Cora's day was not the visit that occurred immediately following Mary's day, and thus, there had to be at least one visit after Mary's. You still don't have a definite fact to write into the chart. Don't lose heart, though, because . . .

. . . clue 3 will start to crack the puzzle! Note that this clue gives you the order of the six visits. Since the days were Monday through Saturday, the only possible way for Jane to be with Louise the day after the zoo visitor and four days before the museumgoer is if the zoo visit took place on Monday, Jane was with Louise on Tuesday, and the museumgoer was with Louise on Saturday. These facts can now be written into the chart — Monday zoo, Tuesday Jane, Saturday museum. Three days have been accounted for. The last part of clue 3 gives you the other three days: with Wednesday, Thursday, and Friday still open, the theatergoer must be the Wednesday friend, Gert is the day after, or Thursday, and Mary saw Louise on Friday. These facts, too, should be written in the chart. Once you've done so, your chart will resemble this one:

	Monday	Tuesday	Wednesday	Thursday	Friday	Saturday
friend		Jane		Gert	Mary	
activity	zoo		theater			museum

Now go back to clue 1 and see what other facts you can establish. There are three blondes — Anna, the museum visitor, and the woman whose day followed the zoo visitor's. The chart shows you that this last woman was Jane. From clue 4 you learn that the woman who took Louise shopping and Anna have the same color hair — blond. The woman who took Louise shopping is not Anna (they're two separate people), nor is she the museum visitor, so she must be the woman whose day followed the zoo visitor's, Jane. That fact can be written in the chart.

You can also, at this point, establish what day Anna spent with Louise. Since you know it's not Monday (clue 1) and Anna is not the museumgoer (also clue 1), the only day left for her is Wednesday, so Anna took Louise to the theater. Clue 2 tells you that Cora's day did not immediately follow Mary's, so Cora's day can't be Saturday, and must be Monday. By elimination, Liz (listed in the introduction) spent Saturday with Louise at the museum.

It may be helpful to make a note of the hair colors mentioned in clue 1, perhaps under the relevant columns in the chart. These hair colors can again be used at this point. We've now established the blondes as Anna, Jane, and Liz; the brunettes are Gert, the concertgoer, and Cora. The only possibility is that Mary is the concertgoer. Everything has now been determined except what Gert did, so, by elimination, Gert must have taken Louise to a ball game (from the introduction).

	Monday	Tuesday	Wednesday	Thursday	Friday	Saturday
friend	Cora	Jane	Anna	Gert	Mary	Liz
activity	zoo	shopping	theater	ball game	concert	museum
	bru	blo	blo	bru	bru	blo

Are all Logic Problems easy to solve? No, of course not. Many of the puzzles in this book are much more complicated than the three examples and should take a great deal more time and thought before you arrive at the solution. However, the techniques you use to solve the puzzles are essentially the same. All the information needed to solve will be given in the puzzle itself, either in the introduction or the clues. As you eliminate possibilities, you will narrow down the choices until, finally, you can establish a certainty. That certainty will usually help narrow down the possibilities in another set of facts. Once you have determined something, you will probably need to return to the clues and reread them, keeping in mind what facts you have now established. Suddenly a sentence in the clues may tell you something you could not have determined before, thus narrowing down the choices still further. Eventually you will have determined everything, and the Logic Problem will be solved.

EASY LOGIC PROBLEMS

1 YARD WARMING

by Jeanne Hurley

Joy recently bought a new home. But as her family and friends already knew and her neighbors soon discovered, it was the garden that really excited her, not the house. So when Ray and six other people brought housewarming gifts, they chose items for her yard. Using the following clues, can you determine each person's first and last name (one last name is Fountain), the gift he or she brought (one was a bird bath), and whether the giver is an old friend, a new neighbor, or Joy's sister or brother?

1. The three old friends who gave Joy gifts for her yard are Daisy, Ms. Foster, and the man who supplied ground cover plants.

2. Olive presented Joy with a bird feeder.

3. Joy's brother brought her perennials.

4. Mr. Finch and Mrs. Flores are Joy's new acquaintances.

5. Glen gave Joy chipped wood mulch.

6. Iris is not Joy's sister Ms. Field, and Basil Funn is not her brother.

7. Joy's old friend Forbes, and her new neighbor June gave her herb plants and money plant seeds, respectively.

Solution is on page 135.

	Field	Finch	Flores	Forbes	Foster	Fountain	Funn	bath	cover	feeder	herb	mulch	peren.	seeds	bro.	fr.	neigh.	sis.
Basil																		
Daisy																		
Glen																		
Iris																		
June																		
Olive																		
Ray																		
bro.																		
friend																		
neigh.																		
sis.																		
bath																		
cover																		
feeder																		
herb																		
mulch																		
peren.																		
seeds																		

2 HAPPY MOTHER'S DAY

by Diane Baldwin

Gail, George, and their brother and sister (who are all in different grades in high school) surprised their mother last Mother's Day. Since gardening is her favorite pastime, they each gave her a flat of a different variety of flower (including marigolds) to plant and each one promised to help with a different garden chore. From the following clues, can you match each teen with the grade he or she is in, the type of flower given, and the chore each promised to do?

1. Larry is one grade ahead of the girl who gave mom petunias and one grade behind the one who promised to do the weeding.

2. The four children are Jane, the sophomore, the boy who gave snapdragons, and the boy who promised to mulch.

3. The boy who promised to mow is a grade behind the teen who promised to trim the hedge.

4. One girl gave her pansies.

Solution is on page 135.

	fresh.	soph.	jr.	sen.	marigolds	pansies	petunias	snapdragons	mow	mulch	trim	weed
Gail												
George												
Jane												
Larry												
mow												
mulch												
trim												
weed												
marigolds												
pansies												
petunias												
snapdragons												

3 RELIVING HISTORY

by Mike Akers

The early history of the Spanish settlement of St. Augustine is tied to the French colony at Fort Caroline in nearby Jacksonville. Southbrook Elementary and three other area schools staged a play based on this period. One boy from each school portrayed one of the characters. The boys appeared onstage, one at a time, and portrayed the the principal French colonists, Jean Ribault and Rene de Laudonierre, as well as the Spanish characters of Juan Ponce de Leon and Pedro Menendez. From the following clues, can you determine the order in which each boy appeared (one boy is Todd), his school and the character he portrayed?

1. Vernon played a Spanish character and appeared before the Eastland Student.

2. The Northridge student appeared before Robert and after Laudonierre.

3. Menendez appeared before Steve and after the Westmill student.

4. The Northridge student played a French character immediately after a Spanish character appeared on stage.

Solution is on page 135.

	1st	2nd	3rd	4th	Jean Ribault	Juan Ponce de Leon	Pedro Menendez	Rene de Laudonierre	East.	North.	South.	West.
Robert												
Steve												
Todd												
Vernon												
Eastland												
Northridge												
Southbrook												
Westmill												
Jean Ribault												
Juan Ponce de Leon												
Pedro Menendez												
Rene de Laudonierre												

4 ALL IN THE FAMILY

by W. Lee Moss

The Marx children grew up in Central City, attended Northeast High School, and excelled throughout in five different sports. Today, you can find each one coaching at one of Central City's five high schools (one of which is their alma mater, Northeast High), each in his or her chosen sport. Last year, each Marx-coached team finished its season ranked at a different spot in the top 5 of its respective sport. From the following clues, can you determine each coach's sport, school, ranking, and length of service as coach (one has six years experience)?

1. Fred is not the man who has coached for eight years.

2. The third-ranked baseball team's coach has two more years' experience than Gail, and four more years' than Southwest High's coach.

3. The four-year male coach's team ranked higher than Southeast High, which ranked higher than Carmen's track team.

4. The fifth-ranked football team's coach has two more years' experience than the Northwest High coach, and four more years' than Mark.

5. The twelve-year coach's team did not finish fourth.

6. Josef's team finished lower than the swimming team, which finished one spot below the ten-year coach's team.

7. The Central High coach's favorite sport has always been basketball.

Solution is on page 135.

	Carmen	Fred	Gail	Josef	Mark	4	6	8	10	12	Cen.	NE	NW	SE	SW	1st	2nd	3rd	4th	5th
baseball																				
basketball																				
football																				
swimming																				
track																				
1st																				
2nd																
3rd																
4th																
5th																
Central											
NE											
NW											
SE											
SW											
4						
6						
8						
10						
12						

5 COPING WITH CABIN FEVER

by Diane Baldwin

Nancy and three others each rent one of the four apartments in the big house perched at the top of Hillcrest Terrace. Friday's ice storm made it impossible for any of them to get out or go to their different jobs for several days. (One of them is the town barber.) To prevent cabin fever, they started different projects they had previously been too busy to do. One of them actually started filling out income-tax forms. From the following clues, can you match each person with his or her apartment, job, and project started?

1. The baker's apartment is one number higher than Nick's and one number lower than the man who painted his bedroom.

2. Ned has the apartment one number lower than the apartment of the bookkeeper, who isn't the woman who cleaned out her closet.

3. Nora isn't the baker.

4. The bookkeeper isn't the one who updated the photo album.

5. Ned isn't the banker.

Solution is on page 136.

	#1	#2	#3	#4	baker	banker	barber	bookkeeper	cleaned closet	did taxes	painted bedroom	updated album
Nancy												
Ned												
Nick												
Nora												
cleaned closet												
did taxes												
painted bedroom												
updated album												
baker												
banker												
barber												
bookkeeper												

6 GOING TO THE ORACLE

by David Champlin

In ancient Greece, persons seeking advice from the gods often went to consult the oracle at Delphi where, at times, a priestess would respond to a questioner's petitions by going into a trance and proclaiming decrees that purportedly were divinely inspired. One day four young men, each from a different city, came to the oracle seeking guidance on a matter he considered to be of great importance. One by one, each went in to consult the oracle, but only the young man who had asked for advice concerning his upcoming marriage received a satisfactory answer. From this information and the following clues, can you determine the home city of each man who came to Delphi, the matter concerning which he wished to receive guidance, and the order in which the four consulted the oracle?

1. The man who asked for guidance in planning his career (who wasn't from Sparta) went into the oracle sometime before Theophilus, who went in sometime before the man from Corinth.

2. Demetrius went in before, but not just before, the man who wanted to know what the future held in store for his newborn son.

3. The four men were, in no particular order: Alexander, the man from Thebes, the man seeking information about the whereabouts of his missing brother, and the third man to ask his question.

4. Lucas was admitted into the oracle's presence just after the man from Athens had asked his question.

5. Demetrius (who was an only child) and Theolphilus didn't consult the oracle consecutively.

Solution is on page 136.

Solution is on page 136.

	Athens	Corinth	Sparta	Thebes	brother	career	marriage	son	1st	2nd	3rd	4th
Alexander												
Demetrius												
Lucas												
Theophilus												
1st												
2nd												
3rd												
4th												
brother												
career												
marriage												
son												

7 WORKING AT HOME

by Lydian Davis

Since Jeanne recently opened a child-care business in her home, five women have enrolled their children. Since she sees the moms five days a week, she's learned quite a lot about each one of them. She knows that each mom works out of her own home in a different occupation — one's an architectural consultant, one a desktop publisher, one a jewelry maker, another a puzzle maker, and the fifth a T-shirt designer. She also recalls that, in addition to contributing to the overall household expenses, each one assumes full responsibility for a different primary budget item and supports a different hobby. Their hobbies, in no particular order, are: collecting art, caring for a horse, maintaining and operating a hot-air balloon, building and flying remote-control airplanes, and traveling. From the following clues, can you determine each woman's first name, occupation, primary financial responsibility, and hobby?

1. Four women are: Andrea; Lyn (who does not make the credit-card payment); the T-shirt designer (who does not collect art); and the one who pays for all of the family's clothing.

2. The desktop publisher, who does not make the car payment, enjoys building and flying remote-control airplanes.

3. Kathy's hobby money goes for the care of her horse, but the jewelry maker does not collect art.

4. Four women are: the architectural consultant; Marian (who does not pay for clothing); the one who makes the car payment; and Cheri.

5. The woman who travels as a hobby, who is not Lyn, also makes the house payment, which is not made by the T-shirt designer.

6. The puzzle maker, who does not collect art or travel as a hobby, pays for the family vacations.

Solution is on page 136.

	arch. consul.	desk. pub.	jewelry maker	puzzle maker	T-shirt designer	car	clothing	credit cards	house	vac.	art col.	horse	hot-air balloon	r/c planes	travel
Andrea															
Cheri															
Kathy															
Lyn															
Marian															
art collecting															
horse															
hot-air ballooning															
r/c airplane															
travel															
car															
clothing															
credit cards															
house															
vacations															

8 MEMORY LANE

by Mary Marks Cezus

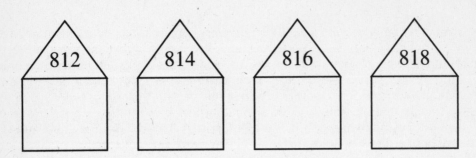

Tiny Memory Lane boasts wooded lots and the advantages of living across from Tribute Park. The gentlemen who live there with their wives wish they had more time to enjoy the serenity. Instead they find themselves leaving memos to their wives and reading memos from their wives. Today was no exception. In each of the houses a note was left on the memo pad, including the romantic message "Clean the bathroom! Please!" No two of the gentlemen received the same message. One of the memo pads was decorated with apples and grapes and each of the other pads was decorated with a different design. From the following clues, can you determine each house owner's first name, house number, memo pad design, and message received?

1. Scott lives directly between the man whose memo pad is decorated with ducks with umbrellas and the man who received the message "Phone your folks."

2. Craig lives to the right of the man whose memo pad is decorated with neckties.

3. Brad (whose memo pad is not decorated with neckties) likes to golf with the man who received the message "Make plane reservations."

4. Scott and the man who received the "Late dinner tonight" message both would like to run businesses from their homes.

5. The man who received the message "Make plane reservations" lives at one end of the of the street and the man whose memo pad is decorated with sports equipment lives at the other.

6. Ted and the man whose memo pad is decorated with ducks with umbrellas have both considered putting pools in their backyards.

7. The man whose memo pad is decorated with sports equipment (who is not Brad) and the man who received the message "Phone your folks" both enjoy yardwork.

Solution is on page 137.

	812	814	816	818	apples/ grapes	ducks w/ umbrellas	necktie	sports equipment	clean bathroom	late dinner	make reser.	phone folks
Brad												
Craig												
Scott												
Ted												
clean bathroom												
late dinner												
make reservations												
phone folks												
apples & grapes												
ducks w/ umbrellas												
necktie												
sports equipment												

9 CAMPAIGN ADS

It was primary time in Megalopolis, and political ads were crowding the airwaves. The day before the primary, no fewer than four political campaign advertisements were shown back-to-back during the first commercial break of the local evening news. Each was for a different candidate running for a different office; one was for a person seeking a nomination for state treasurer. From this information and the clues given below, determine the full name of each hopeful, the nomination each was seeking, and the order in which the four ads were run.

1. Mr. Chin's ad was shown just before the one promoting Grace, which was shown sometime before the one for the candidate running for state's attorney.

2. Nadine's ad was shown sometime before the one for the mayoral candidate, which ran just before the ad supporting Moore's campaign.

3. The four ads were, in no particular order: David's ad, the one urging voters to choose Ortiz, the one for the person seeking the nomination for sheriff, and the second ad to be shown.

4. The ads on behalf of Ronald and Sullivan (who isn't Grace) ran consecutively, but not necessarily in that order.

Solution is on page 137.

	Chin	Moore	Ortiz	Sullivan	Mayor	Sheriff	St. Atty.	St. Treas.	1st	2nd	3rd	4th
David												
Grace												
Nadine												
Ronald												
1st												
2nd												
3rd												
4th												
Mayor												
Sheriff												
St. Atty.												
St. Treas.												

10 THE EASTER BUNNY

by Susan Zivich

The Easter Bunny always makes a special appearance at Uncle Dick's Easter party. The kids are so thrilled with their baskets of goodies that they never notice the bunny comes only after Uncle Dick leaves! After the moms and dads click their last roll of film, it's time to gather up the Easter treats and head for home. Can you help the parents sort out the different color baskets and make sure each child has the right toy, book (one is "Cinderella"), and chocolate treat (one is an egg), while the Easter bunny leaves (and Uncle Dick returns)?

1. Jennifer's basket has the chocolate bunny and Tommy's has "The Three Little Pigs."

2. The boy with the green basket ate half his chocolate chick.

3. Amanda's basket is pink, her favorite color. Michael also has his favorite color.

4. The blue basket came with a jump rope.

5. The basket with "Little Red Riding Hood" also has a chocolate tulip.

6. One of the girls found an airplane in her basket. Her little sister has the purple basket.

7. Julie's Easter basket held a baby doll.

8. The child who received a paint set also has a chocolate heart.

9. "Snow White" came in the basket with a sand bucket. "Jack and the Beanstalk" came in the yellow basket.

Solution is on page 137.

	bl.	gr.	pink	pur.	yel.	plane	doll	rope	paint	bucket	Cin.	Jack	Lit.	Snow	Three	bun.	ch.	egg	heart	tu.
Amanda																				
Jennifer																				
Julie																				
Michael																				
Tommy																				
bunny																				
chickie																				
egg																				
heart																				
tulip																				
Cinderella																				
Jack																				
Little Red																				
Snow White																				
Three Pigs																				
airplane																				
baby doll																				
jump rope																				
paint set																				
sand bucket																				

11 STIR WARS

by Anne Smith

After watching the stir-fry episode of "Cooking with Jules," five women in Small County practiced their stir-fry techniques until they had perfected what each thought was the ideal stir-fry dish. For months, each woman bragged that hers was the tastiest stir-fry food in the county. Tiring of the boasting, the officials of the Small County Fair decided to settle this disagreement by including a stir-fry contest, along with the traditional apple-pie baking contest, in this year's fair. From the following clues, can you determine each woman's full name (one first name is Cheryl; one surname is Sharkey), the type of stir-fry dish she considered her specialty (one was chicken), and where each placed in the county fair competition?

1. The pork stir-fry did not come in last, but it did place somewhere behind the dish prepared by Ms. Rudin, who is not Sue.

2. Barb, who did not win the competition, placed immediately ahead of Kerri, who did not come in last place.

3. The beef stir-fry placed either first or second; the shrimp stir-fry was not third.

4. Lynn's vegetable stir-fry placed two places ahead of her friend, who did not prepare the pork dish.

5. Ms. Brennan won the competition.

6. Ms. Haines' dish placed immediately before the pork dish.

7. Ms. Carlson's culinary preparation placed somewhere after Sue's.

Solution is on page 138.

	Brennan	Carlson	Haines	Rudin	Sharkey	beef	chicken	pork	shrimp	veg.	1st	2nd	3rd	4th	5th
Barb															
Cheryl															
Kerri															
Lynn															
Sue															
1st															
2nd															
3rd															
4th															
5th															
beef															
chicken															
pork															
shrimp															
vegetable															

THE CLOCKMAKER

by W. Lee Moss

George, who has five married daughters, has always prided himself on his chosen hobby, for over 35 years. George is a skilled maker of both clocks and watches. Every year since his oldest daughter got married twelve years ago, he has presented each of his daughters and sons-in-law a new hand-crafted timepiece on the anniversary of their marriage. This past year, for the first time, as his youngest daughter (who is 21) celebrated her first anniversary, George made five timepieces, each a different type (one was a grandfather clock). The five anniversaries fall in January, April, July, October and December. From the following clues, can you determine each woman's full name (one is Clarissa; another is Mrs. Baker), age, gift and month of anniversary?

1. Jennifer is three years older than Mrs. Cox, but three years younger than the woman whose anniversary falls in January.

2. The sundial clock was presented three months before the 24-year-old woman's anniversary, but three months after Mrs. Price's gift was.

3. The three clocks were given to Mrs. Martin, the 30-year-old woman, and Margaret.

4. These three gifts were presented consecutively: The 27-year-old woman's present, the pocket watch, and Gloria's gift.

5. The 33-year-old woman did not receive the calendar watch.

6. The two watches were given to Mrs. Wilson and the woman who married in December.

7. The July bride is three years older than Paula, but three years younger than the woman who got the cuckoo clock.

Solution is on page 138.

	Baker	Cox	Martin	Price	Wilson	calen. watch	cuckoo clock	grand. clock	pkt. watch	sun. clock	Jan.	Apr.	July	Oct.	Dec.	ages		
Clarissa																		
Gloria																		
Jennifer																		
Margaret																		
Paula																		
ages																		
Jan.																		
Apr.																		
July																		
Oct.																		
Dec.																		
calen. watch																		
cuckoo clock																		
grand. clock																		
pocket watch																		
sundial clock																		

MEDIUM LOGIC
PROBLEMS

13 FLIGHT OF FANCY

by Susan Zivich

The Hamilton Junior High Art Club planned an ambitious project for spring, a mural on the library wall showing the joys of reading. Hannigan and four other students volunteered to paint their favorite story characters. After one week, the unicorn and the other four characters were completed, and the art club members began work on the background. As the students watched the trees, shore, and sky take shape, the school newspaper printed a story about the artists. To keep their readers on their toes, however, the news staff printed only a few details and challenged the students to figure out who stayed to paint each day and the figure each student created. The first five students with the correct answers were rewarded with a gift certificate to the school bookstore. From the following clues, can you figure out the winning answers?

1. Each student stayed after after school two days during the week, but none stayed two days in a row.

2. None of the students worked with the same partner twice.

3. Jeff and the student who painted the mermaid finished their artwork on Friday.

4. Emily and the Winegarten child started their pieces on Monday.

5. Dan worked with Coulis earlier in the week than he worked with the student who painted the spaceman.

6. Potter and the student who painted the pirate worked together on Wednesday.

7. Kim and the student who painted the ghost worked on Tuesday.

8. The Matthews child worked with the student who painted the mermaid earlier in the week than Matthews worked with Emily.

9. Kim could not work Thursday, so Meg and the Coulis child took that day.

Solution is on page 138.

	Coulis	Hannigan	Matthews	Potter	Winegarten	M	T	W	Th.	F	ghost	mer.	pir.	space.	unicorn
Dan															
Emily															
Jeff															
Kim															
Meg															
ghost															
mermaid															
pirate															
spaceman															
unicorn															
Mon.															
Tues.															
Wed.															
Thurs.															
Fri.															

14 CELEBRATING ST. PATRICK'S DAY

by Diane C. Baldwin

Clancy and the four other organizers of the St. Patrick's Day parade all found unique ways to celebrate St. Patrick's Day besides the march. The day found each man wearing a different article of green (including the man with the new green sports jacket) and celebrating in a personal way. From the following clues, can you determine each man's full name (one surname is O'Rourk), the green article of clothing, he wore, and the way in which he celebrated?

1. Neither the man who bought the Irish setter pup nor Kelly is the one in the green sweater or tie.

2. Pat, who isn't Mr. O'Day, celebrated by doing an Irish jig.

3. The five are Shawn, Mr. O'Neal, the man who bought the pup, Mr. O'Day, and the man in green pants.

4. Both Mr. O'Neal and Mr. O'Leary often play darts with the man in the green vest.

5. The man who sang Irish songs and the one in the green sweater work at the same company.

6. The three who have visited Ireland are Kelly, the one who celebrated with Irish stew (who isn't O'Leary), and Mr. O'Day.

7. Mr. O'Grady and the man in the green sweater both live on Emerald St.

8. Brian isn't Mr. O'Grady or Mr. O'Day.

9. The man in green pants isn't the one who bought shamrocks or the one who sang.

Solution is on page 139.

	O'Day	O'Grady	O'Leary	O'Neal	O'Rourk	jacket	pants	sweater	tie	vest	jig	setter	shamrock	songs	stew
Brian															
Clancy															
Kelly															
Pat															
Shawn															
jig																
setter																
shamrock																
songs																
stew																
jacket																
pants																
sweater																
tie																
vest																

15 RETURN OF THE RED-EYE

by Anne Smith

After more than a year of offering only daytime flights, Friendly Airlines, based in Chicago, decided to reinstate its (very) early morning trips to nearby cities. In order to promote its new schedule, Friendly offered a different special feature on each flight. One morning, five pilots took off for five different cities at five different times, beginning at 12:30 a.m. with one flight leaving every half hour. From the following, determine each pilot's name (one was Sue), his or her time of departure, the destination of each flight (one was Des Moines), and each flight's special feature.

1. One of the female pilots left earlier than the man flying to Milwaukee. The other female piloted the plane that offered extra legroom.

2. Al made his departure at 2:00 a.m.

3. The last plane to leave was the one offering extra wide seats.

4. The plane with additional overhead storage flew to St. Louis.

5. Walt's flight offered free unlimited coffee and doughnuts.

6. Don flew to either Detroit or St. Louis.

7. Jill did not fly the plane to Indianapolis, which left one hour after the flight offering triple frequent-flyer miles.

Solution is on page 139.

	12:30	1:00	1:30	2:00	2:30	D.M.	Det.	Ind.	Mil.	St.L.	coffee	leg.	miles	seats	storage
Al															
Don															
Jill															
Sue															
Walt															
coffee															
legroom															
miles															
seats															
storage															
Des Moines															
Detroit															
Indianapolis															
Milwaukee															
St. Louis															

16 SIGN HERE

by Susan Zivich

On the last day of school, five close friends celebrated their move to middle school by autographing each others' shirts. Volk and her friends each brought a different color tub of fabric ink to sign her name to the other four shirts. As the shirts dried in the art room, the students admired their handiwork. From the following clues, can you determine each girl's full name, the color shirt she brought (one was blue), the design on her shirt, and the color ink each used to sign her name to the other shirts (one was silver)?

1. Patsy put a teddy bear transfer on her shirt; Goode's had a smiling sun.

2. Angie signed her name with cream fabric ink; Sroka used black.

3. Denise selected a pink shirt.

4. Neither Madeline nor Laura Freed signed in red.

5. The girl with balloons on her shirt signed her name in gold.

6. Nowak collected her friends' signatures on a green shirt.

7. A lacy heart transfer decorated the purple shirt.

8. Denise and Sroka were the first to sign their names on the shirt with the tulips.

9. The girl with the yellow shirt wrote her name in red.

Solution is on page 139.

Solution is on page 139.

	Freed	Goode	Nowak	Sroka	Volk	blue	green	pink	purple	yellow	bal.	heart	sun	teddy bear	tulip	black	cream	gold	red	silver
Angie																				
Denise																				
Laura																				
Madeline																				
Patsy																				
black																					
cream																					
gold																					
red																					
silver																					
balloon																
heart																
sun																
teddy bear																
tulip																
blue						
green						
pink						
purple						
yellow						

17 THE FRENCH COLLECTION

by Diane C. Baldwin

Joyce enjoys fine art, especially French Impressionist paintings. Over the years she has acquired five reproductions of different subjects by five different artists she admires. She framed each painting in a different color and hung them in the hall and four rooms of her house. From the clues supplied, can you match each painting with the right artist, subject, frame, and location, as well as tell the order Joyce acquired them?

1. The country scene is by either Monet or Pissaro.

2. Both the city scene (which doesn't have the white frame) and the Monet painting were acquired after the one in the bedroom.

3. The painting in the black frame was acquired just before the seascape and just after the one by Degas.

4. The first three acquisitions in some order, were: the country scene, the one in the gold frame, and the one in the dining room.

5. The first and last acquisitions, in some order, were the one in the living room and the one by Seurat.

6. The one in the silver frame, which isn't by Pissaro, was acquired just after the Renoir; one of the two is the portrait.

7. The five paintings include the still life, the one by Pissaro, the one in the den, the one with the tan frame, and the first acquisition.

Solution is on page 140.

	Degas	Monet	Pissaro	Renoir	Seurat	black	gold	silver	tan	white	bedroom	den	dining room	hall	living room	1	2	3	4	5
city scene																				
country scene																				
portrait																					
seascape																					
still life																					
1st															
2nd															
3rd															
4th															
5th															
bedroom										
den										
dining room										
hall										
living room										
black					
gold					
silver					
tan					
white					

18   THE UMPIRE
STRIKES BACK

by Anne Smith

Ralph, an umpire for the minor league system, is very upset with today's players. "Such prima donnas," he moaned. "They think they can undermine my authority and question every call I make." With that in mind, Ralph was determined that today he would eject from the game any player who argued his decisions. Thus, in the nine-inning game, Hank and four other players were thrown out of the game, each in a different inning, for a different reason (one was for arguing the ball he hit was a home run, not a foul ball as Ralph had ruled). From the following clues, can you determine each player's full name (one was Mr. Player), the reason he was thrown out of the game, and the inning in which each ejection occurred?

1. Mr. Fielder was thrown out two innings before Lance and two innings after the man who argued he had been hit by a pitch.

2. Rusty was ejected two innings after the man who argued the catcher interfered with his swing and two innings before Mr. Singleton.

3. The man who thought he was safe at home was told to hit the showers two innings before Mr. Walker and two innings after Mick.

4. At least one man was ejected more than two innings after Bubba.

5. Mr. Dinger, who did not argue a called third strike, was ejected in the third inning.

Solution is on page 140.

	Dinger	Fielder	Player	Single.	Walker	called strike	catcher inter.	fair homer	hit by pitch	safe	inning			
Bubba														
Hank														
Lance														
Mick														
Rusty														
inning														
called strike														
catcher inter.														
fair home run														
hit by pitch														
safe at home														

46

19 A SMALL WORLD

by Kevyn Dymond

One day last week, the Dutchess Cruise Lines' luxury flagship was gliding gently through the Caribbean. Five women, all perfect strangers, were on the uppermost sun-deck tanning. They began to chat and quickly found out that they were each staying on a different deck of the ship (each deck was a different color). Soon thereafter, they discovered that they are all not only residents of Montana (each lives in a different county), they had all been born in a different city in California. From the following clues, can you determine each woman's full name, county of residence in Montana (one resides in Lewis & Clark), city of birth in California, and the color of each woman's ship deck?

1. Marie (who isn't Ms. Evans) doesn't live in Missoula County.

2. Ms. Tyler (who didn't stay on the tan deck and wasn't born in Indio) isn't the woman who stayed on the green deck (who doesn't live in Glacier County and isn't Ms. Dunne).

3. The woman born in Indio (who isn't Linda) didn't stay on the blue deck.

4. The woman born in Chico (who doesn't live in Missoula County) isn't Janet.

5. Renee (who was born in Vallejo), Ms. Wolfe, and the woman who lives in Cascade County had berths on the gold, pink and blue decks, in some order.

6. None of the women have the same first and last initials.

7. Ms. Lurie (who was born in Fresno) didn't stay on the tan deck.

8. Linda (who doesn't live in Glacier County) isn't Ms. Evans.

9. The woman who lives in Silver Bow County isn't Marie.

10. The woman born in Novato doesn't live in either Glacier or Cascade County.

11. Ms. Dunne (who didn't stay on the tan deck) and Ms. Tyler are Elyse and the woman who stayed on the pink deck, in some order.

12. The woman who lives in Cascade County wasn't born in Chico.

Solution is on page 140.

first name					
last name					
residence					
birthplace					
deck color					

by Susan Zivich

Five classmates joined the fun when the Museum of Natural History held its annual overnight. Each camper selected two crafts and two late-night tours. The following Monday, the five excited friends tried to share what they learned with their classmates, but they kept interrupting each other. Finally their teacher threw up his hands. "Enough! With what we've learned, we can figure out what each of you enjoyed! Anyone who figures it out will get extra credit!" Can you get the extra points?

1. Each of the five students was paired once with each of the others for either a craft or a tour.

2. Katie and the Brubaker child enjoyed making Mexican tin ornaments.

3. Erin and the VanderWal child spotted many familiar animals on their Walk in the Wild tour.

4. Josh and the Mendoza child showed off the Japanese ribbon fish they made.

5. Katie browsed through the gift shop while Melissa and the O'Connell child toured the South Pacific.

6. Neither of the students who made the Egyptian bookmarks also toured Ancient Egypt.

7. Erin and the Willis child learned to make African corn husk dolls.

8. Katie and the Mendoza child toured Ancient Egypt.

9. Dan and the O'Connell child made Peruvian paper flowers for their classmates.

10. Josh and the Willis child pointed out favorite beasts on the Dinosaur tour.

11. Melissa and the VanderWal child learned to write their names in hieroglyphics when they made Egyptian papyrus bookmarks.

12. Dan and the Brubaker child enjoyed the village on the tour of Africa.

Solution is on page 141.

craft	student		student	
	first name	last name	first name	last name

tour	student		student	
	first name	last name	first name	last name

ROSES OF SUMMER

by Mary Marks Cezus

Blossom Bush, acclaimed artist, created a commemorative plate (as illustrated) to celebrate the family's fiftieth year in the rosebush business. Blossom chose five of the family's favorite roses to illustrate the plate. In choosing the roses she also considered their colors (no two were the same) and their sizes (no two were the same size). From the illustration (indicating position only) and the following clues, can you arrange the roses from smallest to largest and determine the name of each rose (one was Child's Play), its color, and its position?

1. Fairy Godmother was smaller than the white rose.

2. The lavender rose was larger and to the right of at least one other rose.

3. The smallest rose (which was not in position four) was above Regal Veil.

4. The white rose was smaller and below Wedding Bliss.

5. The yellow rose was not in the top row.

6. The pink rose was larger than Fragrant Lady.

7. The rose in position five was smaller than Fairy Godmother.

8. Fragrant Lady was larger than and above the red rose.

Solution is on page 141.

	smallest → largest					lavender	pink	red	white	yellow	1	2	3	4	5
Child's Play															
Fairy Godmother															
Fragrant Lady															
Regal Veil															
Wedding Bliss															
1															
2															
3															
4															
5															
lavender															
pink															
red															
white															
yellow															

22 SCENIC CHECKS

by Mary A. Powell

The Bennington women have always lead colorful lives. On her last birthday, Grandma Bennington became a blonde, one of her daughters bought a motorcycle, and another took up snowboarding. The three were gathered at Grandma Bennington's for a party for a 20-year-old relative (the youngest of them all), when the celebrant bounced in. "Look what I did!" she squealed as she tossed a new checkbook on the table. Her mother said, "But you've had a checking account for years." "Yes, but before I had boring checks. Just look," she said, showing new checks with much zeal. The three older women dug out their own checkbooks. All had fancy checks, but of different designs. The 20-year-old faked a crestfallen expression before she pointed out that her first check was missing. She had used it to pay a month's rent on her first apartment. From the clues, can you find the name and age of each woman, the month of her birth, and the design and background color on each woman's checks?

1. The four women are Olivia, Olivia's mother, the one with green checks, and the one whose checks have rainbows.

2. The cat lover, whose checks depict cats, is twice as old as Tanya and three times as old as the one whose checks are pink.

3. Carla is twice as old as the one whose checks are decorated with roses; neither has the May birthday.

4. Laura is older than both the woman with yellow checks and the one who chose clouds as a design.

5. The one with blue checks has a July birthday; she is neither the oldest nor the youngest.

6. The checks featuring clouds are not pink.

7. Tanya has no children.

Solution is on page 142.

	ages				months				cats	clouds	rainbows	roses	blue	green	pink	yellow
Carla																
Laura																
Olivia																
Tanya																
blue																
green																
pink																
yellow																
cats																
clouds																
rainbows																
roses																
months																

23   A MUSICAL WEEK

by W. Lee Moss

Timothy is a true rock music fan. He owns every CD he can afford and spends hours listening to his favorite rock station and collects memorabilia relating to his passion. So, when Timothy heard that five of his favorite rock stars (including Glynnis Day) were booked into Perishing Auditorium in one week, he was first in line to buy tickets for all five concerts (one each day, Monday through Friday). Can you determine each day's feature performer, opening act, attendance (one day saw 14,201 pack the auditorium), and ticket price (one cost $24)?

1. The concert featuring Winslow Dallas was one day before the one attended by 12,117 people, which was one day before the one costing $30 per ticket.

2. The Monday ticket cost $2.00 less than the one purchased by 13,126 people.

3. Gloria McGraw was the opening act of a concert scheduled earlier in the week than the one opened by Florence Knight; neither of these performers opened for C. C. Queen.

4. Walking Wounded opened to just over 1,000 fewer people than those making up the Tuesday crowd, but just over 1,000 more people than those who paid $26 for their ticket.

5. Thursday's concert was attended by just over 1,000 more people than the concert opened by P D Q, and just over 2,000 more people than those who purchased the $28 ticket.

6. 11,094 people attended the concert opened by Fortune's Wind; the following day's ticket cost $22; the next following day, the Running Dogs were the featured act.

7. The ticket for the concert featuring Nathan Colby cost $4.00 more than the ticket purchased by 10,063 people.

Solution is on page 142.

	Florence Knight	Fortune's Wind	Gloria McGraw	PDQ	Walking Wounded	10,063	11,094	12,117	13,126	14,201	$22	$24	$26	$28	$30	M	T	W	Th	F
C.C.																				
Glynnis																				
Nathan																				
Running																				
Winslow																				
Mon.																				
Tues.																				
Wed.																				
Thurs.																				
Fri.																				
$22																				
$24																				
$26																				
$28																				
$30																				
10,063																				
11,094																				
12,117																				
13,126																				
14,201																				

**BLOCK
PARTY**

by Susan Zivich

When the six houses were completed on Devonshire Drive, the new occupants held a get-acquainted block party. Mr. Vander grilled hot dogs (and plenty of 'em!) in his backyard and each of the other five families brought salads and soda to complete the picnic. The kids beat the adults at softball (well, maybe the adults let them, who knows?) and everyone parted friends. Several nights later, Barbara Chan toted her homework to the Petrie house to babysit. She didn't finish much algebra, though, because she and the Petrie children spent the evening making a map of Devonshire Drive. Can you help them remember where each family lived, the style of each house, the luxury each had added (one family enjoyed a fireplace), and how many children each family has?

1. Andy Petrie remembered that Mr. and Mrs. Morales lived between the Tudor home and the home with the deck.

2. Barbara Chan lives across the street from one of the families with two children. The ranch house is across the street from the other family with two children.

3. Sally Petrie knew that the Levin family and one of the two families with one child were both at the north end of the street.

4. Barbara Chan volunteered that the house with the pool was right across the street from the Colonial style house.

5. The three families on the west side of the street all brought salads. The family with one child brought potato salad, the family with the hot tub brought three-bean salad, and the Hanrahans brought Hawaiian salad.

6. The Petrie children share the south end of the street with the family who lives in the Victorian house.

7. The Manor house is located between the house with the game room and one of the homes with three children.

8. The Vanders grilled hot dogs. The other two families on the east side of the street, the family in the Cape Cod home and the family with the computer center, brought soda. None of these families have two children.

Solution is on page 143.

	1	2	3	4	5	6	Cape Cod	Colonial	Manor	ranch	Tudor	Victorian	comp. center	deck	fire-place	game room	hot tub	pool	children					
Chan																								
Hanrahan																								
Levin																								
Morales																								
Petrie																								
Vander																								

children	1	2	3	4	5	6	Cape Cod	Colonial	Manor	ranch	Tudor	Victorian	comp. center	deck	fire-place	game room	hot tub	pool

	1	2	3	4	5	6	Cape Cod	Colonial	Manor	ranch	Tudor	Victorian
comp. cent.												
deck												
fireplace												
game room												
hot tub												
pool												

	1	2	3	4	5	6
Cape Cod						
Colonial						
Manor						
ranch						
Tudor						
Victorian						

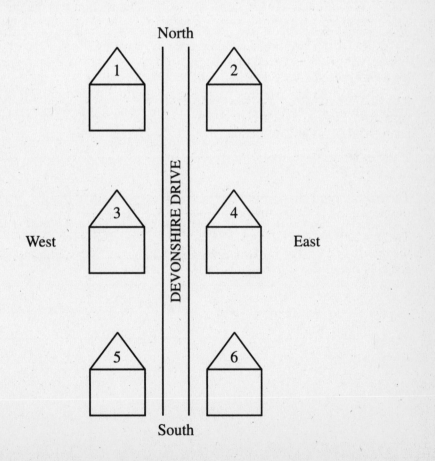

North

1 2

West 3 4 East

DEVONSHIRE DRIVE

5 6

South

25 THE AFTER-SCHOOL PROGRAM

by Evelyn B. Rosenthal

There are four groups in an after-school program that meets Mondays through Thursdays. Each group spends one period at painting, ceramics, nature study, or drama, and a second period at gym, swimming, or dancing. Except for gym, no two groups have any activity at the same time, and again, except for gym — each group has each activity no more than once during the four days. George, Sally, and two other children are in different groups. From the following clues, can you find each child's full name and activities on each day?

1. The two boys do not have gym on the same days.

2. May has painting and swimming on the day the Clarke boy has dance.

3. At least one child has painting later in the week than the Dunn child.

4. The Abbot boy has dance on Thursday, and the Burns girl has dance on Wednesday.

5. John has swimming on the same day as the Dunn child has dance.

6. Every child has gym on two nonconsecutive days, and art — either painting or ceramics — on two other nonconsecutive days.

7. May has drama earlier in the week than at least one of the others.

8. The Dunn child has painting on the same day the Abbot child has ceramics and nature study on the same day as the Burns child has ceramics.

Solution is on page 143.

Solution is on page 143.

first name	last name	Mon.		Tues.		Wed.		Thurs.	
		class 1	class 2	class 1	class 2	class 1	class 2	class 1	class 2

SPRINGFIELD AUTHORS

by Katherine Mondahl

The town of Springfield is justifiably proud of the number of authors who live there. One Saturday the local library featured six of the authors, each of whom gave a brief talk about his or her work, then answered questions from the audience. Can you identify the authors by name (two first names are Betty and Gordon; one last name is Crown), the type of fiction they write (one writes historical fiction), the titles of their latest books (one is "Tiles Underfoot"), and the time at which they appeared (appearances began at 10:00 a.m. and continued at one-hour intervals)?

1. These three appeared in consecutive order: Mr. Bloom, the author of "Drums of Dawn," and the romance writer (who wasn't the woman who wrote "The Moon at Noon.")

2. These three appeared in consecutive order: Frank, the mystery writer, and the author of "On the Shore."

3. The three woman were Karen, Ms. Moore, and the author who spoke at 10:00.

4. The three male authors were Frank, Mr. Flight, and the author who spoke at 1:00.

5. The science fiction author appeared two hours before the author of "The Grotto," who appeared two hours before the man who writes westerns.

6. No two women authors spoke in consecutive order.

7. Isley spoke immediately before Sheppard, and immediately after Donna.

8. The fantasy writer (who didn't write "For the Doves") spoke two hours before Eric.

Solution is on page 144.

first name	last name	type	title	time

27 TV TWIN STARS

by Randall L. Whipkey

A child character on each of five hit television shows is played not by one child star, but by twins who alternate appearing on screen. Using two actors or actresses instead of one allows show directors and writers to have the child characters in more scenes and still obey child labor laws. At the same time, the twins can have show business careers while enjoying the company of their siblings and without sibling rivalry. Can you determine the full names of each pair of twin stars (one surname is Scholl), the character they play, and the show in which they appear?

1. The only girl-boy set of twins plays the infant Rebecca on one show — not "Morning Sun"; the other twins play characters of the same gender as they are.

2. The five pairs of twin stars are Brandon and his twin, Cherise and her twin, the Deluca twins, the twins who play Duane on one program, and the pair who portray a child on "Fool House."

3. Marcus and his twin, who isn't Brian, aren't the ones who play Mikey on one show.

4. One pair of twin girls play the youngest child on "Home Repairs."

5. Teresa and her twin, who isn't Cherise, don't play the baby Rebecca.

6. Marcus and his twin, who aren't the Abbott twins, aren't the ones who act on "Family Matters."

7. Cherise and her twin aren't on "Home Repairs."

8. Shelley and her twin aren't the ones who play the character of Stephanie on one show, nor are they the twins who appear on "Dr. Quaint, Frontier Dentist."

9. Brandon and his twin don't play Mikey, nor do they portray the child on "Family Matters."

10. Micah isn't one of the acting Walsh brothers.

11. Colby and his sibling aren't the twins who work on "Morning Sun."

12. The set of twins who share the role of Jenny aren't on the hit "Family Matters."

13. Shannon and her twin aren't the two who play a role on "Dr. Quaint, Frontier Dentist."

14. Mandy and her twin and the Abbotts have the same agent.

15. The Holmes twins aren't the "Morning Sun" stars.

Solution is on page 144.

	Abbott	Deluca	Holmes	Scholl	Walsh	Duane	Jenny	Mikey	Rebecca	Stephanie	Dr. Quaint	Family Matters	Fool House	Home Repairs	Morn. Sun
Cherise															
Mandy															
Shannon															
Shelley															
Teresa															
Brandon															
Brian															
Colby															
Marcus															
Micah															
Dr. Quaint															
Family															
Fool															
Home															
Morning															
Duane															
Jenny															
Mikey															
Rebecca															
Stephanie															

28 THE DUELING MUSKETEERS

by Evelyn B. Rosenthal

In the days of the musketeers, many French noblemen served under assumed names. On one occasion, M. de Blois and five others were boasting to one another about their prowess in duels, of which each had fought a different number. From the following clues, can you find each man's *nom de guerre* (one was known as Cacomaches), rank (one was a baron), length of service, and the number of duels he had fought?

1. The six men had fought a total of 63 duels; the veteran with the longest service, who was not Skotopsis, had fought 32. The longer a man's service, the more duels he had fought.

2. M. de Poitiers had fought half as many duels as the chevalier and twice as many as Hautophile.

3. Phobopan and M. de Lille, the two with the shortest terms of service, had averaged one duel a month.

4. M. de Bourges had fought twice as many duels as the viscount and half as many as Skotopsis.

5. The marquis had served twice as long as M. de Vannes.

6. Hautophile was neither M. de Bourges not M. de Vannes.

7. Misander was not the count; de Poitiers was not the viscount.

8. Three of the men — M. de Sedan, Misander, and the duke — found they had averaged the same number of duels per month served.

9. Cynides had served more than one month.

10. The numbers of years (all different) served by each of the three who had served the longest turned out to be exactly the same as the numbers of *months* served by each of the other three.

Solution is on page 144.

man	nom de guerre	rank	yrs. of service	# of duels

29   ALIBI, ALIBI, WHO'S GOT AN ALIBI?

by David Champlin

After Janet's Jewelry store was held up during a daring daylight robbery, suspicion fell upon four well-known local characters of less-than-shining repute. When questioned by the police, Scarf Ace and the other three suspects claimed to have an alibi for his whereabouts at the time of the crime. Officer Miller and three fellow police officers were dispatched to check out the stories; each went to a different place to verify whether or not suspect had indeed been where he claimed. The first three officers to return each reported that the alibi he or she had checked out was in fact legitimate, but the fourth officer to return had evidence proving that the story he had investigated was false. The suspect who had given the false story to the officers eventually confessed to the robbery. From this information and the clues given below, determine each suspect's alibi, the officer who investigated each alibi, and the order in which the officers returned with their reports.

1. The officer who checked out a suspect's claim that he was drinking coffee at his favorite restaurant was not the first one to return. Officer Kao wasn't the officer who investigated the coffee alibi.

2. The officer who checked out the story of the suspect who claimed he was getting a shave at the barbershop returned just before the one who checked out Raggedy Sam's story, who returned just before Officer Lewis.

3. The four officers were, in no particular order: Officer Juarez, the one who checked out Bazooka Bob's story, the one who investigated a suspect's claim that he was having his teeth cleaned at his dentist's office, and the 2nd officer to return.

4. The officer who checked out Gorgeous Guy's alibi returned just before Officer Kao, who returned just before the officer who went to investigate a suspect's claim that he was undergoing a tax audit at the time in question.

Solution is on page 145.

30 THE DISTRICTS OF OLBIA

by Evelyn B. Rosenthal

The country of Olbia is divided into four districts by mountains, which run from northeast to southwest, and the two branches of a river, which arises near the middle of the mountain ridge and flows northwest and southeast. Eight cities, of which Tolla is one, are in the numbered locations on the map. From the following clues, can you locate the cities and find which citizen lives in each?

1. From Bibi's point of view, the citizen of Ronda (who is not Bibi) lives on this side of the mountains and on this side of the river; Fifi lives across the river and on this side of the mountains; Dodi lives across the mountains and on this side of the river; and the citizen of Zemba lives across the mountains and across the river.

2. Lili lives north of the river, and due north of Gigi and south of Vanda, which is the city farthest from the source of the river.

3. Judi lives east of the citizen of Sella and due west of Kiki, who lives closest to the source of the river.

4. From Mimi's point of view, the citizen of Pomba lives across the mountains, and the citizen of Walla (who is not Mimi) lives on this side of the mountains and on this side of the river.

5. Yorba is the easternmost city; Gigi lives in the southernmost one.

Solution is on page 145.

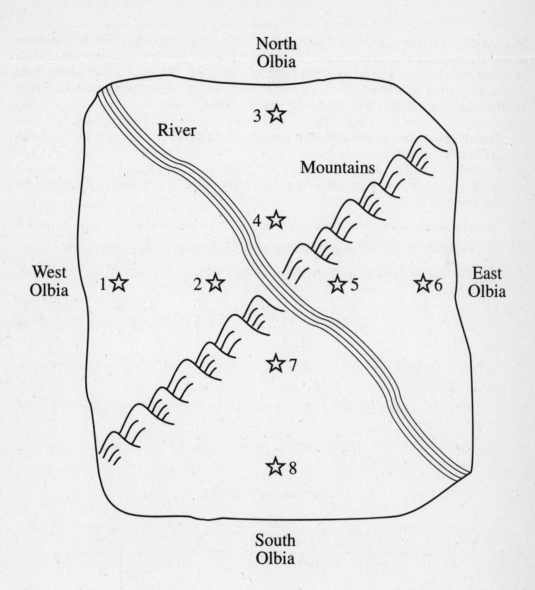

North
Olbia

River

3 ☆

Mountains

4 ☆

West
Olbia

1 ☆   2 ☆   ☆ 5   ☆ 6

East
Olbia

☆ 7

☆ 8

South
Olbia

61

31 THE MODFATHER

by Anne Smith

Mr. Thomas is a very nice gentleman with one major fault. He likes the clothing styles of the disco era so much that he has not updated his wardrobe since the 1970s. Tired of being embarrassed by the way her father dresses, Mr. Thomas's daughter bought him a new article of clothing for his birthday and invited four others to do the same. One of these five astutely purchased Mr. Thomas a new sports coat to replace his Nehru jacket. From the following, can you determine the name of each person, her relationship to Mr. Thomas, the gift each bought, and the order in which Mr. Thomas opened his presents?

1. Betty's gift was not the loafers that were given to Mr. Thomas to replace his platform shoes.

2. Mr. Thomas's mother's present was not the first one opened.

3. Mr. Thomas's wife and sister thought Amy's gift was the best one he received.

4. Mr. Thomas opened Marge's present (which wasn't the pair of dress pants to replace his bell bottoms) immediately after he received the shoes.

5. In consecutive order, Mr. Thomas opened these three presents: the one from Karen, the gift from his boss, and the tie that was given to him to replace his neckchain with the astrological medallion.

6. Gemma's present was not the windbreaker given to Mr. Thomas to replace his fringed jacket.

7. Mr. Thomas opened the gift from his mother immediately before he opened the gift from Gemma.

8. The gift from Mr. Thomas's wife was opened immediately after Betty's gift and immediately before the pants.

Solution is on page 146.

	boss	daughter	mother	sister	wife	pants	shoes	sportscoat	tie	windbreaker	1st	2nd	3rd	4th	5th
Amy															
Betty															
Gemma															
Karen															
Marge															
1st															
2nd															
3rd															
4th															
5th															
pants															
shoes															
sportscoat															
tie															
windbreaker															

32   MR. BELL'S TOLLS

by Michael D. Akers

Mr. Bell takes the turnpike on his daily commute. One morning he forgot to stock up with change for the tollgates. These are automatic tollgates that open only for exact change and, to his dismay, he was at the first of five gates with no change and no way to exit. He parked in the emergency lane and by scrounging through the seat cushions, ashtray, and the glove-compartment came up with fifteen coins (quarters and dimes only) that totalled the exact amount needed to go through all five tollgates. From the clues below, can you determine the amount of toll and the combination of coins required for each tollgate?

1. The toll and combination of coins are not the same for any two tollgates. No fewer than two coins were used at each tollgate.

2. Fewer coins were used at tollgate #5 than at tollgate #2. However, the toll at tollgate #5 is greater than that of tollgate #2.

3. Fewer coins were used at tollgate #1 than at tollgate #2. However, the toll at tollgate #1 is greater than that of tollgate #2.

4. At tollgate #5 (which cost less than $1.00) Mr. Bell used an equal amount of quarters and dimes.

5. The toll at tollglate #4 is twice that of tollgate #2.

6. The toll at tollgate #3 equals that of tollgate #1 and tollgate #2 combined.

Solution is on page 146.

toll	quarters	dimes	total
#1			
#2			
#3			
#4			
#5			

33 MUSICAL CONTESTANTS

by Kevyn Dymond

Every spring, high school students from Summerville and surrounding areas enter the annual classical music competition. The top five finishers are awarded scholarships to the Winters Conservatory of Music. This year, Amy, Nick, and the other three winners each played a different instrument and each performed music in a different key. From the clues provided, can you determine each winner's full name (one last name is Jones), instrument (one was oboe), and the key performed in (one was A major), along with the final order they finished in, first through fifth?

(Note: Voice is considered an instrument.)

1. The student who performed in G major finished higher than Don, who finished higher than the singer, who finished higher than Jane.

2. Harper finished higher than the flute player but not as high as the student who played in F major.

3. No student has the same first and last initial.

4. Young finished one place higher than the boy who played in C major.

5. The cello player's piece was not in G major.

6. Murphy didn't finish as high as the piano player, who didn't finish as high as the girl who played in D major, who didn't finish as high as Perkins.

7. Peggy isn't the singer, who isn't Harper.

Solution is on page 147.

	Harper	Jones	Murphy	Perkins	Young	cello	flute	oboe	piano	voice	A	C	D	F	G	1	2	3	4	5
Amy																				
Don																				
Jane																				
Nick																				
Peggy																				
1																				
2																				
3																				
4																				
5																				
A maj.																				
C maj.																				
D maj.																				
F maj.																				
G maj.																				
cello																				
flute																				
oboe																				
piano																				
voice																				

34 DOG DAYS BEGIN

by Kevyn Dymond

The Barker County Animal Shelter's Adopt-A-Pet program just got underway. On the first day, six formerly lonely dogs found happy new homes with six different couples. For each of the six dogs (including a collie and a German shepherd), can you determine its new owners (three husbands are Carl, Gary, and Larry; four wives are Cathy, Ginger, Lori, and Pam; two last names are Goodman and Taylor), and the color of its new home (two house colors are blue, and green), and the home's street (including Grove, Lincoln, Princeton, and Temple)?

1. For each of the six adoptions the husband's name, the wife's name, their last name, the color of the house, the street it's on, and the breed of dog adopted all begin with different letters of the alphabet.

2. The six couples are the Bunsens, Theresa and her husband, Paul and his wife, Brenda and her husband (who live in a lavender house), Ted and his wife, and the poodle's new owners.

3. The Petrinis didn't adopt the Labrador.

4. The tan house isn't Bob's or Paul's.

5. The poodle's new home isn't charcoal.

6. The Carters didn't adopt the beagle (who isn't the new member of Theresa's Chestnut Street household).

7. There are no pink houses on Broadway.

8. The Landry's didn't adopt the terrier.

9. Bob and Theresa are twins.

Solution is on page 147.

husband	wife	last name	breed	color	street

35 WHAT'S IN THE BASEMENT?

by Mary A. Powell

When the Browns went out of town last week, they hired the 12-year-old twins from next door to feed their fish and watch their house. The day before the Browns' return, the twins heard a strange noise coming from the basement. "Maybe it's a ghost!" said one. "Or a vampire!" "Don't be stupid," countered her brother. "You read too many horror stories. There are no such things as ghosts, and everyone knows vampires don't come out during the day. It's probably a burglar." THAT thought scared both of them. "We have to go tell Mom," said the terrified girl. "No!" countered the boy, who had by then recovered his bravado. "This is our job." Fate intervened in the form of three other neighbor children who were riding by on their bicycles. The twins hailed them and quickly explained their fears. Between them, the children decided to look in all of the basement windows before seeking adult help. But first, each went to his own home and grabbed a useful tool. As they explored, they each had a different idea about what they were seeking (one thought it might be bats). One idea even proved to be right. From the following clues, can you find the full names of the children (one last name is Barber), what each thought might be found, and the tool each carried?

1. The boy who grabbed the flashlight saw something shiny. "Maybe it's gold," said one of the other boys.

2. "I'll bet it's a bunch of giant spiders," shrieked one girl; the other girl carried an umbrella as a weapon.

3. "It could be a baby possum," suggested one child. "We had one in our basement last year." Calvin doesn't live in a house with a basement.

4. "Maybe it's my cat," said another child. "She didn't come home last night." Erica doesn't have a cat.

5. The Farmer child and Bobby live across the street from the twins; neither was the one who had grabbed the hammer.

6. The Weaver boy lives next door to the twins.

7. Neither Jenny nor Jeremy nor the Spinner child guessed what was really in the basement, nor did any of them carry the hoe.

8. Calvin has no sisters.

9. Jenny didn't carry the hammer, and the Farmer child didn't carry the hoe. Jenny is not Farmer.

10. Erica wasn't the child who grabbed the cordless phone and she doesn't live in a house with a basement.

11. The children did not find gold or bats in the basement.

Solution is on page 148.

	Barber	Farmer	Spinner	Weaver	bats	cat	gold	possum	spiders	flashlight	hammer	hoe	phone	umbrella
Bobby														
Calvin														
Erica														
Jenny														
Jeremy														
flashlight														
hammer														
hoe														
phone														
umbrella														
bats														
cat														
gold														
possum														
spiders														

36 RUSH HOUR

by M. F. Gerstell

Every day, rush hour finds Imogene and five of her friends driving home on various freeways, including Freeway 10. Last Thursday was no different. One of the six commuters was driving a white car, and no two cars were the same color. From the clues below, can you determine each commuter's car color, speed, and freeway number?

1. Each commuter was driving at a different speed that was an exact multiple of 5 mph; the slowest was 5 mph and the fastest was 35 mph.

2. The woman in the red car was going faster than the woman on the 405 Freeway, but slower than Harriet, whose speed had no digit in common with Leopold's.

3. The man on the 110 Freeway was going slower than the man in the silver car, but faster than Kenneth.

4. The blue and black cars were on the highest-numbered and lowest-numbered freeways, not necessarily in that order.

5. Michael was going exactly three times as fast as Juliana, who was going exactly twice as fast as the driver of the black car.

6. The green car was going exactly 5 mph faster than the car on the 134 Freeway.

7. The car on the 101 Freeway was going twice as fast as the car on the 210 Freeway.

Solution is on page 148.

	10	101	110	134	210	405	black	blue	green	red	silver	white	speed					
Harriet																		
Imogene																		
Juliana																		
Kenneth																		
Leopold																		
Michael																		
speed																		
black																		
blue																		
green																		
red																		
silver																		
white																		

37 THE AMATEUR ARTISTS

by Frank W. Alward

Each year, usually in late April or early May, The Case City Artists Guild holds a show for aspiring amateur artists. It started out to be just a local event but through the years it has become a state-wide festival. This year over two hundred paintings were on display, and a few of them were from out-of-state entrants. Cory and four other local artists were honored by winning the five top awards. Each painted a different subject, and each has a different full-time occupation (one is an electrician). Your task, using the following clues, is to determine each man's full name, the winning position of his painting, the subject of his work, and his occupation.

1. Neither Dana (who did not paint the floral arrangement) nor Mr. Hayes won first prize.

2. Mr. Pruett (who is not Greg) painted neither the mountain panorama nor the self-portrait.

3. The carpenter (who is not Basil) did not place as high as either Kent or Mr. Torino, but he placed higher than Mr. Baxter (who did not select a floral theme).

4. The automobile mechanic placed higher than Greg, but not as high as Mr. Hayes.

5. Mr. Vaughn placed lower than the man who works in a florist shop and at least one other artist, but higher than the man who painted the seascape.

6. The landscape (which was not painted by Dana) placed higher than both Basil's painting and the self-portrait, but not as high as the plumber's effort.

7. The floral painting (which did not place third) was the work of neither the plumber nor the florist.

Solution is on page 148.

	Baxter	Hayes	Pruett	Torino	Vaughn	carp.	elect.	flor.	mech.	plum.	floral	land.	pan.	sea.	self	1	2	3	4	5
Basil																				
Cory																				
Dana																				
Greg																				
Kent																				
1															
2															
3															
4															
5															
floral										
land.										
pan.										
sea.										
self.										
carp.					
elect.					
florist					
mech.					
plumb.					

38 AUNT MARTHA'S CELLAR

by Susan Zivich

"A canner can can anything that she can," sang Bob and Bonnie as they waltzed into Aunt Martha's steamy, spicy kitchen. "Did you make any of your wonderful jam this year?" Bob asked. But Aunt Martha was not only a superb cook, she was also a first-class tease. "I've canned corn and fifteen other things this summer, and fixed them all up into four rows of four sections. And if you can figure out where everything is without peeking, you can each take home a few jars of your favorite!" Aunt Martha kept them entertained while they gobbled up slices of home-baked bread with her delicious jams. Can you figure out how Bob got his strawberry jam and Bonnie enjoyed her pear butter? Note: All directions indicated are from the viewpoint of a person looking at Aunt Martha's canning.

1. The peach jam is next to the green beans.

2. The tomato sauce is right above the stewed tomatoes and next to the cucumber pickles.

3. The blackberry jam is on the right end of the third row down.

4. The zucchini pickles are not next to the pear butter.

5. The two fruit butters are in the same column.

6. The pickled beets are just to the right of the strawberry jam in the same row.

7. The three vegetables are in the same row.

8. The orange marmalade is right above the carrots.

9. All four jams are in different rows and different columns.

10. The cucumber pickles and zucchini pickles are in the same column, but neither is in the bottom row.

11. The apple butter is to the right of the grape jelly and to the left of the apricot jam, in the same row.

Solution is on page 149.

	A	B	C	D
1				
2				
3				
4				

39 PSYCHIC MISCUES

Five friends (Delta, Gloria, Karen, Nadia, and Tanya) had heard so many good reports about the psychic talents of Madam Zelda, the hostess at the local Gypsy Tea Room, that they had lunch there one day to get their fortunes told. Madam Zelda circulated among the tables and gave patrons free readings based on any one of five psychic processes (astrology, crystal ball, palm reading, tarot cards, or tea leaves); each of the five (Carter, Forrest, Howe, Moran, and Smythe) chose a different one of those methods. Madam Zelda's predictions for them were fairly standard: one would meet a handsome stranger, another was told to expect a minor medical problem, a third would come into unexpected money, a fourth was warned of problems with a family member, and the last would travel soon. A month later, the friends returned to the Tea Room and discussed how accurate Madam Zelda had been. They discovered that although none had experienced the event predicted for her, each of the predictions had come true for another one of the five. The five events (in the comparable sequence of the predictions above) were: meeting a handsome IRS auditor, spraining an ankle, winning $500 in a lottery, having a son accused of vandalism, and being sent on an unexpected business trip. From the following clues, can you identify each woman's full name, psychic process chosen, prediction given, and result experienced?

1. The five friends are: the one who chose astrology, the one for whom a family problem was predicted, the one who sprained her ankle, Nadia, and Mrs. Howe.

2. Tanya's prediction was experienced by Mrs. Moran; Tanya's experience had been predicted for the woman who won the lottery.

3. Neither Delta nor the one who had her palm read had the handsome stranger prediction or the handsome IRS auditor result.

4. The woman for whom money was predicted actually took the unexpected business trip; in some order, Mrs. Carter and Nadia had the travel prediction and the lottery winning result.

5. The woman who had the tarot card reading experienced the result predicted for the woman who had her tea leaves read.

6. The prediction given for Mrs. Forrest (who is not Tanya) was experienced by Gloria; Mrs. Forrest experienced the result predicted for the woman who had the crystal ball-reading.

7. Karen had neither the family problem prediction nor the related result.

8. No two women had direct exchanges of predictions and results.

Solution is on page 149.

		Carter	Forrest	Howe	Moran	Smythe	astrology	crystal ball	palm reading	tarot cards	tea leaves	prediction					result				
												meet stranger	minor/ medical	money	problem/ family	travel	meet auditor	sprain ankle	win $500	son/ vandal	business trip
Delta																					
Gloria																					
Karen																					
Nadia																					
Tanya																					
result	auditor																				
	sprain																				
	$500																				
	vandal																				
	trip																				
prediction	stranger																				
	medical																				
	money																				
	family																				
	travel																				
astrology																					
crystal ball																					
palm reading																					
tarot cards																					
tea leaves																					

HARD LOGIC PROBLEMS

40 TWINS AND MORE TWINS

by Mary A. Powell

It was Twins Day at Memorial Hospital, an annual event at which all twins born at the hospital gather for a picnic with their friends and families. This year, the twins who attended ranged in age from 3 days to 82 years. Although many of the twins are identical, four sets are brother-sister twins, and all eight were named after their grandfathers. Of these, the boys carry the first name of the paternal grandfather and the middle name of the maternal grandfather, while the twin sister has the feminine version of the grandfathers' names in reverse, i.e., the girl's first name is that of the maternal grandfather and the middle name that of the paternal grandfather. (Example: A Phillip George might have a twin sister named Georgina Philippa.) Three of these four sets of twins are related, so the naming practice is family tradition. The parents of the fourth set had read about the other three in the newspaper, and decided to follow their example. This year, there was a newspaper story about all eight twins, accompanied by a photograph of the four female twins. From the following clues, can you find the full *maiden* names of the four in the picture (one maiden name is Brooke; middle names are Christine, Danielle, Olivia, and Ronalda), as well as their ages? (Note: Married women took their husbands' last names, which were then passed on to their children).

1. Claudine and her brother are twice as old as Gabriella and her brother.

2. One Petrillo twin is the mother of the Holcomb twins; one Slater twin is the mother of the Petrillo twins.

3. Cristopher and his sister are 20 years older than Ronald and his sister.

4. Martina and her brother are not the 5-year-old twins.

5. Daniel and his twin are four years younger than Antoinette and her twin.

6. Gabriella's Uncle Oliver made faces at his twin sister while the photo was being taken.

Solution is on page 150.

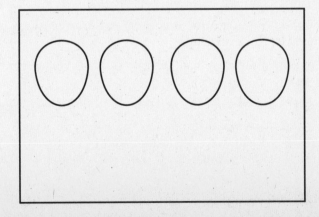

41 THE HALLOWEEN BALL

by Frank W. Alward

Six couples attended a Halloween ball, each in a different costume. One of the husbands dressed as a vampire. Your task, using the following clues, is to determine the first and last names of each of the six couples, and the costume each wife and husband wore.

1. Michael's wife (who was not the woman who wore the cat costume) is not Margie (whose husband is not the man who wore the elephant outfit), Angela, Linda, or Della.

2. Mrs. Coleman (who isn't Beverly) was neither the skunk (whose husband did not dress as an elephant) nor the cat (who was not Yvonne).

3. Neither Mrs. Moore (whose husband is not the man who wore the monster costume) nor Mrs. Wilkins is Della (who is not Willard's wife), Angela, or Margie; nor did Della, Angela, or Margie dress in the cat costume.

4. The man in the dinosaur suit was neither Mr. Kelso (whose wife did not dress as the skunk) nor Mr. Coleman; nor did Mr. Kelso wear the elephant costume.

5. The woman in the skunk costume (who is not Marcus's wife) was neither Mrs. Yemen nor Quinn; nor is the skunk married to either of the men who wore the lion or robot costume.

6. The woman who wore the clown costume is neither Della (whose husband did not dress as an elephant) nor Angela (whose spouse did not wear the robot costume); nor is either Della or Angela Mrs. Coleman.

7. The monster (who is not Della's husband) was not Willard; nor is the clown (who is not Michael's wife) married to the monster.

8. Leonard (who is neither Mr. Quinn nor Kelso) did not wear the robot suit; nor did his wife dress as either a cat or a skunk.

9. Neither Angela (who is not the woman who wore the witch's outfit) nor Linda (who did not dress as a clown) is the woman who disguised herself as a monkey (who is not Howard's wife).

10. Neither Danny (who was not the dinosaur) nor Marcus (who was not the elephant) is either Mr. Kelso or Quinn.

11. Neither Mrs. Yemen (who is not Della) nor Mrs. Quinn is the woman who dressed as a ghost.

12. Neither Beverly (who was not the skunk) nor Linda is Mrs. Yemen.

13. Mrs. Moore (who is not Beverly) did not wear the cat outfit.

Solution is on page 150.

42 MOVIE RATINGS

by Evelyn B. Rosenthal

The movie critic in the "Daily Bugle" rates films on a scale of one to ten points. Recently, five movies of different types opened at different theaters around town and all received different ratings. From the following clues, can you find the theater and rating for each film?

1. The comedy was rated one point higher than the science-fiction film.

2. The romance was not at the Plaza.

3. The film at the Adelphi was rated twice as high as the spy film, which did not get the lowest rating of the five.

4. The film at the Rialto was rated one point higher than the one at the Plaza.

5. No film was rated eight or higher.

6. The romance was rated twice as high as the horror film.

7. The film at the Tower was rated one point above the one at the Bijou.

Solution is on page 151.

	Adelphi	Bijou	Plaza	Rialto	Tower	ratings				
comedy										
horror										
sci-fi										
spy										
romance										
ratings										

43 TRIVIAL RISK

by David Champlin

Competition on "Trivial Risk" is keen, and the daily championship is often decided on the "Ultimate Risk" category that ends the program. During this round, the contestants wager any or all of their day's winnings on their ability to answer a trivia question on a specific subject. Last week, a different champion was crowned on each of the five shows that aired Monday through Friday, and in each case that champion won the game by being the only contestant able to answer the "Ultimate Risk" question correctly. Each champion won a different amount of money. From this information and the clues, determine the full name of each champion (one first name is Cathy), the category that helped each winner triumph, the amount of money each won, and the order in which the five won their games.

1. Mr. Gonzalez won the championship the day before Althea, who won her game before the person who gave the correct answer in African history.

2. Monday's champion won $2,000 more than Brian, who won $2,000 more than the person who correctly answered the TV Commercials of the Past question. Jones won $2,000 more than Foster. (Note: All five champions are listed in this clue.)

3. Eric won $1,000 more than Thursday's winner. Ives won more money than the person who answered the question on inorganic chemistry. (Note: Four different people are mentioned in this clue.)

4. The five daily champions were David, Jones, the woman who answered the question about Italian opera, the person who won $11,000, and Friday's winner.

5. The person who correctly answered the question about the American Revolution, who didn't win on Monday, won earlier in the week than the one surnamed Han.

6. Both Althea and Foster are schoolteachers.

7. Both Eric and Han (who didn't answer the questions about TV commercials or African history) read an encyclopedia before competing on the show.

Solution is on page 151.

first name	last name	subject	amount won	day

44 PAPER NICKEL WEST

by Kevyn Dymond

Paper Nickel Restaurant became quite successful by offering "the Paper Nickel combo" (choice of sandwich, side dish and beverage) for $5. So successful was this strategy that a second restaurant recently held its grand opening. As a promotional ploy, the first five people in line outside Paper Nickel West when it opened each got to order a paper nickel combo for five cents. Furthermore, each of the five ordered a different type of sandwich, a different type of side dish, and a different type of beverage. From the clues below, can you determine each patron's first name, last name (one is Glass), their place in line (first through fifth) and their choice of sandwich, side dish (one had corn on the cob), and beverage (one had cola)? Note: Ann is a woman. Lee, Pat, Sal, and Viv could be either men or women; part of the problem is to determine the gender of each.

1. The person who had a baked potato (who didn't have lemonade) stood in line immediately between two women.

2. The person who had a patty melt (who isn't Zabel) stood in line immediately between two men.

3. The person who had a BLT and the person who had root beer are both women.

4. Chase and the person who had onion rings are both men.

5. Viv stood somewhere ahead of the person who had a cheeseburger and somewhere behind Whyte.

6. The person who had chili stood somewhere behind Miles (who isn't Sal) and somewhere ahead of the person who had fruit punch.

7. Lee was the fourth person in line.

8. The first person in line was a woman.

9. The person who had chocolate milk stood immediately ahead of the person who had a tuna melt; these two are of different sex.

10. Sal (who didn't have a hamburger) stood immediately ahead of the person who had fries, who stood somewhere ahead of the person who had root beer.

Solution is on page 152.

#	first name	last name	sandwich	side dish	beverage
1					
2					
3					
4					
5					

45 THE MOBILE GROCER

by Frank W. Alward

Grocery-deliverer Bill Gorman Sr. began serving the rural area of Case County in 1950. The first summer was difficult but as people got to know him and depend on him, his business picked up, and by the following summer he was operating well into the black. He took special requests for hard-to-find items, whether they were in the grocery line or not, and the farmers liked that. His first six customers on Tuesday morning were a little hard to get to know, but eventually, they turned out to be the best ones on his route. He overcame the growing popularity of the supermarkets by offering his customers superior quality of both his products and service. None of his customers objected to paying slightly more as all of them figured he was worth it. Mr. and Mrs. Crocker laughingly called him "the best want-ad section in the county." When he retired, his son took over and continued running the business. Bill Gorman Jr. had been his dad's right-hand man for several years and all the farmers both knew and liked him, and the first six stops on Tuesday morning were still the best ones. Your task, using the following clues, is to determine each customer's first and last name, the main product of each couple's farm, and the sequence of Bill's first six Tuesday morning stops.

1. Bill stops at the Perkins farm (which is not the cherry orchard) immediately before he visits Melanie and her husband (who do not grow peaches), which is one stop before the dairy farm.

2. Bill calls on Bert and his wife (who do not raise corn) after he stops at the Atkins place and before he does business with the Putnams.

3. Dirk and his wife (who is not Mitzie) are not his sixth stop.

4. Neither Mitzie (who is not Hugh's wife) nor Laurie is married to Lucas (who does not raise apples).

5. Carrie and her husband do not grow corn, wheat, or cherries.

6. Bill stops at Tangie's (who is not Mrs. Atkins) immediately after he leaves the Durhams' (whose crop is not peaches) and immediately before he sees the cherry orchard owners (who are not Melanie and her husband).

7. The dairy farmer (who is not Mr. Durham) is married to neither Candice nor Tangie.

8. Neither Bert (who does not grow wheat) nor Walter is Mr. Rutgers.

9. Bill visits Walter before he calls on Claude (who does not grow corn); however, neither's farm is either his first or sixth stop.

10. Three of Bill's stops, in consecutive order, are the Atkinses (who do not own the cherry orchard), Candice, and the couple who raise peaches.

Solution is on page 153.

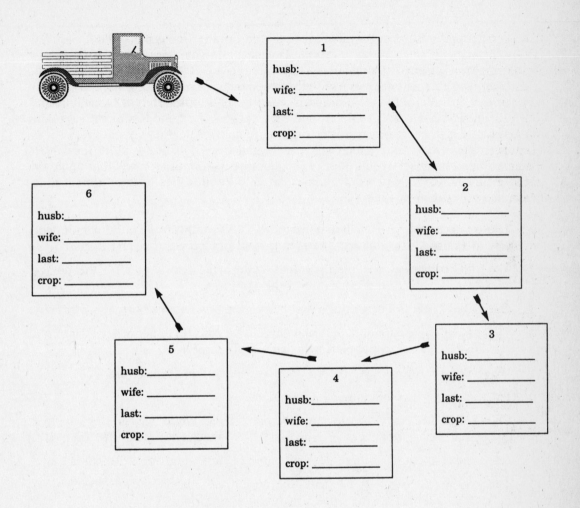

1

husb:_____

wife: _____

last: _____

crop: _____

2

husb:_____

wife: _____

last: _____

crop: _____

3

husb:_____

wife: _____

last: _____

crop: _____

4

husb:_____

wife: _____

last: _____

crop: _____

5

husb:_____

wife: _____

last: _____

crop: _____

6

husb:_____

wife: _____

last: _____

crop: _____

46 GLITCH-FREE VACATIONS

by Kevyn Dymond

One of the conditions of employment at the Glitch Corporation is a mandatory annual (all-expenses-paid) three-week vacation. During a six-day period last August, six Glitch employees, each of whom holds a different job at Glitch, departed on vacations, all to European destinations. Each of the six people departed on a different day (Monday through Saturday), flew to a different country, and took different color luggage. From the clues below, can you determine each person's first and last name (one surname is Quinn), whether male (as is George) or female (as is Mary), vacation destination (one person flew to Greece), color of luggage, and job title (one is the CMP: cafeteria-menu planner). Note: Four of the employees have first names that could be either men's or women's (Chris, Frankie, Pat, and Robin); part of the problem is to determine the gender of each.

1. These four people departed on consecutive days (in this order): the person who flew to Finland, Ms. Zimmer, the person with orange luggage, and Robin.

2. The VSC (vacation-schedule coordinator) departed two days after the person who flew to Ireland; these two are of the same sex.

3. One person flew to Portugal the day before the one with red luggage departed.

4. These two people did not depart on consecutive days (in either order): The CCR (child-care-center receptionist), who did not fly to Sweden, and Hartke.

5. Wong departed three days before the man with yellow luggage did.

6. Pat was the SPA (swimming-pool attendant).

7. The OPD (office-party director) and the person with white luggage were the first and last to depart (not necessarily in that order); these two are of different sexes.

8. Chris departed at least three days after the person who flew to Romania did.

9. The woman who was the FLP (front-lobby pianist) departed the day after Valdez did and the day before the person with blue luggage did.

10. Frankie and Aames departed on consecutive days, though not necessarily in that order.

11. The person with green luggage departed two days before George did.

Solution is on page 153.

47 HOUSE AND GARDEN SHOW

by Mary A. Powell

The annual home and garden show was a popular event in Ridley, a wonderful day for buyers and sellers alike. The following Monday, the teachers at Ridley Middle School discussed the show over coffee. Five had attended for an entire morning or afternoon or evening, and each bought a product from an acquaintance. From the clues, can you find the full names (one first name is Marsha and one last name is Rodeno) of the five buyers and the five sellers, and the five items purchased (one was a fancy screen door)?

1. Norma and Mr. Taylor each bought something from a man.

2. Willard (a first name), Ms. Gavin, and the woman who sold a garden hoe all sold something to a man.

3. The porch swing and the item Mr. Bishop bought were sold in the morning; Carolyn sold something in the evening.

4. Pamela, Ms. Levy, Eric, and Mr. Young were at the show only during the afternoon.

5. These three sellers were never at the show at the same time — Fred, the woman who sold the blender, and Ms. Smith.

6. Jack, Mr. Vogel, and the person who sold the mop were never at the show during the same time.

7. Doris sold something in the morning; Ms. Hanson bought something in the evening.

8. Richard bought something in the morning; it was not the item Mr. King sold in the morning.

Solution is on page 154.

Solution is on page 154.

	buyer	item	seller
morning			
afternoon			
evening			

48 SANDY BAY FAMILIES

PART I: SANDY BAY CHILDREN

Gwen Emerson shook her head in amazement as she watched the group of children playing together. "I remember when my son Geoff was born and I worried because there were no children for him to play with. Soon the Dodges and the McKays moved in with their kids and then there was a baby boom in the neighborhood. Now, twelve years later, there are fifteen children in these seven homes!" Can you figure out to which family each child belongs and then determine their ages (all ages are in whole numbers)?

1. Every family, including the Simpsons, has from one to four children, with siblings at least two years apart in age.

2. Matt Dodge is the oldest child at 15; Spencer is the youngest at 3.

3. The five Montgomery children are cousins; Joey is the only boy.

4. Every girl has one sister.

5. Hannah is the oldest of the four McKay children.

6. Only the following pairs of children are the same ages: Hannah and Brett; Josh and Alan; Cameron and Joey; Cindy and Nicole.

7. Brett has an older brother. Geoff is younger than Brett.

8. Greg Robinson and Geoff are the only two who have no siblings.

9. Only one child has the same first and last initial. No siblings share a first initial.

10. Kate's older brother Alan likes to play with Sherry (Joey's sister), who is only a year younger than he.

11. Greg is midway in age between the Simpson children.

12. Kate is older than Cindy who is older than Joey who is older than Christine.

13. Sherry is five years older than Christine.

Now that you've met the children of Sandy Bay, it's time to meet their parents, including Jim, Norm and Brenda. Each family has a husband and wife with the same last name. Using the information you've gleaned from Part I, plus the information below, can you figure out each couple and determine who their children are?

1. There are two Rick's, but neither is married to Debbie.

2. Helen has two daughters, as do Debbie and Lynn.

3. Andy, Al, Dave and one of the Rick's have only sons.

4. Three of the mothers have the same initials as their sons; one mother has the same initials as her daughter. None of the fathers share the first initial of any of his children.

5. Debbie is Joey's mom; Marlene is not Matt's.

6. Dave is Geoff's godfather; Helen is not related to either Rick.

7. Dave has only one child, as does one of the Rick's.

8. Sheila is not married to Andy.

Solution is on page 154.

girls	boys	last name	mom	dad

49 MIS-MATCHMAKER, MIS-MATCHMAKER

by Randall L. Whipkey

After being hired to his first job as a computer programmer with Matchmaker, Matchmaker Dating Service, Morey Messabout immediately improved the program designed to pair clients based on their backgrounds and interests. Unfortunately, Morey didn't notice a bug in the program that caused men and women to be matched purely at random — sometimes even when they were total opposites. Fortunately, the couples didn't seem to notice, as the first five paired by Morey's program fell madly in love at first sight, and Morey earned a bonus for his creative mis-matchmaking. Can you find the full names (one surname is O'Hara) of each paired couple, their occupations (one person is a used-car dealer), and the one thing each likes to do most in his or her spare time (one loves an all-night party)?

1. Morey's program mismatched the woman employed as a tattoo artist with the man who enjoys quiet country walks.

2. Ms. Eastman is neither the person who is a pediatrician nor the person who is a history professor.

3. The man who works as a chimney sweep isn't paired with the woman who enjoys weekends in Las Vegas or the woman who enjoys playing in a string quartet.

4. Ula and the plumbing contractor are so pleased that Morey "matched" them that they have invited the programmer to their planned June wedding.

5. Ms. Chan wasn't mismatched with the man who enjoys racing motorcycles in his spare time.

6. Neither the woman who works as a television producer nor the woman who is a golf pro was paired with Julio.

7. Ms. Eastman and the man who enjoys watching professional wrestling are one happy couple.

8. The woman who enjoys heavy-metal concerts isn't the tattoo artist.

9. Ms. Berger's mismatched mate isn't the man who works as a choir director.

10. Huey, who is a patent attorney, was mismatched with Ms. Dove, who enjoys reading romance novels.

11. Miss Chan is neither the woman who enjoys weekends in Las Vegas nor the woman who enjoys playing in a string quartet.

12. Greg, who isn't the history professor, wasn't paired with the woman who is a television producer.

13. Mr. Lopez' mismatched partner, who enjoys heavy-metal concerts, convinced him to accompany her to a show by her favorite group, the DedHeds; he liked the concert but still prefers his own pastime.

14. The person who enjoys a lonely beach at sunset isn't the plumbing contractor.

15. Neither Frank nor Greg is the choir director.

16. Sally Adams is now engaged to her mismatch, the man who enjoys an evening with the film "Casablanca."

17. Ms. Eastman, who isn't Ula, isn't the heavy-metal enthusiast.

18. Mr. Lopez contacted Matchmaker, Matchmaker Dating Service at the urging of his best friend, the plumbing contractor.

19. The pediatrician was paired with Ian Nicks.

20. Ms. Berger and her mismatch are very happy together but have not made any wedding plans.

21. Ms. Dove isn't the tattoo artist.

22. The plumbing contractor isn't the man who enjoys quiet country walks.

23. Mr. King, who isn't Frank, isn't the man who enjoys watching professional wrestling.

24. Neither Frank nor Julio is Teresa's mismatch by Morey.

25. Ricki wasn't paired with the pro-wrestling fan.

26. Val, who isn't the woman who enjoys weekends in Las Vegas, isn't the one who was mismatched with Mr. Marinovich.

Solution is on page 155.

woman	job	enjoys	man	job	enjoys

50 HOUSE PAINTING

by Mary A. Powell

Last summer, Josh and Jerome were 15-year-old twins with big plans and little money. Summer jobs were scarce and they dreamed of a fancy car. Then serendipity intervened. Their enterprising uncle bought a train load of salvage, which included a truck load of house paint. "Here's your chance, boys," he said. "I'll sell you this paint for my cost and you can paint houses for the summer." Their hopes were dampened only slightly when they discovered there were only seven colors, one of which was black, but they were as enterprising as their uncle. First, they painted their parents' home, partly for practice and partly for public relations. Next, they made up flyers with pictures of houses in various three-tone color combinations and tacked them up all over town. Third, they called everyone in the phone book whose last name was the same as one of the colors they had available and offered them a special discount. Their first five customers, including the Greens, were so lavish with their praise and recommendations that by mid-summer the boys had to hire helpers. From the following clues, can you find the names of their first five customers and the three colors (main color plus two trim colors) each chose?

1. Of the six colors used for trim, three houses have white trim, two have cream, two have green. One main color is gray.

2. No two houses have more than two colors in common.

3. The Whites' house color is the same as a trim color on the Browns' house.

4. The Grays' house color is the same as a trim color on the white house and the brown house.

5. No one chose both green and blue.

6. One family chose neither white nor gray.

7. The Blacks chose one color no one else chose.

8. The Whites do not have the white house.

9. The green house has no more than one color in common with any other house; the green and blue houses have no colors in common.

Solution is on page 156.

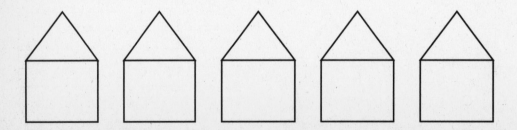

51 GUESS WHO'S COMING TO DINNER

by Mary Marks Cezus

Five new brides gave their first dinner parties last month. Each used her new silver, no two of the same pattern or of the same cost. No two dinner parties had guests having the same relationship with the bride and no two parties were on the same date. Using the clues below can you determine each woman's first name, her silver pattern, her guests, the date of her party (the 4th, 10th, 16th, 25th, or 27th), and the cost of her silver ($245, $285, $440, $650, or $830)?

1. The woman who used the Toccata silver (which cost less than the silver used at the party at which the bride's grandparents were her guests) scheduled her party for later in the month than Edith's party.

2. There were more than ten days between the party at which the Vivace was used and the party with the bride's boss.

3. Cara's silver (which was not used when the in-laws were guests) cost more than twice as much as the silver used at the dinner party on the 4th.

4. The dinner party with the neighbors (at which the Rose Gold silver was not used) was later than the party given by Gwen (who did not use the Toccata silver).

5. The college roommate and her husband were guests at a dinner party later in the month than the party at which the Vivace silver was used.

6. Amelia's silver (which was not Toccata) cost more than that used on the 16th.

7. The Satin Frost silver cost more than the total of the cost of the silver owned by Inez (who did not invite her boss to dinner) added to the cost of the silver used at the dinner party with the neighbors.

8. The woman who used the Rose Gold silver (which did not cost $440) did not invite her boss to dinner.

9. The dinner party with the in-laws was earlier than the party at which Grande Plume (which is not Amelia's silver) was used, but later than the dinner party using the least expensive silver.

Solution is on page 156.

bride					
silver pattern					
guests					
date					
cost					

THE CONFUSING QUADRUPLETS

by Evelyn B. Rosenthal

The identical Smith quadruplets are usually very cooperative and help people tell them apart by wearing blouses and skirts of colors whose initials match the girls' names. For instance, Rose regularly wears a red blouse and a red skirt, Greta a green blouse and a green skirt. One week, however, they decided to mix things up as much as possible. After three days they had to stop, as they ran out of new ways to dress according to those rules. From the following clues, can you find how each girl dressed for those three days?

1. No girl was to wear her own color blouse or skirt or a blouse and a skirt of the same color; no one was to wear the same color blouse or skirt more than once; no blouse and skirt were to be worn together more than once; and on any one day, no two of the girls were to wear the same color blouses or the same color skirts.

2. On Monday, Tina wore a blue blouse; Greta did not wear a tan one.

3. On Tuesday, Betty wore a tan skirt; Rose did not wear a blue one.

4. On Wednesday, Greta did not wear a blue skirt.

Solution is on page 157.

girl	reg. color	Mon.		Tues.		Wed.	
		skirt	blouse	skirt	blouse	skirt	blouse

"SWAP MEET"

by David Champlin

The game show "Swap Meet," which airs Monday through Friday, attracts crowds of spectators because all the contestants are chosen from the studio audience. In order to attract the attention of host Travis Trader people dress in outlandish costumes. Creativity, ingenuity, and the willingness to make fools of themselves on national TV paid off last week for five people (including the one whose last name is Fox), as Travis not only noticed them, but gave them the chance to win the big prize! Each day's lucky contestant wore a different costume and won a different prize. From this information and the clues below, determine the full name of each winner, the costume each wore, the prize won, and the day each appeared on the show.

1. The man who wore the butterfly costume (who didn't appear on Monday's show) didn't win either the car or the boat.

2. The contestant who dressed as a rag doll was the big winner the day before the one who won new kitchen appliances. Elaine appeared on the show at least two days earlier than Hobson. (Note: Four different people are mentioned in this clue.)

3. Betty (who didn't appear on Wednesday's show) was neither the contestant who won new living room furniture nor the person who dressed up as an Egyptian mummy (who didn't win the boat).

4. The contestant who wore the clown costume appeared on the show earlier in the week than Chris, who appeared earlier than the contestant who won the car.

5. The five winners were, in no particular order: Allan, Guyarre, the one who dressed as a space alien, the one who won a vacation in Hawaii, and Friday's winner.

6. Mr. Indy didn't win either furniture or kitchen appliances.

7. Neither Chris nor Hobson had ever won anything before in their lives.

8. The contestant who won the boat appeared on the show the day before Ms. Jinn, who appeared the day before Dan.

9. The contestant dressed as the clown (who didn't win furniture) and the contestant dressed as the space alien didn't appear on consecutive shows.

Solution is on page 158.

first name	last name	costume	prize	day

54 THE ELKS' FLEA MARKET

by Frank W. Alward

Each year, the Case City Elks Lodge holds its annual Monday-through-Saturday flea market. This year gate prizes were awarded to some of the lucky visitors, which spiced up the attendance a bit. Mr. and Mrs. Ludden and five other couples decided to spend a day browsing to pick up a bargain or two. Each couple attended on a different day of the week and each pair was lucky enough to win a gate prize. Using the clues, discover each husband's and wife's first name (one wife is Glenda), surname, the day each couple attended, and the gate prize each pair won.

1. The portable tool grinder was not Mr. and Mrs. Dudek's gate prize.

2. Antonio and his wife attended one day before Tonyia and her husband, which was one day before the Dudeks.

3. The electric weeder was given away later in the week than the portable mixer (which was not Vincent's prize) but earlier than the oriental throw rug (which Tonyia and her husband did not win).

4. Malcolm and his wife attended later in the week than Carla and her husband.

5. Mr. and Mrs. Wooten shopped the day before Forrest and his wife but the day after the Yaklitzes attended, which was the day after the grinder was given away.

6. Both Sylvia and Connie admired the floor lamps a third couple won.

7. Rollo and his wife attended one day after Maxine and her husband and one day before Connie and her spouse.

8. Tonyia is not Mrs. Wooten.

9. Harvey is not Mr. Saddler.

10. The his-and-her leather jackets were a gate prize the day after the Neidays attended, which was the day after Sylvia and her husband shopped.

11. Connie is not Mrs. Yaklitz.

Solution is on page 158.

husband	wife	last name	prize	day

55 CLYDE'S BIRTHDAY POTLUCK

by Kevyn Dymond

Clyde Persiflage orchestrated a party in honor of his own 38th birthday. Not wishing to be swallowed up in a sea of faces, Clyde limited the invitations to five of his closest friends (one was Tina). Not wishing to cook, Clyde asked the five guests to bring a dish for potluck. At the conclusion of the festivities, Clyde patted himself on the back, for it was a fine birthday bash. From the clues below, can you determine the first and last names of each of the five guests (one first name was Phil), hair color, transportation to the party, the type of food each guest brought (one brought cheese), the type of gift each guest gave Clyde, and each guest's profession?

1. Mr. Rudman and his sister-in-law both have blond hair.

2. The person who gave Clyde cologne has red hair and walked to the party.

3. Harris and the dentist both rode bicycles to the party.

4. The person who brought salad and the person who gave Clyde slippers are both the same sex.

5. Fred and the person who gave Clyde the video both rode the bus to the party.

6. Ms. Kelly gave Clyde a CD.

7. The engineer and the person who brought bread both have brown hair.

8. North, deSilva, and the lawyer each took different types of transportation to the party.

9. The person who brought soup (who didn't take the bus) was neither Margo nor the tailor.

10. Sandra (who didn't give Clyde the board game) and deSilva have the same color hair.

11. The accountant and the one who brought pasta both took the same type of transportation to the party.

Solution is on page 159.

56 MIDNIGHT SNACKERS

by David Champlin

There were lights on in the kitchens of five different houses on Main Street late last night, each of which stands on a different corner between 1st Street and 5th Street inclusively. In each, a resident had been awakened for a different reason (one had a bad dream), and went to the kitchen for a snack. Each ate something different; one had cheese and crackers. From this information and the clues below, determine the full name of each snacker, the snack each enjoyed, the reason each woke up, and the numbered street on which each lives. Note: 1st Street is the furthest north, and 5th Street is the furthest south of the five streets.

1. Neither the man named Jay nor Ruiz ate ice cream.

2. None of the five has the same first and last initials.

3. The two male snackers (who do not live on consecutively numbered streets) were Mr. Martin and the man who was awakened by a wrong-number phone call.

4. The five persons in question were, in no particular order, Faye, Jackson, the one who ate a piece of pie, the one awakened by a barking dog, and the one who lives on 5th Street.

5. The man named Ray lives somewhere to the north of Flood, who lives one block north of the person who ate ice cream.

6. Mae lives one block north of the person who was awakened by a truck backfiring. The man who ate a sandwich lives at least two blocks north of Koji. (Note: Four different persons are mentioned in this clue).

7. Kaye doesn't live on 4th Street.

8. The person who ate a cupcake lives directly north of the woman who was awakened by her crying baby, who lives directly north of Ruiz.

Solution is on page 159.

	Flood	Jackson	Koji	Martin	Ruiz	cheese	cupcake	ice cr.	pie	sand.	baby	dog	dream	phone	truck	1st	2nd	3rd	4th	5th
Faye																				
Jay																				
Kaye																				
Mae																				
Ray																				
1st																				
2nd																				
3rd																				
4th																				
5th																				
baby																				
dog																				
dream																				
phone																				
truck																				
cheese																				
cupcake																				
ice cr.																				
pie																				
sand.																				

57 GREEN THUMBS

by W. Lee Moss

The Mendezes have seven children, all of whom like working in the family vegetable garden. This past Sunday through Saturday, all nine family members took part in planting this year's nine crops; each planted one crop; every day found at least one Mendez working his or her selected plot of ground. From the diagram provided and the clues, find each child's age and crop of choice, Mom and Dad's crop of choice, the day of the week each family member exercised the Mendez "green thumb" and the plot of ground where each crop will grow.

1. The oldest Mendez child planted the carrots in plot #6 two days before Anita planted the turnips; these two and their brothers and sisters are all of different ages; all seven children were born two years apart.

2. No two children worked a plot on the same day of the week; Mom worked the same day as the 19-year-old girl did and Dad worked the same day of the week as Ramona.

3. Gabriela's plot is between the cauliflower and the plot worked on Wednesday; the peas are between Carmen's plot and Dad's plot; none of these six different plots was planted by Mom.

4. The four corner plots are: the two plots planted on Tuesday, the one planted by the 7-year-old girl, and the radish plot; none of these is Mom's plot.

5. The girl who planted on Monday is six years older than Juan; the boy who planted on Sunday is two years older than the girl who planted on Thursday (Note: There are four different persons mentioned in this clue).

6. These three planted on consecutive days, in this order: Raphael, the one who planted the asparagus and Jose.

7. Julio's plot is adjacent to the eggplant; he planted three days after the 11-year-old did and four days after Rosita did.

8. Both the squash (which was planted by the 9-year-old) and the bean crop (which is not adjacent to the cauliflower) are adjacent to Mom's plot and both are on plots the numbers of which are higher than the number of the eggplant plot.

9. The child who planted the beans is younger than the child who planted the peas.

Solution is on page 160.

1	2	3
4	5	6
7	8	9

58 THE ROMANTIC LINE

by Randall L. Whipkey

Summerset Steamship Ltd. bills itself as "The Romantic Line" and backs up its pledge to foster love that lasts by making a unique offer: couples who get married aboard one of the company's five cruise ships receive a complimentary second honeymoon on any of the line's other four voyages. The first five couples who took advantage of this offer each were married on a different cruise and then enjoyed a second honeymoon on a different one of the cruises on which another couple had wed; one wedding and one second honeymoon were on board the *S. S. Guinevere*. Can you determine the full names (including the bride's maiden name) of each romantic couple, the cruise ship and its destination on which their wedding took place, and the cruise on which they took their second honeymoon?

1. Mr. & Mrs. Chedworth second-honeymooned aboard the ship on which Cary and his wife were married.

2. Judd's shipboard wedding wasn't to Bridget.

3. Dixie and Bob had their second honeymoon on the cruise on which Allison and her husband were married; the cruise isn't the one to Alaska.

4. Cary and his wife aren't the couple who wed on the Rio de Janeiro cruise.

5. The *S. S. Venus,* on which Rick and his wife have never cruised, sails to Hawaii.

6. Mr. North has never been on the Rio de Janeiro-bound boat.

7. The former Miss Goldman had her second honeymoon on the cruise on which Tara had her wedding.

8. Mr. & Mrs. Mullins, who weren't married on the Mediterranean cruise, didn't have their wedding on the *S. S. Cupid.*

9. Ted Valdez and his wife, who isn't the former Miss Jeffcoat, were married on the Alaskan cruise.

10. The former Miss Powell and her husband didn't take their second honeymoon on the Yucatan-bound liner.

11. Tara, who isn't Mrs. Chedworth, didn't marry Cary.

12. The former Miss Beaulieu has never been on the *S. S. Juliet.*

13. The former Wanda South and her husband, who isn't Mr. Butkus, second-honeymooned on the cruise to beautiful Rio de Janeiro.

14. Dixie and Bob were on two different cruises than the Chedworths.

15. No two of the couples were on the same two ships.

16. The former Miss Jeffcoat, who isn't Bridget, didn't have her wedding on the *S. S. Cleopatra.*

17. Mr. & Mrs. Butkus didn't get married aboard the *S. S. Juliet.*

18. The *S. S. Cupid* isn't the Summerset Steamship plying the Rio de Janeiro route.

The second honeymoon of

Mr. _____ _____

and Ms. _____ nee _____

who were married aboard the _____

en route to _____

will take place aboard the _____

en route to _____

The second honeymoon of

Mr. _____ _____

and Ms. _____ nee _____

who were married aboard the _____

en route to _____

will take place aboard the _____

en route to _____

The second honeymoon of

Mr. _____ _____

and Ms. _____ nee _____

who were married aboard the _____

en route to _____

will take place aboard the _____

en route to _____

The second honeymoon of

Mr. _____ _____

and Ms. _____ nee _____

who were married aboard the _____

en route to _____

will take place aboard the _____

en route to _____

The second honeymoon of

Mr. _____ _____

and Ms. _____ nee _____

who were married aboard the _____

en route to _____

will take place aboard the _____

en route to _____

Solution is on page 160.

59   COIN BRACELET

by Mark Marks Cezus

Penny's parents recently gave her a bracelet on which hung coins from six imaginary lands. No two coins were decorated with the same design and no two had the same date. Using the clues below, can you determine for the coin in each position, its land of origin, its decorative design, and the date on the coin (1897, 1910, 1921, 1944, 1952, or 1974)?

1. The coin from Zomoly (which was not decorated with the dolphin design) was older than both the one directly to the left of it and the one directly to the right of it.

2. There were exactly three coins between the coin from Cameria and the coin with the knight design.

3. The coin in #3 was newer than the coin with the pine cone design (which was not on the coin from Marita).

4. The coin with the castle design (which was not from Cameria) was older than all three coins to the left of it.

5. The #4 coin was older than the coin with the wolf design.

6. There were exactly two coins between the 1952 coin and the coin from Repona (which was newer than #2).

7. The coin with the castle was somewhere to the left of the coin from Kleinland.

8. Neither the oldest coin nor the newest coin was at either end.

9. The coin from Marita (which was not #2) was newer than the coin which had the dolphin design.

10. The design on the coin from Zomoly was neither the castle nor the pine cone.

11. The coin from Joraco (which was not the 1921 coin) was newer than and was the next coin directly to the left of the coin with the obelisk.

Solution is on page 161.

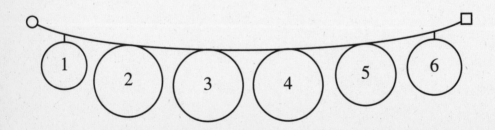

60 FLATBUSH FLYERS

by Robert Nelson

The Flatbush Flyers are a touring professional women's basketball team patterned after the Harlem Globetrotters. As part of their warm-up before each game, the five starting players on the team (Bobbi Block, Dora Dunk, Joni Jumper, Paula Pass, and Rona Rebound) do a ball-handling and passing routine. Standing in a circle, each player handles the ball three times, does some sort of stunt with it, and passes it to another player for a total of 15 steps. From the following clues, can you establish the sequence in which the players perform this routine?

1. The team's captain is both the first and last player to handle the ball.

2. Each player passes the ball to a different player each time she handles it and never returns the ball to the player she received it from.

3. Dora never passes the ball to nor receives it from Paula.

4. In the last five steps of the routine, each player holds the ball once; this is not true of the first five steps.

5. Rona never passes the ball to Joni, Joni never passes it to Bobbi, and Bobbi never passes it to Dora.

6. One player handles the ball for steps 3, 7, and 11; another handles it for steps 4, 10, and 13.

Solution is on page 162.

1: _____	6: _____	11: _____
2: _____	7: _____	12: _____
3: _____	8: _____	13: _____
4: _____	9: _____	14: _____
5: _____	10: _____	15: _____

61 MARJORIE MOVIESTAR

by David Champlin

To the great disappointment of her millions of fans all over the world, famous film actress Marjorie Moviestar recently announced her retirement from the screen. Marjorie's career has been short but brilliant; all five of her movies (each of which was a different type of film) have been huge box-office hits. In each film, Marjorie had as her costar a different handsome leading man. When asked for her reasons for leaving the cinema, Marjorie joked "So I can remember what color my hair really is" — a reference to the fact that she has been able to display her own naturally beautiful light brown hair in only one of her movies. In each of her other films, the producers insisted that she dye her tresses some other color; in no two of her movies did she have the same hair color. From this information and the clues given below, determine the order in which Marjorie's five movies were made, the actor who appeared opposite Marjorie in each movie, the title of each film, the genre of each film, and the color Marjorie's hair was for each role.

1. Marjorie played the title role in "Candy Rapper" just before she made her film with Lionel Limelight as her leading man, which she completed just before she started work on the film for which she dyed her hair black (which wasn't the science-fiction film).

2. Marjorie starred in the mystery just before she turned in an award-winning performance in "Barb Dwyer." She made the movie in which her costar was Richard Rolepadder sometime before she made the movie for which she dyed her hair platinum blonde. (Note: Four different films are mentioned in this clue.)

3. Marjorie's five films are: the musical (which wasn't her first film), "Donna Blitzen," the one for which she dyed her hair red, the one in which she costarred with Simon Scenestealer (who wasn't in the comedy), and her last movie.

4. Marjorie made the comedy just before she portrayed the title role in "Amber Wayves." She made the film for which she dyed her hair dark brown before, but not immediately before, she made the film in which she played opposite Greg Greasepaint. (Note: Four different films are mentioned in this clue.)

5. Marjorie once commented to an interviewer that she had loved making both the western movie and "Elda Barry," but that she had gotten little pleasure out of making either her fourth film or the one in which she had to work with vain and temperamental actor Brad Broadway.

6. Marjorie's two biggest box-office successes were "Amber Wayves" and the science fiction movie.

7. Marjorie didn't work with Simon Scenestealer (who wasn't in the western) and Richard Rolepadder (who wasn't in the comedy) in consecutive movies.

8. Marjorie's hair wasn't dark brown in "Candy Rapper."

9. "Barb Dwyer" wasn't the western.

Solution is on page 162.

102

Marjorie Morningstar appeared with
_____ hair

in her FIRST hit film _____

costarring _____

in the genre _____

Marjorie Morningstar appeared with
_____ hair

in her SECOND hit film _____

costarring _____

in the genre _____

Marjorie Morningstar appeared with
_____ hair

in her THIRD hit film _____

costarring _____

in the genre _____

Marjorie Morningstar appeared with
_____ hair

in her FOURTH hit film _____

costarring _____

in the genre _____

Marjorie Morningstar appeared with
_____ hair

in her FIFTH hit film _____

costarring _____

in the genre _____

62 MIXED DOUBLES TENNIS

by Randall L. Whipkey

In this year's Summerset Court Club's mixed doubles tennis tournament, Lisa and her partner, along with seven other female-male pairs, reached the quarterfinals. Against all odds, since no husband and wife are allowed to form a team by tournament rules, the elite eight pairs who reached the last rounds of the tournament were composed of eight married couples, including Ben and his wife. Given the information below about results in the last three rounds of tournament action, can you determine the full names of each pair of players reaching the quarterfinals and who defeated whom in the quarterfinals, semifinals, and finals of the net event?

1. Not only were no husband and wife paired as a team, but no husband and wife of the elite eight played against each other in the event.

2. Mr. Miller and Mrs. Clay played together last year but changed partners for this year's tourney.

3. In the quarterfinals, Carol and her partner played Hank and his.

4. In one round of play, Mr. Wright and his partner defeated Alice and her partner, 6-2 6-3, while Mrs. Minelli and her partner eked out a 7-6 6-7 6-4 win over Jay and his teammate.

5. In one match, Mark, who isn't Mr. Clay, and his partner opposed Debbie and her partner, whose serve was timed at 75 m.p.h.

6. Betsy and Mrs. Wright were partners in the Court Club's women's doubles, where they lost in a first round upset.

7. Mrs. Clay and Mr. Wright weren't partners in the mixed doubles.

8. In one match, Les Miller and his partner stopped Hank Finn and his.

9. In one round of action, Mrs. Clay and her partner upended Mr. Lieber and his and Mr. Brophy and his teammate handled Mrs. Finn and her partner.

10. Ron and his playing partner defeated Betsy and hers in one match.

11. Tanya is Mrs. Miller.

12. Mr. Brophy and his mixed doubles partner, who wasn't Alice, and Mrs. Minelli and hers won their way into the quarterfinals without losing a game.

13. Hank didn't partner Mrs. Wright in the event.

14. Ron and Mr. Minelli paired to win the Court Club's men's doubles.

15. In one match, Susan and her partner played against Mr. Plummer and his.

16. Tom and his mixed doubles teammate lost to Carol and her partner in one tournament match.

17. Steve's partner in the tourney wasn't Betsy.

18. Penny didn't pair with Mark for the event.

QUARTERFINALS

_____ _____   &   _____ _____   &   _____ _____   &   _____ _____ &

_____ _____   _____ _____   _____ _____   _____ _____

defeated   defeated   defeated   defeated

_____ _____   &   _____ _____   &   _____ _____   &   _____ _____ &

_____ _____   _____ _____   _____ _____   _____ _____

SEMIFINALS

_____ _____   &   _____ _____ &

_____ _____   _____ _____

defeated   defeated

_____ _____   &   _____ _____ &

_____ _____   _____ _____

FINALS

_____ _____ &

_____ _____

defeated

_____ _____ &

_____ _____

Solution is on page 163.

63 SHARED MEALS

by Mary A. Powell

While many restaurants recognize lighter appetites by permitting people to share a single meal, the Dining Palace actively encourages it. "No one likes to see food wasted," said the restaurant's manager, "so we decided to do something about it." Their new ads read: "Save room for dessert. Share a dinner with a friend." Since the new ad campaign began, their business has doubled, and nearly everyone orders dessert. Last Tuesday night, which is typically a slow business night, there were five couples who shared a dinner and a dessert. From the following clues, can you find the names of each pair, and the meat, vegetable (one was corn), and dessert each shared?

1. Susan and her companion were served after the steak dinner was served, but before the dinner which included cheesecake.

2. Bruce's table was served after Nancy's table, but before Rosalie's.

3. Jello was served before ice cream, which was served before cheesecake.

4. Clara and her friend dined together; Kristine ate with her mother.

5. Susan, Steve, and Bruce were seated at three different tables; none of them ordered fish.

6. Rosalie's dinner was served after the chicken dinner, but before the dinner which included green beans.

7. The pair who ordered ice cream were served after the two who ate peas, who were not served first.

8. The man who shared broccoli with his wife did not have meatloaf.

9. Robert and his companion did not have cheesecake.

10. Rosalie did not have pie, which was not served with peas.

11. Hilda and her companion didn't order chicken or steak.

12. Linda, who has no children, did not have pie or cake.

13. The two sisters ordered spinach; the two brothers ordered ham.

14. None of the men had jello or ice cream, neither of which was served with green beans.

15. Hilda has no sisters and no children.

16. Neither the meatloaf dinner nor the dinner which included spinach was served to the pair who ordered ice cream.

Solution is on page 164.

	bros.	friends	hus. & wife	mom & dau.	sist.	beans	broc.	corn	peas	spin.	cake	cheese cake	ice cr.	jello	pie
chicken															
fish															
ham															
meatloaf															
steak															
cake															
cheesecake															
ice cream															
jello															
pie															
beans															
broccoli															
corn															
peas															
spinach															

brothers		
friends		
husband & wife		
mom & daughter		
sisters		

64 HAPPY'S BIRTHDAY PRIZES

by David Champlin

When Henry "Happy" Happelmeyer celebrated his sixth birthday, the party included a number of games and contests enjoyed by the birthday boy and his friends. Happy's mother awarded the winner of each game a brand-new coloring book and crayons as a prize. The Lopez child and the other four winners each received a book about a different subject. No game was played more than once, and no child won more than one prize. From this information and the clues given below, determine the full name of each child who won a prize (one first name was Mary), the subject of each child's coloring book, the game each child won, and the order in which the five games were played.

1. None of the winners has the same first and last initials.

2. Nick, who is not Miyoshi, was neither the child who came closest to guessing the number of pennies in a jar nor the child who won the game of musical chairs.

3. The book about astronauts in space was awarded before at least one other book.

4. The children played darts just before they played the game won by the Miyoshi child. The game Leo won was played before, but not just before, the game won by the girl who received the coloring book about trolls. (Note: Four different games are mentioned in this clue.)

5. The five winners were, in no particular order, Karen, the Nash child, the one who won the musical chairs game, the boy who received a coloring book about dinosaurs, and the last one to win a prize.

6. The Kellogg child received a coloring book just before the child who won Pin the Tail on the Donkey, who won just before the child who received the book "Middle-Aged Wizard Lizards" (who was not Nick). None of these three children is Jeff.

7. The child who received the coloring book about tropical birds won the game played just before the one won by the Jordan child, whose win came just before that of the boy who won Drop the Clothespin.

Solution is on page 164.

65 HAPPY ACRES B'BALL

by Robert Nelson

Happy Acres High is a small school that has only seven players on this year's basketball team. Besides the five who start at the center, forward (2), and guard (2) positions, there is one substitute forward and one substitute guard; as necessary, one of the forwards relieves the center. By chance, the uniform numbers of the seven players use each of the ten numerical digits one time. From the following clues, can you identify each player's full name, position, and uniform number?

1. Stan's number plus Tower's number equals the substitute forward's number.

2. Jojo's number plus Young's number equals the higher starting guard number.

3. The sum of the two starting forwards' numbers is the same as the sum of the two starting guards' numbers.

4. In increasing (not necessarily sequential) numerical order, Nolan's number plus Tyrone's number plus White's number equals Lew's number.

5. The substitute guard's number is the next higher than Locke's number which is the next higher than Doug's number.

6. Buck and Craig (whose number is higher than Buck's) are, in some order, the center and Butcher.

7. The sum of all seven numbers is 99; the 0 is not used alone or as a first digit.

8. Aspin has the highest number, but the sum of his digits is the lowest of all players.

9. The sum of the digits of the substitute guard's number is the same as the sum of the digits of the substitute forward's number (one possibly being a single-digit number).

10. The seven players are: the one with #4, Buck, Craig, Aspin, Tower, and the two substitutes.

Solution is on page 165.

CHALLENGER LOGIC
PROBLEMS

66 FINAL STANDINGS

by Randall L. Whipkey

Last year, the four teams in the Summerset League battled through July for the Mayor's Trophy, awarded to the regular-season champion and prominently displayed by the winning team's business sponsor for the next twelve months. Each team played the other three teams four times during the month, with no two teams ending the season with the same won-loss record. Can you determine the final standings of the Summerset League, the sponsor and nickname of each team, its coach's full name (one first name is Ben), and the team's regular-season record?

1. Only the Mayor's Trophy-winning Morton's Feed Store team finished the season with a winning record; the champions swept all four games from the Yankees and split their series 2–2 with Coach Axelrod's squad.

2. The Dodgers lost their season series 1–3 to both the team coached by Cindy and the Loyal Order of Beavers nine.

3. The teams placing second and third in the standings went 2–2 against each other.

4. The Cubs won three of the four against the Readem & Weep Attorneys team, which isn't the one coached by Mike.

5. Axelrod didn't coach the Jeff's Gas & Go entry.

6. The Phillies coach, who isn't Mike, and Wallingford coached the league all-star team in post-season play.

7. Grabowsky didn't coach the Morton's Feed Store team.

8. The Loyal Order of Beavers squad wasn't coached by Wallingford.

9. Walt and Coach Bodine are the league's president and treasurer.

10. The Yankees and Grabowsky's team had the most heated rivalry, with all four games settled by two runs or fewer.

Solution is on page 166.

67 SUSSEX COUNTY FOOTBALL

by Robert Nelson

During football season, the nine high schools in Sussex County (Alton, Bakersville, Carbona, Dahlia Glen, Evanstown, Five Forks, Gardenia, Hogan's Hill, and Inkberry) all play one another. The team with the best record is crowned county champion. Each school has an animal nickname (Badgers, Bears, Bulldogs, Eagles, Hawks, Lions, Panthers, Rattlers, and Tigers) and the school's coaches are: King, Logan, Marx, Nolan, Osborn, Parker, Queen, Rather, and Shultz. From the following clues, can you identify each school's won-loss record, nickname, and coach?

1. No two teams had identical W–L records and no games ended in ties.

2. The nine teams are: Alton, Gardenia, the Rattlers, the Tigers, Coach Logan's, Coach Rather's, and the ones with 6–2, 4–4, and 2–6 records.

3. Inkberry beat the Lions and Coach Osborn's team, but lost to Carbona and Coach Marx's team.

4. The Badgers beat the Bulldogs, Hogan's Hill, and Coach Parker's teams; the Panthers lost to those three teams.

5. Bakersville won as many more games than Coach Shultz's team as it won less than the Eagles.

6. Evanstown lost the same number of games the Bears won and the Hawks won the same number that Coach Queen's team lost; the Bears won more than Queen, but fewer than the Hawks.

7. Coach Nolan's team won two more games than Coach King's and two fewer than Coach Rather's; among the other six teams, Dahlia Glen won two more than the Rattlers and two fewer than Five Forks.

8. The two teams with bird names (Eagles and Hawks) had more combined wins than the three teams with "B" mascot names (Badgers, Bears, and Bulldogs) who had more wins than the three cat mascot teams (Lions, Panthers, and Tigers).

9. The four pairs of teams whose combined win totals were nine were: the Hawks and Coach Parker's (neither of which is Gardenia); Inkberry and the Rattlers; Bakersville and Coach Logan's; and those with 2–6 and 7–1 records.

Solution is on page 167.

school	nickname	coach	w/l record

PUBLIC TELEVISION PLEDGES

by David Champlin

Recently, public television station KTTC in the city of Megalopolis had a pledge drive to raise funds for new programming. Among those who pledged their support for the first time were six people from Megalopolis and five surrounding communities. Each of these people was so impressed by a special program telecast during the pledge drive that he or she phoned in a pledge the very night the show was on. Each new subscriber phoned in on a different night (Monday through Saturday inclusive) and each made a different monthly pledge. From this information and the clues given below, determine the full name of each caller, each caller's home town, the show each caller was impressed by, the evening on which each patron phoned in a pledge, and the monthly amount pledged by each caller.

1. The caller who made the smallest pledge (which was $5 per month) phoned in the evening before Art, who called the evening before Ms. Bacon. The caller from Lakeview called in earlier in the week than the person who liked the documentary. (Note: Five different people are listed in this clue.)

2. Helen, who isn't from Bigg City or Farmville, didn't watch the opera.

3. The six callers were, in no particular order: Dorothy, Mr. Stone, the caller from Woodlawn, the one who liked the international animation special, the one who pledged $15 per month, and the one who phoned in on Saturday night.

4. The caller who liked the ballet best (who wasn't the last to call in) pledged $10 per month more than Monday's caller (who isn't from Woodlawn).

5. The caller who made the largest pledge (who didn't care for the Shakespeare play) called in earlier in the week than the Smallburg resident, who called in earlier than the man who liked *Whodunit?*. Loretta phoned in the night before Moore. (Note: Five different persons are mentioned in this clue.)

6. The person who phoned in on Tuesday night pledged twice as much per month as the person who liked the opera. The caller who lives in Farmville pledged twice as much as Walter, who pledged $5 per month more than Flores. (Note: Five different persons are listed in this clue.)

7. Ted pledged earlier in the week than Zander (who isn't from Lakeview), who pledged before, but not just before, the caller who lives in Bigg City.

8. The caller whose last name is Kato pledged more per month than Helen, (who pledged two days later than Kato). Neither of them liked the Shakespeare play.

9. The Farmville resident's pledge was larger than Ted's.

Solution is on page 167.

first name	last name	town	show	$	day

69 AUNT LORRAINE AND THE BRIDES

by Mary A. Powell

Aunt Lorraine is the relative who has traveled all over the world, has several ex-husbands, and has caused more than a few scandals. Her escapades are legendary and her charm is compelling, but she is so busy, she rarely returns to her home state. Nonetheless, Serena sent her a wedding invitation. "I'll be there with bells on," Aunt Lorraine wrote back. Serena was delighted, as was everyone else in the family. Then came the inquiries. "Would you mind if I held my wedding the same weekend rather than wait until spring?" Serena's cousin asked. "After all, Aunt Lorraine doesn't come around that often." "Oh, how fun. We can make plans together," Serena replied. Then Serena's only sister asked the same question, as did another aunt, and Serena's fiance's only sister. So five happy brides-to-be knocked on the door of Betty's Dressmaking Shop with "rush" orders. Betty's first reaction was to faint, but the brides were eager to make everything as easy as possible. Some gowns could be worn by more than one attendant. By the weekend of the weddings, Betty and her crew had made four white bridal gowns and ten attendants' gowns. Aunt Lorraine arrived on Thursday night, expecting to attend one wedding. Instead she heard about five! Fortunately the gown that was made for her fit perfectly. Then came the weekend of weddings — one on Friday evening, one Saturday afternoon, one Saturday evening, one Sunday afternoon, and one Sunday evening. The local newspaper covered it as a front-page event. From the following clues, can you find when each wedding was held, the full names of the bride and attendants (including Ann and Ms. Winchell) in each wedding, and the colors of the gowns in each wedding? (Note: Maids of honor are single women who have never been married; matrons of honor are women who are or have been married. Although brides took their husbands' names, only pre-wedding names are used here. Each woman mentioned was in one or more of the weddings.)

1. Lorraine's only sister was both a bride and a mother of the bride; this was her second marriage; the other brides had never been married before.

2. Pamela and Janine each had a maid of honor and three bridesmaids; Serena and Ms. Ripley each had a matron of honor and two bridesmaids; the other bride had a matron of honor and no bridesmaids.

3. Aunt Lorraine was in both the first and the fourth wedding.

4. Three brides chose their sisters to serve as maid (or matron) of honor.

5. In three consecutive weddings, Janine wore Valerie's green gown, her own white gown, and her own pink gown.

6. Ms. Taylor wore her new rose gown in the first wedding; someone else wore the same gown in the third wedding.

7. Blythe, Michele, and Ms. Cole all wore the same color in one wedding.

8. Ms. Fitzgerald and Diane were in one afternoon wedding; Cheryl was in the other.

9. Ms. Palmer was in two weddings; both took place in the evening.

10. In one evening wedding, Ms. Goodhue, a lady in a rose gown, Janine, and a Ms. Knight marched down the aisle — in that order. (Note: This was a traditional wedding; the bridesmaids were first and the bride was last; the bride may or may not be mentioned here.)

11. Ellen was a bridesmaid in two weddings; Serena and her sister were each in three weddings.

12. The two Knight brides were in each other's weddings; neither of the Hamilton brides was in the other's wedding.

13. Pamela wore Janine's pink gown as matron of honor in one wedding.

14. Green was worn in four weddings; Serena and Aunt Lorraine both wore green in one wedding.

15. Maids (or matrons) of honor did not wear the same color as the bridesmaids in any of the weddings.

16. One of the brides wore yellow as a bridesmaid in another bride's wedding; it was not Serena.

17. Either Michelle or Lorraine was in each of the five weddings; neither is Ms. Fitzgerald.

18. One bride is an only child.

19. The bride who wore her grandmother's champagne gown was in only one wedding.

Solution is on page 168.

bride					
maid/matron of honor					
color					
attendants					
color					
day					

70 LOST AND FOUND KIDS

by David Champlin

The Megalopolis Mall hired six security guards to patrol the walkways outside the stores. Though the guards' main duty was to deter and apprehend shoplifters, they also were called upon to help find children separated from their parents — and a good thing, too! In one week, a missing-child alert went out over the guards' walkie-talkies each day between Monday and Saturday inclusive. Fortunately, the Dodge child and the other five missing kids were quickly located by the guards and returned unharmed to their worried parents; one reason the children were discovered so quickly was that each was wearing a brightly colored nylon jacket that made them easy to spot (no two children wore the same color jacket). As it happened, each child was found in a different location by a different security guard. From this information and the clues below, determine the full name of each lost child (one first name is Francine), the color of his or her jacket, the day he or she got lost at the mall, the name of the security guard who found that child, and the place in which each was found.

1. No child had the same first and last initials, and no security guard located a child whose first or last name began with the same letter as the guard's last name.

2. The child brought back by Ms. Clay was located the day before the Fuentes child wandered off, which was the day before the child wearing the blue jacket was found. Eric was located before, but not the day before, the child who was found reading comic books at the bookstore. (Note: Five different children are mentioned in this clue.)

3. The child found at the toyshop and the child located watching cartoons at the video store (who was neither Betsy nor the Easton child) didn't get lost on consecutive days.

4. The child who was located at the pet store was found two days before the Akimoto child; the child found by Mr. Burns was located two days before the child wearing the orange jacket. (Note: Four different children are mentioned in this clue.)

5. The six children were Donna, the Collins child, the child wearing the purple jacket, the child found by Mr. Endo, the one who was located at the toyshop, and the one who got lost on Saturday.

6. Neither Ms. Diaz nor Mr. Foster was the guard who found the child in the video store.

7. The girl wearing the green jacket was located the day before the child found by Ms. Anderson (who didn't work on Saturday). The child who fell asleep in a chair at the furniture showroom was located earlier in the week than Craig, who was located earlier than the Birdsong child. (Note: Five different children are mentioned in this clue.)

8. The child found waiting in line for a soda was located the day before the child wearing the red jacket, who was found the day before Andy. The Easton child

was located earlier in the week than the child Ms. Diaz found. (Note: Five different children are mentioned in this clue).

9. The three boys who got lost were the one wearing the yellow jacket, the one found by Mr. Foster, and the one found on Thursday.

10. Andy wasn't at the bookstore.

Solution is on page 169.

Solution is on page 169.

first name	last name	jacket	guard	place	day

71 DECK THE CAKE WITH SPRIGS OF HOLLY

by Robert Nelson

Since their son's birthday was on Dec. 21, the Goren's party for him had a Christmas theme. For example, one game the birthday boy and his six guests played was a treasure hunt for hidden Christmas candies. The Gorens hid 12 candy canes and 24 foil-wrapped chocolate candies; the chocolates were shaped like Christmas tree decorations and were wrapped in three foil colors — eight each in red, green, and silver. The children found all of the candies. From the following clues, can you determine each child's full name and how many candies of each type and foil color he/she found?

1. No child had the same first and second initials.

2. The seven children were: Evan, Gene, the Forrey child, the only child who found a combination of two canes and three decorations, the only child who found three green decorations, the only child who found decorations of just one color, and the birthday boy.

3. Colleen found the same total number of candies as the Dawson boy, but none of the same color decorations as he did.

4. Andy found more decorations than the Birch boy, but they had the same total number of candies.

5. Dirk found more total candies than the Anderson girl, but fewer than the only child who found three silver decorations.

6. Beth, the English child, and the only girl with two red decorations found the same number of candy canes (more than Gene), but one of those three found the same number of decorations as the other two combined.

7. Andy, one of only two children who found decorations in all three colors, had the same number of red as Evan, the same number of greens as Beth, and the same number of silvers as Gene.

8. Fran found more candy canes than the Carson boy, but had a smaller total number of candies than him.

9. The only girl who found three decorations had two red and one green; the only boy who found three decorations had one red and two silver.

10. The only girl who found five decorations had the same number of silver ones as the only boy who found five decorations had green.

11. All children found at least one candy cane and at least two decorations.

12. The birthday boy was the only child who found a unique number of decorations not equalled by some other child.

13. One of the two children who found only two decorations found more candy canes than any other child.

Solution is on page 170.

first name	last name	# canes	# decs.	# red	# green	# silver

72 FIGURING WITH FIGURINES

by Mary Marks Cezus

Clara Winters is an avid collector of Cherished Children figurines. She just checked their worth in her latest collectors' guide and arranged her nine favorites as illustrated. No two figurines are engaged in the same activity and no two are worth the same amount. Using the clues below can you determine for each position the figurine's name, activity, and value ($30, $45, $60, $80, $110, $150, $260, $275, or $300)?

1. The figurine shown folding laundry was valued at exactly twice Hallie's value.

2. Bertina was worth less than both the one directly above Bertina and the one directly below Bertina.

3. Isadore (which was not the figurine folding laundry) was worth less than the figurine shown kissing a doll.

4. The figurine named Felicia (which was in one of the corners) was not shown chasing a butterfly.

5. The figurine named Arabella (which was not shown playing the piano) was in the space directly below the figurine shown mailing letters (which was worth more than the figurine in position four).

6. The figurines with the two greatest values were in the same column.

7. The figurine shown eating blackberries was worth less than the figurine in position eight but more than the figurine which was in the space directly above the figurine shown eating blackberries.

8. Felicia (which was not worth $275) was shown neither mailing letters nor holding the puppy.

9. Gwyneth was worth more than the one immediately to the left of Gwyneth and less than the one immediately to the right of Gwyneth.

10. Together, the figurine shown kissing a doll, Evangeline (which was not shown chasing a butterfly), and the figurine in position seven total the value of the figurine shown picking wildflowers.

11. One row consisted of these figurines: Bertina, the one worth $110, and the one shown feeding ducks.

12. The figurine shown playing the piano (which was worth more than Clementine) was in the space directly below the $45 figurine.

13. Together the figurine shown folding laundry and Dominique are worth less than the figurine in position two.

Solution is on page 170.

1	2	3
name _____	name _____	name _____
activity _____	activity _____	activity _____
value _____	value _____	value _____
4	**5**	**6**
name _____	name _____	name _____
activity _____	activity _____	activity _____
value _____	value _____	value _____
7	**8**	**9**
name _____	name _____	name _____
activity _____	activity _____	activity _____
value _____	value _____	value _____

73   PIZZA, ANYONE?

by Mary A. Powell

When Wanda Johnson opened a new pizza shop across from the college campus, it became an instant success with the students. The prices were good, the company was great, and the pizza was the best in town. To keep prices down and quality high, Wanda limits service and keeps choices to a minimum. The menu is posted on a board above the order counter: mini pizza $3 (serves 1); small $6 (1–2); medium $8 (2–3); large $10 (3–4); extra large $12 (4–6); all include cheese and tomato sauce; toppings 50¢ each. Toppings: Canadian bacon, green peppers, ground beef, ham, mushrooms, olives, pepperoni, pineapple, sausage. Although it is mostly a self-service establishment, yesterday afternoon Wanda had time to serve and chat with groups at three different tables. From the following clues, can you find the full names of the students (one was Ms. Edelman) at these three tables, what they ate, and how much each student spent? (Note: The three groups did not intermingle.)

1. Each student bought a $1 drink; each table spent the same total amount, including drinks. Altogether the three tables ordered at least one of everything on the menu.

2. No one spent more than $5 or less than $3.50. Those who shared a pizza did so within the limits suggested on the menu and divided the cost evenly.

3. Three pizzas had sausage; two had mushrooms.

4. Anthony spent exactly $1.00 more than everyone else at his table; Anthony and Mr. Leffler were at different tables.

5. Johann shared a pizza with two or more women; Mr. Kingery shared a pizza with three or more women.

6. Mark and Mr. Tillet shared in a pizza topped with Canadian bacon and green peppers.

7. The pizza with ham and pineapple was larger than the one Kimberly shared, but smaller than the one Ms. Vincent shared.

8. Rick sat between Yolanda and Mr. Watkins; they all spent the same amount.

9. Sylvia sat between Ginger and Ms. Bradshaw; the pizza they shared in had Canadian bacon.

10. Jolene sat between Ms. Armani and Mr. Harrigan; they all ate a pizza with toppings including both ground beef and green peppers.

11. Rosa and Ms. Fetters each spent 50¢ less than Mr. Olson, who spent 50¢ less than Mr. Marshall; Rosa and Ms. Fetters both had sausage.

12. Peter and Ms. Price each ate pizza that had no more than two toppings; Peter's bill was 50¢ more than that of Ms. Price.

13. Ms. Croft sat between Tyler (a first name) and Olivia; they all enjoyed sausage, pepperoni, and olives.

14. Donald and Nathan (a first name) both ate pizza topped with olives; Donald and Mr. Leffler both ate pizza topped with pepperoni; these three men sat at three different tables. Donald spent less than either of the other two.

15. Lynette spent 50¢ more than Mr. Serrano, but 50¢ less than those who shared the small pizza.

16. Jolene spent $3.50.

17. Kimberly is not Bradshaw; Ginger is not Ms. Juarez.

Solution is on page 171.

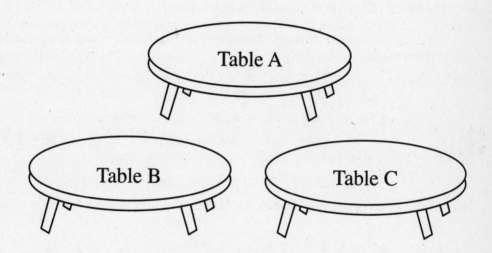

FRIDAY NIGHT SPECIAL

by Robert Nelson

Every Friday evening, the Kountry Kitchen has a Mix-N-Match special; for $6.95, a diner gets a choice of any one of four entrees, four styles of potato (including baked), four vegetables (including broccoli), and four desserts (including ice cream). One recent Friday evening, six married couples sat at one large table and made their choices from that assortment. From the following clues, can you determine the full name and meal order of each of the six wives and six husbands?

1. No person has the same first and last initial and no husband and wife have the same first initial.

2. Three people ordered each item offered; no two had more than one item in common and no husband and wife had any items in common.

3. Adam, Cheryl, Mr. Farmer, and Mrs. Engel had four different entrees.

4. Frank, Dixie, Mr. Cloud (who did not have au gratin potatoes), and Mrs. Baker had four different potatoes.

5. Bob, Flo, Mr. Engel, and Mrs. Cloud had four different vegetables.

6. Don, Edna (who is not Bob's wife), Mr. Baker, and Mrs. Farmer had four different desserts.

7. Clyde Dash had pork, french fries, peas, and pie.

8. Earl had the same entree as Beth, the same potato as Anna, the same vegetable as Mrs. Cloud, and the same dessert as Mrs. Dash; neither he nor his wife had anything that matched either of the Aspens.

9. Three wives had one type of entree, three wives had one type of potato, three wives had one type of vegetable, and three wives had one type of dessert; no item was ordered by three husbands.

10. Adam and Beth enjoyed their carrots, but Mr. Aspen found his carrots too sweet.

11. Anna sampled her husband Don's chicken and he sampled her fish.

12. Adam sampled his wife's cake, but she knew she wouldn't like his pudding.

13. Bob and Frank both complained about lumps in their mashed potatoes.

14. One woman had beef, french fries, beans, and cake.

Solution is on page 173.

first name	last name	entree	potato	veg.	dessert

75 THE BIRDLAND MAZE

by Mary A. Powell

At the intersection of Bluebird Drive and Blackhawk Road in the city of Rockland, the Wayward Development Company designed a circular subdivision around a round park. Since both Bluebird Drive and Blackhawk Road come to a dead end at Robin Park, those wishing to go through town must take Goldfinch Circle, which surrounds the subdivision. In each quarter of the development (which was promptly nicknamed Birdland), the company installed four short courts from Robin Park to Goldfinch Circle, making Birdland look like a giant pie cut into eight pieces. Six houses face each court (three on each side of the street) as well as each section of Bluebird Drive (north and south) and Blackhawk Road (east and west). These 48 houses are numbered from 1 to 6, with lower numbers on the Robin Park end. Odd numbers on Bluebird Drive are on the west side; odd numbers on Blackhawk Road are on the north. Before all of these houses were finished, Wayward Development acquired a permit for eight more houses — one in each segment — to face Goldfinch Circle. Starting at the segment between South Bluebird Drive and Hummingbird Court and going clockwise, these houses were numbered 10, 20, 30, etc. through #80. Before these were finished, the company bought more land and added 32 more houses along the outside perimeter of Goldfinch circle. There seemed to be no way to add numbers to these houses that wouldn't drive postal employees crazy, so all suggestions were stuffed into a hat, and the first one drawn out was used. The four houses opposite 10 Goldfinch Circle were numbered 11, 12, 13, and 14, going clockwise. Across from 20 Goldfinch Circle, the four new houses were numbered 21, 22, 23, and 24, and so on, with the highest number being 84 Goldfinch Circle. Into this numerical maze came some brave new buyers. The first eight are all professional couples who share the same last name. Because each husband works at or near the same place as his wife, each couple drives to work together. As would be expected, each couple uses the street entrance(s) nearest to their home. From the following clues, can you find the full names and street addresses of the eight couples?

1. Among these eight families, the local postman sees eight different street numbers and seven different street names.

2. Barbara's street number is 16 times as high as Lester's.

3. The Montgomerys' street number is twice as high as Keith's; neither of these two families lives on Mockingbird Court.

4. Rosemary and her husband always drive home from the west and make a left turn, then a right before turning right into their driveway; they pass no other occupied house in the subdivision.

5. The Kirbys and Isabelle and her husband make no turns before turning into their driveway; Steven and his wife make one.

6. Michael and his wife sometimes turn left into Birdland and go past Patricia's house, then make a right before reaching home; at other times, they take a right, then a left, passing no occupied houses.

7. Mr. and Mrs. Hopkins and David and his wife require east, west, north, or south designations in their addresses.

8. Without using Robin Park or passing the end of a court, Lillian can visit both John's wife and Mrs. Anderson without crossing a street; Lillian has the lowest street number of the three.

9. Whipporwill Court is due north of the court where Joyce lives.

10. Oriole Court is due north of the court where Andrea lives.

11. Without going to Robin Park, Tony can visit the Bakers without crossing a street.

12. The Pattersons' street number is five times that of Brian's.

13. The Gallaghers' side yard faces Robin Park; Madeline's side yard faces Goldfinch Circle.

14. The Trimmers cannot visit any other family without crossing a street.

15. No one has the same first and last initial.

16. John is not Baker; neither Steven nor Tony is Anderson.

Solution is on page 174.

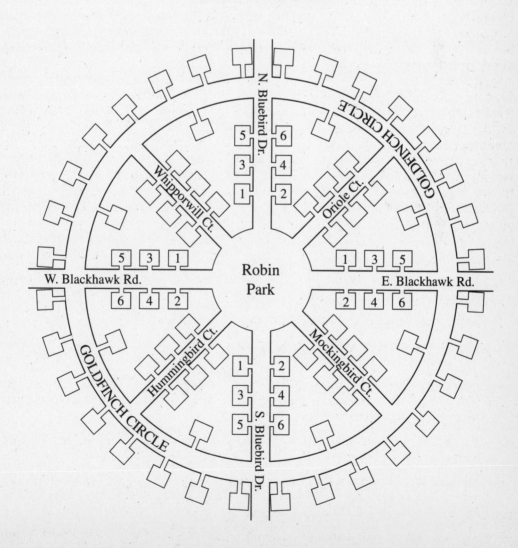

131

SOLUTIONS

1. YARD WARMING

There were gifts from three old friends (clue 1), one sister and one brother (clue 6), so there were two new neighbors. Ms. Field is the sister (clue 6). Mr. Finch and Mrs. Flores are the new neighbors (clue 4). Ms. Foster is an old friend (clue 1), as is Forbes (clue 7). Basil Funn is not her brother (clue 6); he is an old friend, while Fountain is her brother. Fountain gave her perennials (clue 3). Glen gave her chipped wood (clue 5), so he is not the brother; Ray is. June is a new neighbor (clue 7); she is Mrs. Flores. She gave money plant seeds (clue 7). Old friend Basil Funn gave her ground cover (clue 1). Daisy, then, is Forbes (clue 1), who gave her herb plants (clue 7). Mr. Finch is the only remaining man, Glen. Olive gave a bird feeder (clue 2), so Iris gave a bird bath. Iris is not the sister (clue 6); she is old friend Mrs. Foster. By elimination, Olive is the sister, Mrs. Field. In summary:

> Basil Funn, ground cover, friend
> Daisy Forbes, herb plants, friend
> Glen Finch, chipped wood mulch, neighbor
> Iris Foster, bird bath, friend
> June Flores, money plant seeds, neighbor
> Olive Field, bird feeder, sister
> Ray Fountain, perennials, brother

2. HAPPY MOTHER'S DAY

By clue 2, Gail is the sophomore. Larry isn't the senior or freshman (clue 1); he is the junior. Also by clue 1, the senior promised to weed and Gail gave the petunias. By clue 3, George is the freshman who promised to mow and Gail promised to trim the hedge. By elimination, Jane is the senior, who, by clue 4, gave her mother pansies. By clue 2, George gave her snapdragons and Larry promised to mulch. By elimination, Larry gave her marigolds. In summary:

> Gail, sophomore, petunias, trimming
> George, freshman, snapdragons, mowing
> Jane, senior, pansies, weeding
> Larry, junior, marigolds, mulching

3. RELIVING HISTORY

The French character played by the Northridge student was not Laudonierre (clue 2); it was Ribault. The Northridge student was neither first nor fourth (clue 2) nor was he second (clue 4); he was third, so by clue 2, Robert was fourth. By clue 4, a Spanish character was second and, by clue 2, Laudonierre was first. By elimination, a Spanish character was fourth. He was not Menendez (clue 3); he was de Leon and Menendez was second. Vernon was not fourth (clue 1); he was second and the Eastland student was fourth (also clue 1). By clue 3, Steve was third and the Westmill student was first. By elimination, Todd was first and the Southbrook student was second. In summary:

> Robert, 4th, Eastland, Juan Ponce de Leon
> Steve, 3rd, Northridge, Jean Ribault
> Todd, 1st, Westmill, Rene de Laudonierre
> Vernon, 2nd, Southbrook, Pedro Menendez

4. ALL IN THE FAMILY

The baseball team ranked 3rd (clue 2). The football team ranked 5th (clue 4). Carmen's track team did not rank 1st or 2nd (clue 3), so it ranked 4th. She has not coached for 8 (clue 1), 4 (clue 3), 12 (clue 5) or 10 years (clue 6); she has coached for 6 years. The swimming team did not rank 1st (clue 6); by elimination, it ranked 2nd. Also by elimination, the 1st-ranked team was the basketball team, of Central High (clue 7). The 8-year coach is a man (clue 1); by clue 2, the baseball coach has 12 years on the job, Gail 10 years, and the 8-year male coach works at Southwest High. By clue 4, he is the football coach, Carmen works at Northwest High, and Mark is the 4-year coach. Fred does not coach football (clue 1); he is the 12-year baseball coach. Josef, by elimination, coaches the football team. By clue 6, Gail is the 1st-place basketball coach at Central High. Mark, by elimination, is the swimming coach. By clue 3, Fred works at Southeast High; by elimination, Mark works at Northeast High. In summary:

> 1st: Gail, basketball, 10, Central
> 2nd: Mark, swimming, 4, Northeast
> 3rd: Fred, baseball, 12, Southeast
> 4th: Carmen, track, 6, Northwest
> 5th: Josef, football, 8, Southwest

5. COPING WITH CABIN FEVER

By clue 1, Ned is the man who painted his bedroom and who lives in either apartment #3 or #4. By clue 2, he lives in #3 and the bookkeeper lives in #4. By clue 1, Nick is in #1 and the woman who is the baker is in #2. By clue 2, the baker cleaned her closet. Since Nora isn't the baker (clue 3), she is the bookkeeper and Nancy is the baker. Nora isn't the one who updated the photo album (clue 4); by elimination, she worked on her taxes and Nick updated the album. Ned isn't the banker (clue 5); by elimination, he is the barber and Nick is the banker. In summary:

> #1: Nick, banker, updated photo album
> #2: Nancy, baker, cleaned closet
> #3: Ned, barber, painted bedroom
> #4: Nora, bookkeeper, did taxes

6. GOING TO THE ORACLE

Theophilus was either the 2nd or 3rd man to consult the oracle (clue 1). By clue 5, then, Demetrius wasn't 2nd or 3rd to see the oracle. By clue 2, Demetrius wasn't the last to see the oracle; therefore, he was 1st. By clue 5, Theolphilus wasn't 2nd, he was 3rd, and by clue 1, the man from Corinth was the last of the four to enter. By clue 5, Demetrius wasn't the man who consulted the oracle about his brother. By clue 3, Demetrius was the man from Thebes. By clue 4, Lucas wasn't the 2nd to consult the oracle; Lucas was 4th, and, by elimination, Alexander was 2nd. By clue 4, Theophilus was from Athens, and, by elimination, Alexander was from Sparta. The man who asked about his brother wasn't Alexander or Theophilus (clue 3); he was Lucas. Alexander didn't consult the oracle about his career (clue 1) or his son (clue 2); he asked about his marriage. Demetrius didn't ask about his son (clue 2); he asked about his career, and, by elimination, Theophilus asked about his son. In summary:

> 1st, Demetrius, Thebes, career
> 2nd, Alexander, Sparta, marriage
> 3rd, Theophilus, Athens, son's future
> 4th, Lucas, Corinth, brother's whereabouts

7. WORKING AT HOME

The desktop publisher builds remote-control airplanes (clue 2). Kathy's hobby is her horse (clue 3). The traveler makes the house payment (clue 5). The puzzle maker pays for vacations (clue 6). The art collector isn't the T-shirt designer (clue 1), jewelry maker (clue 3), or puzzle maker (clue 6); she is the architect. The traveler isn't the T-shirt designer (clue 5) or puzzle maker (clue 6); she makes jewelry. The one who pays for the car isn't the desktop publisher (clue 2) or architect (clue 4); she is the T-shirt designer. By clue 1, the T-shirt designer isn't Andrea or Lyn; by clue 4, she isn't Cheri or Marian; she is Kathy. By elimination, the puzzle maker's hobby is hot air balloons (introduction). By clue 1, the one who pays for clothing isn't Andrea or Lyn; she isn't Marian (clue 4); she is Cheri. The one who pays for clothing isn't the architect (clue 4); she is the desktop publisher. By elimination, the architect makes credit card payments. Lyn pays for neither the credit cards (clue 1) nor the house (clue 5); she pays for vacations. Marian isn't the architect (clue 4); she is the jewelry maker. By elimination, Andrea is the architect. In summary:

> Andrea, architectural consultant, credit cards, art collecting
> Cheri, desktop publisher, clothing, remote control airplanes
> Kathy, T-shirt designer, car, horse

Lyn, puzzle maker, vacations, hot air ballooning
Marian, jewelry maker, house, travel

8. MEMORY LANE

Scott's message was not "Phone folks" (clue 1) or "Late dinner" (clue 4). Since Scott lives on neither end (clue 1), his message was not "Make reservations" (clue 5); Scott's message was "Clean bathroom." The message on the sports pad was not "Clean bathroom" or "Make reservations" (clue 5), or "Phone folks" (clue 7); it was "Late dinner." The message on the ducks pad was neither "Clean bathroom" nor "Phone folks" (clue 1); it was "Make reservations." The ducks pad was neither Brad's (clue 3) nor Ted's (clue 6); it was Craig's. The man who lives at 812 is not Scott (clue 1) or Craig (clue 2). Since the pads at the two end houses were the ones with the "Make reservations" message and the sports pad (clue 5) and Brad's pad had neither the "Make reservations" message (clue 3) nor the sports design (clue 7), Brad lives at neither 812 nor 818. By elimination, Ted lives at 812. Scott does not live at 818 (clue 1). By elimination, Craig lives at 818. Scott lives at 816 (clue 1). By elimination, Brad lives at 814. The "Phone folks" message was at 814 (clue 1). By elimination, the "Late dinner" message was at 812. Brad's pad did not have neckties (clue 3); Brad's pad had apples and Scott's had neckties. In summary:

> Brad, 814, apples and grapes, "Phone your folks."
> Craig, 818, ducks with umbrellas, "Make plane reservations."
> Scott, 816, neckties, "Clean the bathroom! Please!"
> Ted, 812, sports equipment, "Late dinner tonight."

9. CAMPAIGN ADS

The 2nd ad run wasn't Moore's (clue 2) or Ortiz's (clue 3); it was either Chin's or Sullivan's. Grace isn't Chin (clue 1) or Sullivan (clue 4), so Grace's ad didn't run 2nd. Nor did Grace's ad run 1st or 4th (clue 1); it ran 3rd. By clue 1, Mr. Chin's ad ran 2nd and the ad for the state's attorney candidate ran 4th. Grace isn't Sullivan (clue 4), so Sullivan's ad didn't run 3rd. By clue 4, Ronald's ad didn't run 4th. Nor was the 4th ad Nadine's (clue 2); it was David's. David isn't Chin (clue 1), Ortiz (clue 3) or Sullivan (clue 4); he is Moore. By clue 2, the ad for the mayoral candidate ran 3rd and is Grace; by elimination, she is Ortiz. Nadine isn't Mr. Chin (clue 1); she is Sullivan and, by elimination, Ronald is Mr. Chin. By clue 4, Nadine Sullivan's ad ran 1st. The ad for the sheriff hopeful didn't run 2nd (clue 3) it ran 1st and was Nadine Sullivan's. By elimination the ad for the candidate for treasurer ran 2nd, and was Ronald Chin's. In summary, the ads ran in this order:

> 1st, Nadine Sullivan, sheriff
> 2nd, Ronald Chin, state treasurer
> 3rd, Grace Ortiz, mayor
> 4th, David Moore, state's attorney

10. THE EASTER BUNNY

The green basket, which belongs to either Michael or Tommy, had a chocolate chick (clue 2). It did not have the jump rope (clue 4), airplane (clue 6), doll (clue 7), or paint set (clue 8); it had the sand bucket and "Snow White" (clue 9). It is not Tommy's basket (clue 1); it is Michael's. Tommy's basket has "The Three Little Pigs" (also clue 1). His basket is not pink (clue 3), purple (clue 6), or yellow (clue 9); it is blue and came with a jump rope (clue 4). His chocolate treat was not the bunny (clue 1), tulip (clue 5), or heart (clue 8); it was the chocolate egg. The basket with the paint set also had a chocolate heart (clue 8). It is not Jennifer's basket (clue 1) or Julie's basket (clue 7); it is Amanda's basket and is pink (clue 3). It did not have "Little Red Riding Hood" (clue 5) or "Jack and the Beanstalk" (clue 9); it has "Cinderella." Jennifer's basket had a chocolate bunny (clue 1). By elimination, Julie's had a chocolate tulip, "Little Red Riding Hood" (clue 5), and a doll (clue 7). By elimination, Jennifer's basket had the airplane and "Jack and the Beanstalk." Her basket is yellow (clue 9) and, by elimination, Julie's is purple. In summary:

> Amanda: pink, paint set, Cinderella, chocolate heart
> Jennifer: yellow, airplane, Jack and the Beanstalk, chocolate bunny
> Julie: purple, baby doll, Little Red Riding Hood, chocolate tulip

Michael: green, sand bucket, Snow White, chocolate chick
Tommy: blue, jump rope, The Three Little Pigs, chocolate egg

11. STIR WARS

The last-place finisher was not Barb or Kerri (clue 2), Lynn (clue 4), or Sue (clue 7); Cheryl finished last. The pork stir-fry was not last, but it finished behind Ms. Rudin (clue 1), Ms. Haines (clue 6), and Ms. Brennan, who won the competition (clue 5); the pork dish came in fourth. Ms. Haines placed third (clue 6), so Ms. Rudin placed second. Ms. Rudin is not Sue (clue 1), Kerri (clue 2), or Lynn (clue 4); she is Barb and Kerri is Ms. Haines (clue 2). Lynn, the preparer of the vegetable stir-fry, is Ms. Brennan (clue 4), so, by elimination, Sue came in fourth and Cheryl is Ms. Carlson (clue 7). By elimination, Sue is Ms. Sharkey. The beef stir-fry came in second and the shrimp dish placed last (clue 3). By elimination, the chicken stir-fry placed third. In summary:

first, Lynn Brennan, vegetable
second, Barb Rudin, beef
third, Kerri Haines, chicken
fourth, Sue Sharkey, pork
fifth, Cheryl Carlson, shrimp

12. THE CLOCKMAKER

The December gift was a watch (clue 6), but it wasn't the pocket watch (clue 4); it was the calendar watch. By clue 6, Mrs. Wilson received the pocket watch. The December bride is not 24 (clue 2), 30 (clue 3), 27 (clue 4) or 33 (clue 5); she is 21. By clue 2, the 24-year-old woman was married in either July or October. If it was in July, by clue 2, the April gift would have been the sundial clock. By clue 7, the 27-year-old woman would have received the cuckoo clock. By clue 4, the April gift would have been the pocket watch, which would contradict clue 2. Therefore, the 24-year-old woman was married in October, and by clue 2, the sun-dial clock was the July gift and Mrs. Price's anniversary is in April. By clue 4, then, Mrs. Wilson is 24, the 27-year-old woman received the sundial clock and Gloria is 21. By clue 7, the 30-year-old received the cuckoo clock and Paula is Mrs. Wilson. By clue 1, the January bride is 33, Jennifer Price is 30 and Mrs. Cox is 27. By clue 3, Mrs. Martin is 33 and Margaret is Mrs. Cox. By elimination, Mrs. Martin is the woman who got the grandfather clock, Gloria is Mrs. Baker and Clarissa is Mrs. Martin. In summary:

Clarissa Martin, 33, grandfather clock, January
Gloria Baker, 21, calendar watch, December
Jennifer Price, 30, cuckoo clock, April
Margaret Cox, 27, sundial clock, July
Paula Wilson, 24, pocket watch, October

13. FLIGHT OF FANCY

Emily and the Winegarten child worked on Monday (clue 4). Kim and the student who painted the ghost worked on Tuesday (clue 7). The Potter child and the student who painted the pirate worked on Wednesday (clue 6). Meg and the Coulis child worked on Thursday (clue 9), and Jeff and the student who painted the mermaid worked on Friday (clue 3). Since no student worked two days in a row (clue 1), Jeff is not the Coulis child. The Coulis child is also not Dan (clue 5), or Meg or Kim (clue 9); she is Emily, who worked Monday (clue 4) and Thursday (clue 9). Emily did not paint the pirate on Wednesday, the ghost on Tuesday, or the mermaid on Friday (clue 1). Since no students were paired more than once (clue 2), Emily also did not paint the spaceman (clue 5); she painted the unicorn. The Winegarten child who painted on Monday is Dan (clue 5). He did not paint the ghost on Tuesday (clue 1) or the spaceman (clue 5). Since Emily Coulis and her unicorn was Dan's first partner, Dan also did not paint the mermaid (clue 8); he painted the pirate on Monday (clue 5) and Wednesday (clue 6). By clue 5, the Potter child painted the spaceman. The Potter child is not Kim, who painted on Tuesday, or Meg, who painted on Thursday (clue 1); he is Jeff, who also painted his spaceman on Friday (clue 3). Kim did not paint the ghost (clue 7); she painted the mermaid on Tuesday (clue 7) and Friday (clue 3). The Matthews child painted the ghost on Tuesday (clue 8). Since she also painted with Emily on Thursday (clue 8), her first name is Meg. By elimination, Kim's last name is Hannigan. In summary, the schedule figured out by the five prize winners was:

Monday: Dan Winegarten (pirate) & Emily Coulis (unicorn)
Tuesday: Kim Hannigan (mermaid) & Meg Matthews (ghost)
Wednesday: Dan Winegarten (pirate) & Jeff Potter (spaceman)
Thursday: Emily Coulis (unicorn) & Meg Matthews (ghost)
Friday: Jeff Potter (spaceman) & Kim Hannigan (mermaid)

14. CELEBRATING ST. PATRICK'S DAY

Mr. O'Day isn't Pat (clue 2), Shawn (clue 3), Kelly (clue 6), or Brian (clue 8); he's Clancy. Pat did the jig (clue 2). The man who bought the Irish setter pup isn't Kelly (clue 1), or Shawn or Clancy (clue 3); he's Brian. The man who ate Irish stew isn't Kelly or Clancy O'Day (clue 6); he's Shawn. The man in green pants didn't buy the pup and isn't Shawn who ate the stew (clue 3); he also didn't sing songs or buy shamrocks (clue 9), so, he did the jig and is Pat. Mr. O'Neal isn't Shawn, Clancy O'Day, Brian with the pup, or Pat (clue 3); he's Kelly. Kelly didn't wear the green sweater or tie (clue 1) or vest (clue 4); he wore the green jacket. By clue 1, Brian with the pup didn't wear the green sweater or tie; he wore the vest. Brian isn't Mr. O'Leary (clue 4) or Mr. O'Grady (clue 8); he is Mr. O'Rourk. By clue 6, Shawn, who ate the stew, isn't Mr. O'Leary; he is Mr. O'Grady and Pat, by elimination, is Mr. O'Leary. By clue 7, Shawn didn't wear the green sweater; by elimination, he wore the green tie and Clancy had on the green sweater. By clue 5, Clancy didn't sing the Irish songs. By elimination, Kelly sang and Clancy bought the shamrocks. In summary:

> Clancy O'Day, green sweater, shamrocks
> Shawn O'Grady, green tie, Irish stew
> Pat O'Leary, green pants, Irish jig
> Kelly O'Neal, green jacket, Irish songs
> Brian O'Rourk, green vest, Irish setter

15. RETURN OF THE RED-EYE

Al, the man who left at 2:00 (clue 2), didn't fly the plane with extra legroom (clue 1), wide seats (clue 3), coffee & doughnuts (clue 5), or triple miles (clue 7); he piloted the plane with extra storage, and flew to St. Louis (clue 4). By clue 6, then, Don flew to Detroit; the man who flew to Milwaukee (clue 1), by elimination, is Walt. Jill didn't fly to Indianapolis (clue 7), so Sue did and Jill, by elimination, flew to Des Moines. The 2:30 flight featured wide seats (clue 3); that flight was not piloted by either of the women (clue 1) or by Walt, whose flight featured coffee & doughnuts (clue 5). Don flew the 2:30 flight to Detroit. Sue's flight to Indianapolis was not at 12:30 or 1:00 (clue 7); it was at 1:30. By clue 1, then, Jill is the female pilot who left earlier than Milwaukee-flyer Walt while Sue's flight featured extra legroom; Jill flew to Des Moines at 12:30 and Walt at 1:00. Jill's flight featured triple miles (clue 7). In summary:

> Al: 2:00 to St. Louis, storage
> Don: 2:30 to Detroit, wide seats
> Jill: 12:30 to Des Moines, triple miles
> Sue: 1:30 to Indianapolis, legroom
> Walt: 1:00 to Milwaukee, coffee & doughnuts

16. SIGN HERE

The girl who signed her name in red brought a yellow shirt (clue 9). Her first name is not Angie (clue 2), Denise (clue 3), Laura (clue 4), or Madeline (clue 4); it is Patsy. Her shirt was decorated with a teddy bear (clue 1). Patsy is not Goode (clue 1), Sroka (clue 2), Freed (clue 4), or Nowak (clue 6); she is Volk. The Sroka girl signed her name in black ink (clue 2). She is not Angie (clue 2), Laura (clue 4), or Denise (clue 8); she is Madeline. Her shirt did not have the sun (clue 1), balloons (clue 5), or tulip (clue 8); it had the lacy heart and was purple (clue 7). The Nowak girl had a green shirt (clue 6). Her first name is not Denise (clue 3) or Laura (clue 4); it is Angie, who signed her name in cream (clue 2). Her transfer was not the sun (clue 1) or balloons (clue 5); it was the tulips. Denise brought a pink shirt (clue 3). By elimination, the blue shirt belonged to Laura, whose last name is Freed (clue 4). By elimination, Denise's last name is Goode and she used the sun transfer (clue 1). By elimination, Laura's shirt had the balloons and she signed her name in gold (clue 5). By elimination, Denise wrote her name in silver. In summary:

Angie Nowak: green shirt with tulips and cream ink
Denise Goode: pink shirt with smiling sun and silver ink
Laura Freed: blue shirt with balloons and gold ink
Madeline Sroka: purple shirt with heart and black ink
Patsy Volk: yellow shirt with teddy bear and red ink

17. THE FRENCH COLLECTION

The first acquisition wasn't by Monet (clue 2) or Pissaro (clue 7), so by clue 1, it also wasn't the country scene. It also wasn't the city scene (clue 2), seascape (clue 3), or still life (clue 7); it was the portrait. By clue 6, then, it was by Renoir and the second acquisition was in the silver frame. By clue 5, the first acquisition hung in the living room and the fifth was by Seurat. By clue 2, the Monet was either the third or fourth acquisition. Since the Pissaro wasn't the second acquisition with the silver frame (clue 6), it, too, was either the third or fourth acquisition. Since, by clue 4, the country scene was second or third, by clue 1, it was third. By clue 4, the one in the gold frame was first, the dining room acquisition second, and by clue 2, the bedroom acquisition was third. By elimination, the Degas was second and, by clue 3, the painting in the black frame was third and the seascape fourth. By clue 2, the city scene was fifth and the still life, by elimination, second. Also, by clue 2, the city scene isn't in the white frame; by elimination, it is in the tan, and the seascape has the white frame. Again, by clue 2, the Monet was the fourth acquisition and the Pissaro, by elimination, the third. By clue 7, the painting in the den was the fourth acquisition and the one in the hall, by elimination, fifth. In summary:

> 1st: Renoir portrait, gold, living room
> 2nd: Degas still life, silver, dining room
> 3rd: Pissaro country scene, black, bedroom
> 4th: Monet seascape, white, den
> 5th: Seurat, city scene, tan, hall

18. THE UMPIRE STRIKES BACK

Since there are five players, at least one person mentioned in clues 2 and 3 is the same person. Since each player was ejected in a different inning, there are only two possibilities. One is that the one arguing catcher interference was ejected third and the one arguing being called out at home was ejected two innings earlier. By clue 1, then, the man claiming he was hit by a pitch would have been thrown out in the first inning and Fielder would have been ejected in the third inning. However, this contradicts clue 5. Therefore, it was Walker who was thrown out last (in the ninth inning), the one who argued he was safe at home was ejected in the seventh inning, Singleton (who is Mick) in the fifth inning, Rusty in the third inning, and the one who argued catcher interference in the first inning. By clue 1, Fielder argued he was safe at home, Singleton argued he was hit by a pitch, and Walker is Lance. By clue 5, Dinger is Rusty and argued he had hit a home run. Bubba was the first player ejected (clue 4). By elimination, Player was ejected in the first inning, Lance argued a called third strike, and Hank is Fielder. In summary:

> Lance Walker, 9th inning, called third strike
> Hank Fielder, 7th inning, safe at home
> Mick Singleton, 5th inning, hit by pitch
> Rusty Dinger, 3rd inning, fair home run
> Bubba Player, 1st inning, catcher interference

19. A SMALL WORLD

Renee (from Vallejo), Ms. Wolfe, and the woman who lives in Cascade County stayed on the gold, blue, and pink decks (clue 5), so the other two women stayed on the green and tan decks. The woman who stayed on the tan deck wasn't Ms. Tyler (clue 2), Ms. Wolfe (clue 5), Ms. Lurie (clue 7) or Ms. Dunne (clue 11); she was Ms. Evans. Ms. Evans isn't Marie (clue 1), Elyse (clue 6), Linda (clue 8) or Renee; she is Janet. The woman who stayed on the green deck wasn't Ms. Tyler or Ms. Dunne (clue 2), she was Ms. Lurie, who, by clue 7, was from Fresno. By elimination, Ms. Dunne and Ms. Tyler are Renee and the woman who lived in Cascade County, in some order. By clue 11, Ms. Dunne and Ms. Tyler are also Elyse and the woman who stayed on the pink deck, in some order. Therefore, in some order, Renee and the woman who lived in Cascade County are Elyse and

140

the woman who stayed on the pink deck. By elimination, Renee was the woman who stayed on the pink deck and the woman who lives in Cascade County was Elyse. Linda isn't Ms. Lurie (clue 6); she's Ms. Wolfe. Marie, by elimination, is Ms. Lurie. The woman from Chico isn't Janet (clue 4) and doesn't live in Cascade County (clue 12); she is Linda. Elyse isn't from Novato, (clue 10), so Janet is, and Elyse, by elimination, was born in Indio. Ms. Tyler wasn't born in Indio (clue 2), so she's Renee. Ms. Dunne, by elimination, is Elyse. The woman who stayed on the blue deck wasn't from Indio (clue 3) so she is Linda. By elimination, Elyse stayed on the gold deck. The woman who lives in Glacier County isn't Marie (clue 2), Linda (clue 8) or Janet (clue 10); she is Renee. The woman who lives in Missoula County isn't Marie (clue 1) or Linda (clue 4); she is Janet. The woman who lives in Silver Bow County isn't Marie (clue 9); she is Linda. Marie, by elimination, lives in Lewis & Clark County. In summary:

> Renee Tyler, Vallejo, Glacier County, pink deck
> Linda Wolfe, Chico, Silver Bow County, blue deck
> Elyse Dunne, Indio, Cascade County, gold deck
> Janet Evans, Novato, Missoula County, tan deck
> Marie Lurie, Fresno, Lewis & Clark County, green deck

20. FUN AT THE FIELD MUSEUM

Katie toured Ancient Egypt (clue 8). Her other tour was not the South Pacific (clue 5). Her last name is not Brubaker (clue 2), so she did not tour Africa (clue 12). Since she toured Egypt, she did not make the bookmarks (clue 6), thus her last name is not VanderWal (clue 11), so she did not go on the Walk in the Wild tour (clue 3). She went on the Dinosaur tour and her last name is Willis (clue 10). Katie Willis made an African corn husk doll (clue 7) and a Mexican tin ornament (clue 2). The Brubaker child was Katie's partner for the Mexican tin ornaments (clue 2). Each student was paired with the others once (clue 1), so Katie's partner for the Mexican tin ornaments was not Erin (clue 7) or Josh (clue 10). Dan is not the Brubaker child (clue 12), so Melissa is. Melissa Brubaker also made Egyptian bookmarks (clue 11). She toured the South Pacific (clue 5) and Africa (clue 12). Erin was Katie's partner for the African corn husk dolls (clue 7), so she was not paired with Katie for the tour through Ancient Egypt (clue 1), thus she is not the Mendoza child (clue 8). She is also not the VanderWal child (clue 3); her last name is O'Connell. Erin O'Connell made the Peruvian paper flowers (clue 9). She went on the Walk in the Wild (clue 3) and the South Pacific tours (clue 5). Josh is not the Mendoza child (clue 4); he is the VanderWal child. He made the Japanese ribbon fish (clue 4) and Egyptian bookmarks (clue 11). He toured the Walk in the Wild (clue 3) and the Dinosaurs (clue 10). By elimination, Dan is the Mendoza child. He made the Japanese ribbon fish (clue 4) and Peruvian paper flowers (clue 9). He toured Ancient Egypt (clue 8) and Africa (clue 12). In summary:

CRAFTS

> African corn husk dolls: Erin O'Connell & Katie Willis
> Egyptian papyrus bookmarks: Josh VanderWal & Melissa Brubaker
> Japanese ribbon fish: Dan Mendoza & Josh VanderWal
> Mexican tin ornaments: Katie Willis & Melissa Brubaker
> Peruvian paper flowers: Dan Mendoza & Erin O'Connell

TOURS

> Africa: Dan Mendoza & Melissa Brubaker
> Ancient Egypt: Dan Mendoza & Katie Willis
> Dinosaurs: Josh VanderWal & Katie Willis
> South Pacific: Erin O'Connell & Melissa Brubaker
> Walk in the Wild: Erin O'Connell & Josh VanderWal

21. ROSES OF SUMMER

The rose in position five was not the smallest (clue 3). The rose in five was smaller than Fairy (clue 7), which was smaller than the white rose (clue 1), which was smaller than Wedding (clue 4). The rose in five was the second smallest. Fairy was third smallest, the white rose was second largest, and Wedding was the largest. The rose in one was not lavender (clue 2), white (clue 4), yellow (clue 5), or red (clue 8); it was pink. The rose in two was not white (clue 4), yellow (clue 5), or red (clue

8); it was lavender. The smallest rose was neither lavender (clue 2) nor pink (clue 6). By clue 3, the smallest rose was in the middle row and Regal was in five. The smallest rose was not in four (clue 3); the smallest rose was in three. The smallest rose was not Fragrant (clue 8); by elimination, Fragrant was second largest and Child's was smallest. The pink rose was largest (clue 6). By elimination, the white rose was in four and the lavender in two was Fairy. The red rose was in five (clue 8). By elimination, the yellow rose was in three. In summary (from smallest to largest):

> Child's Play, yellow, three
> Regal Veil, red, five
> Fairy Godmother, lavender, two
> Fragrant Lady, white, four
> Wedding Bliss, pink, one

22. SCENIC CHECKS

The four women are Grandma Bennington, her two daughters, and her 20-year-old granddaughter, who is the youngest of the four. The youngest is not Tanya (clue 2), Carla (clue 3), or Laura (clue 4); Olivia is youngest. The oldest woman doesn't have pink checks (clue 2), yellow checks (clue 4), or blue checks (clue 5); hers are green. Green checks don't have rainbows (clue 1), roses (clue 3), or clouds (clue 4); they have cats. The checks depicting clouds are not yellow (clue 4) or pink (clue 6); they are blue. The youngest woman does not have blue checks (clue 5), so Olivia has neither clouds nor rainbows (clue 1); Olivia chose roses. Tanya has no children (clue 7), so she is not Olivia's mother, nor is she the oldest (clue 2) with green checks, so Tanya is the one in clue 1 who chose rainbows. Tanya's rainbow checks are not pink (clue 2); they are yellow. By elimination, Olivia chose pink checks. Laura's checks don't have clouds (clue 4), so hers have cats, and Carla chose blue checks with clouds. Laura is three times as old as Olivia (clue 2), so Laura is 60. Tanya is half as old as Laura (also clue 2), so Tanya is 30. Carla is twice as old as Olivia (clue 3), so Carla is 40. The four birthdays are in consecutive months, with Olivia's being last. One birthday is in May (clue 3) and Carla's is in July (clue 5), so one is in June and Olivia's in August. Since Grandma Bennington's birthday was first, and Tanya has no children (clue 7), Laura's is in May. By elimination, Tanya's is in June. In summary:

> Carla, 40, July birthday, clouds on blue checks
> Laura, 60, May birthday, cats on green checks
> Olivia, 20, Aug. birthday, roses on pink checks
> Tanya, 30, June birthday, rainbows on yellow checks

23. A MUSICAL WEEK

Monday's ticket did not cost $30 (clue 1) or $22 (clue 6). It cost $2 less than the concert attended by 13,126 people (clue 2). That concert did not cost $26 (clue 4) or $28 (clue 5). By elimination, Monday's cost $28 and, the concert that drew 13,126 cost $30. The $30 concert was not on Tuesday (clue 1). Fortune's Wind opened before 11,094 people (clue 6). By clue 4, then, 14,201 people attended Tuesday's concert, Walking Wounded opened before 13,126 people, and 12,117 people attended the $26 concert. The $30 concert was on Thursday, P D Q opened the $26 concert, and Monday's concert was attended by 11,094 people (clue 5). Tuesday's concert featured Winslow Dallas and P D Q opened Wednesday's concert (clue 1). By elimination, Friday's concert was attended by 10,063 people. Tuesday's concert cost $22 and the Running Dogs were the feature act on Wednesday (clue 6). By elimination, Friday's concert cost $24. Nathan Colby was Monday's featured artist (clue 7). Gloria McGraw opened for Winslow Dallas, Florence Knight opened Friday's concert, and Thursday's concert featured C.C. Queen (clue 3). By elimination, Glynnis Day was Friday's featured act. In summary:

> Monday: Nathan Colby, Fortune's Wind, 11,094, $28
> Tuesday: Winslow Dallas, Gloria McGraw, 14,201, $22
> Wednesday: Running Dogs, P D Q, 12,117, $26
> Thursday: C.C. Queen, Walking Wounded, 13,126 $30
> Friday: Glynnis Day, Florence Knight, 10,063, $24

24. BLOCK PARTY

One of the families on the west side of the street has one child (clue 5). None of the families on the east side of the street has two children (clue 8), so they have, in some order, 1 child, 3 children, and 3 children. Thus the families on the west side of the street have, in some order, 1 child, 2 children, and 2 children. The Manor house is between the game room and a house with three children (clue 7), so it is house #4. The house across the street, #3, is not the Tudor (clue 1), ranch (clue 2), Victorian (clue 6), or Cape Cod (clue 8); it is the Colonial and house #4 has the pool (clue 4). This house is owned by the Vander family (clue 8). Since they are neither the Chan family nor the family with the ranch (clue 2), the family in house #3 has one child (clue 2) and, by elimination, the families in house #1 and house #5 both have 2 children. House #1 is not the ranch (clue 2), Victorian (clue 6), or Cape Cod (clue 8); it is the Tudor. The Morales family lives in house #3 and the family in house #5 has a deck (clue 1). Houses #1, #3, and #5 are, in some order, the family with 1 child, the family with the hot tub, and the Hanrahans (clue 5). The family in house #3 has 1 child. Since house #5 has a deck, they are the Hanrahans and, by elimination, house #1 has a hot tub. Since house #1 has 2 children, they are the Levin family (clue 3), and house #2 has one child (clue 3). By elimination, house #4 and house #6 both have 3 children. House #2 is not the Petrie family (clue 6); it is the Chan family. They do not live in the ranch (clue 2) or Victorian (clue 6); they live in the Cape Cod and have a game room (clue 7). By elimination, the Petrie family lives in house #6. They do not have the Victorian house (clue 6); they have the ranch with the computer room (clue 8). By elimination, house #5 is the Victorian and house #3 has the fireplace. In summary, the six families and their homes are:

> House 1: Levin, Tudor, hot tub, 2 children
> House 2: Chan, Cape Cod, game room, 1 child
> House 3: Morales, Colonial, fireplace, 1 child
> House 4: Vander, Manor, pool, 3 children
> House 5: Hanrahan, Victorian, deck, 2 children
> House 6: Petrie, ranch, computer center, 3 children

25. THE AFTER-SCHOOL PROGRAM

The Abbott boy has dance Thursday and the Burns girl has it Wednesday (clue 4). By clue 6, then, the Abbott boy's gym classes are on Monday and Wednesday. By elimination, his swim class is Tuesday. Clarke is the surname of the other boy (clue 2), so his gym classes are on Tuesday and Thursday (clue 1). The Clarke boy then swims and dances, in some order, on Monday and Wednesday; since the Burns girl dances Wednesday, the Clarke boy dances Monday and swims Wednesday. By elimination, the Dunn girl dances Tuesday. By clue 5, then, the Abbott boy is John, so by elimination, the Clarke boy is George. May has painting and swimming Monday (clue 2). By clue 6, John Abbott has painting and ceramics, in some order, on Tuesday and Thursday, so the Dunn girl does not have painting on Monday (clue 8); May, then, is Burns. By elimination, Sally is the Dunn girl, and her swimming class is Thursday. By clue 6, then, her gym classes are on Monday and Wednesday. Also by elimination, May Burns' gym classes are on Tuesday and Thursday. By clue 6, May's ceramics class is Wednesday. She does not have drama Thursday (clue 7); she has it Tuesday, while her Thursday class is nature study. Sally has nature study on Wednesday (clue 8). She has painting and ceramics, in some order, Tuesday and Thursday (clue 6). She does not have painting Thursday (clue 3); she has is Tuesday, and has ceramics Thursday. By elimination, she has drama Monday. By clue 8, John has ceramics Tuesday. By clue 6, he has painting Thursday. Since Sally has nature studies Wednesday, John has it Monday. By elimination, John has drama Wednesday, while George has ceramics Monday, nature studies Tuesday, painting Wednesday, and drama Thursday. In summary:

	Monday	Tuesday	Wednesday	Thursday
John Abbot	nature study gym	ceramics swimming	drama gym	painting dancing
May Burns	painting swimming	drama gym	ceramics dancing	nature study gym
George Clarke	ceramics dancing	nature study gym	painting swimming	drama gym
Sally Dunn	drama gym	painting dancing	nature study gym	ceramics swimming

26. SPRINGFIELD AUTHORS

The three women are Karen, Ms. Moore, and the one who spoke at 10 (clue 3). The three men are Frank, Mr. Flight, and the one who spoke at 1 (clue 4). Since no two women spoke consecutively (clue 6), one woman spoke at 12 and the other at either 2 or 3, while a man spoke at 11 and the other man spoke at 2 or 3. Frank didn't speak at 1 (clue 4); so by clue 2, he spoke at 11, the mystery writer at 12, and the author of "On the Shore" at 1. Since the woman who spoke at 12 writes mysteries, the fantasy author spoke at 11 or 1, and is a man (clue 8). Since the author of "Shore" spoke at 1, the author of "Grotto" spoke at noon, and is the mystery author, the science fiction author spoke at 10, and the man who writes westerns spoke at 2 (clue 5). The man who writes westerns, then, is Mr. Flight. By clue 8, Frank writes fantasy and Eric is the man who spoke at 1. By elimination, Mr. Flight is Gordon. By clue 7, Donna spoke at 10 and writes science fiction, Mr. Isley spoke at 11 and is Frank, and Ms. Sheppard spoke at 12 and writes mysteries. Ms. Sheppard, then, is Karen. By elimination, Ms. Moore is Betty, and she spoke at 3. By clue 1, Mr. Bloom is Eric, Mr. Flight wrote "Drums at Dawn," and Betty Moore writes romances. By elimination, Eric Bloom writes historical fiction, and Donna is Crown. By clue 1, a woman wrote "The Moon at Noon," but not Betty; Donna wrote that. Frank didn't write "For the Doves" (clue 8), so he wrote "Tiles Underfoot" while, by elimination, Betty wrote "For the Doves." In summary:

10: Donna Crown, science fiction, "The Moon at Noon"
11: Frank Isley, fantasy, "Tiles Underfoot"
12: Karen Sheppard, mystery, "Grotto"
1: Eric Bloom, historical fiction, "The Shore"
2: Gordon Flight, western, "Drums of Dawn"
3: Betty Moore, romance, "For the Doves"

27. TV TWIN STARS

By clue 2, the five sets of TV twin stars are Brandon and his twin, Cherise and her twin, the Deluca twins, the twins who play Duane on one show, and the two who appear on "Fool House." There is only one boy-girl set of twins and they play Rebecca on one show, while the other sets play characters who are the same gender they are (clue 1); there are thus two female—playing Stephanie (clue 8) and Jenny (clue 12)—and two male—playing Duane (clue 2) and Mikey (clue 3)—sets. Since Brandon isn't one of the twins who plays Duane (clue 2) or Mikey (clue 9), he must be one of the twins who play Rebecca. By clue 4, one set of girl twins play a child on "Home Repairs." Since Cherise and her twin aren't on "Home Repairs" (clue 7), the child on "Home Repairs" is played by the Deluca twins (clue 2). Teresa doesn't share the role of Rebecca with Brandon, nor is she Cherise's twin (clue 5); Teresa is one of the Delucas. The role of Mikey is on "Fool House." By clue 3, then, Marcus and his twin play Duane, and Brian is one of the two who play Mikey. Neither Marcus and his twin (clue 6) nor Brandon and his (clue 9) are on "Family Matters"; Cherise and her twin are on that program. The Deluca twins, then play the role of Jenny on their show (clue 12), and Cherise and her twin share the Stephanie role. By clue 1, Brandon and his twin play Rebecca on "Dr. Quaint, Frontier Dentist"; Marcus and his twin are Duane on "Morning Sun." Neither Shelley (clue 8) nor Shannon (clue 13) is Brandon's twin, so Mandy is. Shelley is Teresa's twin and Shannon is Cherise's (clue 8). Colby is Brian's twin and Micah is Marcus's twin (clue 11). By clue 10, Brian and Colby are the Walsh brothers. Neither Marcus and Micah (clue 6) nor Brandon and Mandy (clue 14) are the Abbotts, so Cherise and Shannon are. Brandon and Mandy are the Holmes twins and Marcus and Micah are the Scholls (clue 15). In sum, the TV twin stars are:

Cherise & Shannon Abbott, Stephanie on "Family Matters"
Shelley & Teresa Deluca, Jenny on "Home Repairs"
Brandon & Mandy Holmes, Rebecca on "Dr. Quaint, Frontier Dentist"
Marcus & Micah Scholl, Duane on "Morning Sun"
Brian & Colby Walsh, Mikey on "Fool House"

28. THE DUELING MUSKETEERS

By clue 2, the chevalier fought twice as many duels as de Poitier, who fought twice as many duels as Hautophile. By clue 4, Skotopsis fought twice as many as de Bourges, who fought twice as many as the viscount. Since all six fought different numbers of duels, both clues do not mention the same three men. Hautophile was not de Bourges (clue 6), and de Poitiers was not the viscount (clue 7), so three different men are mentioned in each clue. Since all six men are mentioned in the two clues, either Skotopsis or the chevalier fought the most duels. By clue 1, then, the chevalier fought the most with 32 duels. By clue 2, de Poitiers fought 16 duels and Hautophile fought 8. These three men fought a total of 56 duels, so the other three fought a total of seven duels (clue 1). By clue 4, then, Skotopsis fought four duels, de Bourges two, and the viscount one. By clue 1, ranking the men in order from highest to lowest number of duels fought also ranks them in order from longest to shortest length of service. De Bourges and the viscount, then, served the two shortest lengths of service; by clue 3, de Bourges is Phobopan and the viscount is de Lille, while de Bourges had served two months and de Lille one month. De Vannes was neither the chevalier (clue 5) nor Hautophile (clue 6); he was Skotopsis. By clue 10, Hautophile had served one year and de Poitiers two years. De Vannes had served more than two months and less than a year, while the marquis had served either one or two years, and twice the length of de Vannes' service (clue 5); the marquis had served one year, and was Hautophile, while de Vannes had served six months. The chevalier, then, had served six years (clue 10). By clue 8 and by dividing the number of duels fought by the number of months served for each man (1.5 per month), Hautophile was de Sedan, de Poitiers was Misander, and de Vannes was the duke. By elimination, the chevalier was de Blois. De Lille was not Cynides (clue 9); he was Cacomaches while, by elimination, de Blois was Cynides. De Poitiers was not the count (clue 7); he was the baron while, by elimination, de Bourges was the count. In summary:

de Blois, Cynides, chevalier, 6 years, 32 duels
de Poitiers, Misander, baron, 2 years, 16 duels
de Sedan, Hautophile, marquis, 1 year, 8 duels
de Vannes, Skotopsis, duke, 6 months, 4 duels
de Bourges, Phobopan, count, 2 months, 2 duels
de Lille, Cacomaches, viscount, 1 month, 1 duel

29. ALIBI, ALIBI, WHO'S GOT AN ALIBI?

Clue 2 mentions three people in order from first to last: the officer checking out the shave, the one checking out Raggedy Sam, and Lewis. Clue 4 mentions three people in order from first to last: the one checking out Gorgeous Guy, Kao, and the one checking the tax audit. Since there are only four officers, at least two must be mentioned in both clues. Either all three mentioned in clue 2 are also mentioned in clue 4, or the four in order were the one checking out Gorgeous Guy, Kao who was checking out the shave, the one checking Raggedy Sam's claim of a tax audit, and Lewis. If the same three were mentioned in both clues, Gorgeous Guy would have claimed the shave, Kao would have been checking Raggedy Sam, and Lewis would have been checking the tax audit. Kao would not have been checking the coffee alibi (clue 1); he would have been checking the dentist. He would not have been second (clue 3); he would have been third. This, however, would leave the coffee alibi as the first checked, contradicting clue 1. Therefore, the same three men were not mentioned in both clues 2 and 4, so the four in order were the one checking Gorgeous Guy, Kao checking the shave, the one checking Raggedy Sam's claim of a tax audit, and Lewis. The coffee alibi was not checked first (clue 1); it was checked fourth and the dentist alibi was checked first. Kao was not checking on Bazooka Bob (clue 3); he was checking on Scarf Ace, while Lewis was checking on Bazooka Bob. Juarez was not checking Gorgeous Guy's dentist alibi (clue 3); he was checking Raggedy Sam's tax audit while, by elimination, Miller was checking Gorgeous Guy's dentist alibi. In summary:

1: Miller, Gorgeous Guy, dentist
2: Kao, Scarf Ace, shave
3: Juarez, Raggedy Sam, tax audit
4: Lewis, Bazooka Bob, coffee

30. THE DISTRICTS OF OLBIA

By clue 5, Yorba is city #6 and Gigi lives in city #8. By clue 2, Lili lives in city #4 and Vanda is city #3. By clue 3, since only cities #2, #5, and #6 have cities due west, Kiki lives in city #5, Judi in city #2, and Sella is city #1. Mimi's city and Walla are in the same district (clue 4), as are Bibi's city and Ronda (clue 1). Mimi does not share a district with either Fifi or Dodi; since Fifi's district is adjacent on one side with Bibi's and Dodi's is adjacent on the other (clue 1), Mimi's district is across the mountains and across the river from Bibi's. By clue 1, then, Mimi lives in Zemba and Walla and Zemba are in the same district; Zemba is city #7 and Walla is city #8. By clue 1, then, Bibi lives in Vanda, Ronda is city #4, Fifi lives in Sella, and Dodi lives in Yorba. By clue 4, Pomba is city #2 so, by elimination, Tolla is city #5. In summary:

1:	Sella,	Fifi	5:	Tolla,	Kiki
2:	Pomba,	Judi	6:	Yorba,	Dodi
3:	Vanda,	Bibi	7:	Zemba,	Mimi
4:	Ronda,	Lili	8:	Walla,	Gigi

31. THE MODFATHER

Three different gifts are mentioned in clues 5 and 8, so there is some overlap. If Karen's present were followed by boss Betty's present, the wife's tie, and the pants, by clue 4 Betty's gift would be the shoes. This contradicts clue 1. If Betty's present were followed by wife Karen's present, the boss's pants, and the tie, by clue 4 Marge's gift would be the pants. This contradicts clue 4. Therefore, Karen's and Betty's gifts are, in some order, the first and third ones opened. If Betty's gift were first, she couldn't be the mother (clue 2), so, by clue 7 Karen would be and Gemma would be the boss. Since Betty did not give Mr. Thomas the shoes (clue 1), Gemma would have and Marge's present would be the tie (clue 4). By elimination, Amy would be the wife, which would contradict clue 3. Therefore, Karen's gift was opened first, the boss's gift was second, Betty's tie was third, the wife's gift was fourth, and the pants were last. Since the mother's gift was not first (clue 2), it is the third gift and Gemma is Mr. Thomas's wife (clue 7). Since Marge did not give Mr. Thomas the pants (clue 4), she is his boss and, by clue 4, Karen's gift was the shoes. By elimination, Amy's gift was fifth. Amy is not the sister (clue 3), so Karen is and, by elimination, Amy is Mr. Thomas's daughter. Gemma's present is not the windbreaker (clue 6), so it is the sports coat and, by elimination, Marge's present was the windbreaker. In summary:

First, Karen, sister, shoes
Second, Marge, boss, windbreaker
Third, Betty, mother, tie
Fourth, Gemma, wife, sports coat
Fifth, Amy, daughter, pants

32. MR. BELL'S TOLLS

By clue 4, #5 was either 35¢ (one dime and one quarter) or 70¢ (two dimes and two quarters). If #5 costs 70¢, there are three possible combinations for #2 (clue 2). The first is six dimes ($.60). This combination can be eliminated because after adding the four coins used at #5 there would be only five coins remaining that cannot be distributed among the remaining three gates without contradicting clue 1. The other two combinations each require 5 coins; five dimes ($.50) and four dimes and one quarter ($.65). Six coins would then remain to be distributed among the remaining three gates at two coins apiece. However, this contradicts clue 3, which says that Mr. Bell used fewer coins at #1 than #2. Therefore, the toll at #5 is 35¢ and the only combination of coins greater in number but less in value for #2 (clue 2) is three dimes (30¢). Therefore, there are two possibilities for #1 (clue 3) 35¢ and 50¢. It cannot be 35¢ (one quarter and one dime) because this combination is already used at #5 (clue 1). Therefore, 50¢ (two quarters) is the toll for #1. The toll for #3 is 80¢ (clue 6). Without using quarters, eight dimes would be required. However, the fifteen-coin limit would then be exceeded. An odd number of quarters would leave a remainder that is not a multiple of ten. Therefore, #3 required two quarters and three dimes. Toll #4 is 60¢ (clue 5). The three remaining coins required for #4 is two quarters and one dime.

IN SUM:

Tollgate #1	.... 2 quarters	....	50¢
Tollgate #2	....	3 dimes	30¢
Tollgate #3	.... 2 quarters/	3 dimes	80¢
Tollgate #4	.... 2 quarters/	1 dime...........	60¢
Tollgate #5	.... 1 quarter /	1 dime...........	35¢

33. MUSICAL CONTESTANTS

The top two finishers did not sing (clue 1) or play flute (clue 2) or piano (clue 6); they played cello and oboe in some order. The student who finished fifth did not sing (clue 1) or play piano (clue 6); he or she played flute. The fourth and fifth finishers did not play in G major (clue 1), F major (clue 2), or D major (clue 6); they played in A major and C major in some order. A boy played C major (clue 4). Don finished second or third and Jane fourth or fifth (clue 1), so the boy who played C major was Nick, and Jane played A major. Don did not play G major (clue 1) or D major, which was played by a girl (clue 6); he played F major. He didn't finish first (clue 1), nor did the girl who played D major (clue 6); the one who played in G major, who by elimination is a girl, finished first. She did not play cello (clue 5); she played oboe, and the cello player finished second. If Don had finished third, by clue 1 the singer would have finished fourth and Jane would have finished fifth and played flute. By clue 2, Harper would have finished fourth; but this would make Harper the singer, contradicting clue 7. So Don didn't finish third; Don finished second and played cello in F major. The girl who played D major, then, finished third; by clue 6, the piano player finished fourth, and Murphy is the flute player who finished fifth. By elimination, the third-place finisher sang. She is therefore not Peggy (clue 7); she is Amy, and Peggy is the oboe player who finished first. Peggy's last name is not Perkins (clue 3), so Don's is (clue 6). Harper finished lower than Don Perkins (clue 2), but is not the third-place singer (clue 7); Harper finished fourth and played piano. By clue 4, Young is Amy who finished third, Nick who played C major finished fourth, and Jane, by elimination, finished fifth. By elimination, Peggy is Jones. In summary, in order of finish:

> Peggy Jones, oboe, G major
> Don Perkins, cello, F major
> Amy Young, voice, D major
> Nick Harper, piano, C major
> Jane Murphy, flute, A major

34. DOG DAYS BEGIN

Clue 2 lists the six couples: the Bunsens, Theresa and her husband, Paul and his wife, Brenda and her husband, who own a lavender house, Ted and his wife, and the couple who adopted the poodle. Theresa lives on Chestnut (clue 6). Bob is not Mr. Bunsen or Brenda's husband (clue 1), or Theresa's husband (clue 9); he adopted the poodle. His house is not blue or pink (clue 1), tan (clue 4), or charcoal (clue 5); it's green. The tan house is not Ted's or Theresa's (clue 1), or Paul's (clue 4); it is the Bunsens'. Theresa did not adopt the beagle (clue 6) so, by clue 1, the item beginning with B for her is her house color, which is blue. Paul's house is not pink (clue 1); it is charcoal while, by elimination, Ted's house is pink. The remaining items beginning with B are the beagle and Broadway, and they, in some order, are Paul's and Ted's (clue 1). Ted does not live on Broadway (clue 7), so he adopted the beagle, while Paul lives on Broadway. The remaining items beginning with P are Pam, Petrini, and Princeton Street, and they belong, in some order, to the Bunsens, Theresa, and Brenda (clue 1). Theresa, then, is Mrs. Petrini, Pam is Mrs. Bunsen, and Brenda lives on Princeton. Theresa did not adopt the Labrador (clue 3), so her item beginning with L is Larry, her husband. By elimination, her item beginning with G is her dog, so she adopted the German shepherd. Ted is not Mr. Carter (clue 6), so his wife is Cathy (clue 1). Bob's house is green, so his wife is not Ginger (clue 1); she is Lori. By elimination, Paul's wife is Ginger. By clue 1, Bob lives on Temple and he is Mr. Carter. Paul's remaining letters are L and T (clue 1), and they are, in some order, his last name and the dog he adopted. He is not Mr. Landry who didn't adopt the terrier (clue 8); he is Mr. Taylor, who adopted the Labrador. Brenda's house is lavender, so her last name is not Landry (clue 1); she is Goodman, while Ted and Cathy are the Landrys. By clue 1, then, the Landrys live on Grove, the terrier was adopted by the Goodmans, and Gary is Mr. Bunsen. By elimination, Carl is Mr. Goodman, the Bunsens adopted the collie, and they live on Lincoln. In summary:

> Gary & Pam Bunsen, collie, tan, Lincoln
> Larry & Theresa Petrini, German shepherd, blue, Chestnut
> Paul & Ginger Taylor, Labrador, charcoal, Broadway
> Carl & Brenda Goodman, terrier, lavender, Princeton
> Ted & Cathy Landry, beagle, pink, Grove
> Bob and Lori Carter, poodle, green, Temple

35. WHAT'S IN THE BASEMENT?

The twins are a boy and a girl (introduction); their last name is not Farmer (clue 5), Weaver (clue 6), or Spinner (clue 7); it is Barber. The Barber boy is not Bobby (clue 5) or Calvin, who has no sisters (clue 8), so Jeremy is Barber. Jenny is not Weaver (clue 6), Spinner (clue 7), or Farmer (clue 9): Jenny is the Barber girl. Bobby is not Farmer (clue 5), or Weaver (clue 6); Bobby is Spinner. Calvin, then, is the Weaver boy, and Erica is Farmer. Erica didn't carry the flashlight (clue 1), hammer (clue 5), hoe (clue 9) or phone (clue 10); Erica carried the umbrella. Jenny, then, was the girl who dreaded to see spiders (clue 2). Jenny didn't carry a flashlight (clue 1), hoe (clue 7) or hammer (clue 9); Jenny carried the phone. Neither Jeremy nor Bobby Spinner carried the hoe (clue 7), so Calvin did. Bobby didn't carry the hammer (clue 5), so Jeremy grabbed the hammer and Bobby carried the flashlight. Neither Calvin (clue 3) nor Erica (clue 10) has a basement, so neither expected to find the possum (clue 3). Erica also didn't expect gold (clue 1), nor does she have a cat (clue 4); Erica feared finding bats. One child guessed right (introduction); it was not Jeremy, Jenny or Bobby Spinner (clue 7), nor Erica, who guessed bats (clue 11). Calvin made the right guess. Calvin, then, didn't expect gold (clue 11), so Calvin found his cat. Bobby didn't expect gold (clue 1), so Jeremy guessed gold and Bobby guessed the possum. In summary:

Jenny Barber guessed spiders and carried the phone
Jeremy Barber guessed gold and carried the hammer
Erica Farmer guessed bats and carried the umbrella
Bobby Spinner guessed possum and carried the flashlight
Calvin Weaver found his cat and carried the hoe

36. RUSH HOUR

By clue 1, one driver was going 5 mph and another 35, and the other possible speeds driven are 10, 15, 20, 25, and 30. By clue 5, Juliana was driving 10, Michael 30, and the driver of the black car was going 5. The one going 35 was not on Freeway 405 (clue 2), 110 (clue 3), 134 (clue 6), or 210 (clue 7). Since 35 is not divisible by 2, the driver on the 101 was not going 35 (clue 7); the fastest driver was on Freeway 10. The black car was on either Freeway 10 or 405 (clue 4), so it was on 405. By clue 4, then, the blue car was on Freeway 10. The person in the black car going 5 mph on Freeway 405 was a woman, but not Harriet (clue 2); she was Imogene. Juliana, then, has a red car (clue 2). By clue 3, Michael was in the silver car, the man on the 110 was going 25 or 20, and Kenneth was going 20 or 15. By elimination, Leopold as on the 110 and Harriet was going 35. By clue 2 then, Leopold was going 20; by clue 3, Kenneth was going 15. By clue 7, Michael was on the 101 and Kenneth was on the 210. By elimination, Juliana was on the 134. By clue 6, then, Kenneth has the green car. By elimination, Leopold has the white car. In summary:

5: Imogene, black, 405
10: Juliana, red, 134
15: Kenneth, green, 210
20: Leopold, white, 110
30: Michael, silver, 101
35: Harriet, blue, 10

37. THE AMATEUR ARTISTS

Fifth place was not won by the carpenter (clue 3), mechanic (clue 4), florist (clue 5), or plumber (clue 6); it was won by the electrician. The first-place painting was not the seascape (clue 5), landscape or self-portrait (clue 6); it was either the floral or the mountain. The carpenter did not place first or second (clue 3). Since Mr. Hayes did not place first (clue 1), the mechanic did not place first or second (clue 4); the plumber and the florist placed, in some order, first and second. The floral painting was by neither the plumber nor the florist (clue 7), so it did not place first; the mountain panorama placed first. The second-place painting was not the seascape (clue 5), self-portrait (clue 6), or floral (clue 7); it was the landscape. By clue 6, then, the plumber placed first and the florist second. The third-place painting was not the seascape (clue 5) or the floral (clue 7); it was the self-portrait. The painter who took first with the mountain panorama was not Hayes (clue 1), Pruett (clue 2), Baxter (clue 3), or Vaughn (clue 5); he was Mr. Torino. Torino is not Dana (clue 1), Kent (clue 3), Greg (clue 4), or Basil (clue 6); he is Cory. The one who took second with the landscape was not Greg (clue 4), Dana or Basil (clue 6); he was Kent. Hayes is not Dana (clue 1) or Greg (clue 4). Hayes did not win fourth or fifth (clue 4). Basil won either fourth or fifth (clue 6),

148

so he is not Hayes; by elimination, Kent is Hayes. The man who placed third was not Pruett (clue 2) or Baxter (clue 3); he was Vaughn. Baxter did not paint the floral (clue 3); he painted the seascape, while Pruett painted the floral. Pruett is neither Dana (clue 1) nor Greg (clue 2); he is Basil. By clue 3, the carpenter is neither Basil Pruett nor Mr. Baxter; he is Vaughn. By elimination, the auto mechanic placed fourth. By clue 4, then, Greg placed fifth. Basil Pruett, then, placed fourth, and is the auto mechanic, while Greg is Baxter. By elimination, Vaughn is Dana. In summary:

1: Cory Torino, plumber, panorama
2: Kent Hayes, florist, landscape
3: Dana Vaughn, carpenter, self-portrait
4: Basil Pruett, auto mech., floral
5: Greg Baxter, electrician, seascape

38. AUNT MARTHA'S CELLAR

The blackberry jam is in space 3-D (clue 3). The apricot jam is not in column A or B (clue 11) or D (clue 9); it is in column C. In some order, the strawberry jam and peach jam are in columns A and B (clue 9). Since the apricot jam is in column C, space 4-D is not the grape jelly or apple butter (clue 11). Space 4-D is also not the pear butter (clue 5). Since the strawberry jam is in column A or B, space 4-D is not the pickled beets (clue 6). Since the peach jam is in column A or B, space 4-D is not the green beans (clue 1). Space 4-D is not the tomato sauce or stewed tomatoes (clue 2), or orange marmalade or carrots (clue 8). It is not the cucumber or zucchini pickles (clue 10); it is the canned corn. The remaining spaces in column D are not the carrots or green beans (clue 7), orange marmalade (clue 8), or grape jelly or apple butter (clue 11). Since the apple butter is not in that column, neither is the pear butter (clue 5). As established, the peach and strawberry jams are in columns A and B. Thus the pickled beets are not in column D (clue 6). The two spaces in column D are thus either the cucumber and zucchini pickles (clue 10) or tomato sauce and stewed tomatoes (clue 2). The two items that are not in column D are in column C (also clue 2). Therefore, space 3-A is not filled with the cucumber or zucchini pickles, tomato sauce or stewed tomatoes. The apricot jam is not in row 3 (clue 9), so space 3-A is not the grape jelly or apple butter (clue 11) or pear butter (clue 5). Space 3-A is not the pickled beets (clue 6), carrots or green beans (clue 7), or strawberry jam or peach jam (clue 9); it is the orange marmalade. Space 4-A is the carrots (clue 8). Spaces 4-B and 4-C are, in some order, the green beans (clue 7) and peach jam (clue 1). As established, the peach jam is in column A or B, so the peach jam is in space 4-B and the green beans are in space 4-C. As established, column B does not have the cucumber or zucchini pickles, or tomato sauce or stewed tomatoes. Space 3-B does not have apricot or strawberry jam (clue 9), pickled beets (clue 6), or grape jelly or apple butter (clue 11); it holds pear butter. Space 3-C is not the tomato sauce or cucumber pickles (clue 2), zucchini pickles (clue 4), apple butter (clue 5), strawberry jam or pickled beets (clue 6), or apricot jam or grape jelly (clue 11); it is stewed tomatoes. Space 2-C is the tomato sauce (clue 2). The cucumber pickles are in space 2-D (clue 2). The zucchini pickles are in space 1-D (clue 10). As established, the apricot jam is in column C. By elimination, the apricot jam is in space 1-C. The grape jelly is in space 1-A and the apple butter is in space 1-B (clue 11). The strawberry jam is not in space 2-B (clue 9); it is in space 2-A. By elimination, the pickled beets are in space 2-B. In summary, Bob and Bonnie discovered that the canned goods are as follows:

	A	B	C	D
1	grape jelly	apple butter	apricot jam	zucchini pickles
2	strawberry jam	pickled beets	tomato sauce	cucumber pickles
3	orange marmalade	pear butter	stewed tomatoes	blackberry jam
4	carrots	peach jam	green beans	corn

39. PSYCHIC MISCUES

No two women exchanged predictions and results (clue 8), and no woman had the result predicted for her. Therefore, by clue 2, Tanya, Mrs. Moran, and the lottery winner were three different women. Mrs. Forrest, Gloria, and the woman who had the crystal-ball reading were three different women (clue 6). At least one woman has to be common to both clue 2 and clue 6. Tanya is not Mrs. Forrest (clue 6); she also can't have had the crystal-ball reading since that woman's result was experienced by Mrs. Forrest (clue 6) rather than by Mrs. Moran (clue 2). Mrs. Moran is not Gloria (who experienced Mrs. Forrest's prediction rather than Tanya's); she also can't have had the crystal-ball reading since that would have involved a direct exchange of predictions and results with Tanya. Thus, clue 2's lottery winner has to be one of the three cited in clue 6. She can't be Mrs. Forrest (whose result was experienced by Gloria rather than by Tanya) or the one who had the crystal-ball reading (since Tanya is not Mrs. Forrest); she is Gloria. Thus, the crystal-ball prediction was experienced by Mrs. Forrest, Mrs. Forrest's prediction was experienced by Gloria (the lottery winner), Gloria's prediction was experienced by Tanya, and Tanya's prediction was experienced by Mrs. Moran; and by elimination, Mrs. Moran's prediction was experienced by the woman who had the crystal-ball reading. Since Gloria had the money result, that was Mrs. Forrest's prediction; by clue 4, Gloria is Mrs. Carter. Clue 4 also identifies Mrs. Forrest as the woman who took the business trip and Nadia as the one who had the crystal-ball reading and travel prediction. Nadia is not Mrs. Howe (clue 1); she is Mrs. Smythe, and Tanya is Mrs. Howe. From clue 1's remaining identifications, Mrs. Forrest is the one who had the astrology reading. Gloria Carter did not sprain her ankle, so she had the family problem predicted (giving Tanya that result); this leaves Mrs. Moran as the one who sprained her ankle (giving Tanya the medical problem prediction). Mrs. Moran is left as the woman predicted to meet a handsome stranger and Nadia as the one who actually met the IRS auditor. Delta is Mrs. Forrest (clue 3), and Karen is Mrs. Moran; also by clue 3, Karen did not have her palm read. Clue 5 excludes Karen as the one who had her tea leaves read, so she had the tarot-card reading, Tanya had the tea-leaf reading, and Gloria had the palm reading. In summary:

> Gloria Carter—palm reading—family problem/lottery winner
> Delta Forrest—astrology—money/business trip
> Tanya Howe—tea leaves—medical problem/son accused of vandalism
> Karen Moran—tarot cards—handsome stranger/sprained ankle
> Nadia Smythe—crystal ball—travel predicted/met IRS auditor

40. TWINS AND MORE TWINS

By clue 2, three generations of the same family (oldest to youngest) are the Slaters, Petrillos, and Holcombs. The unrelated twins, who are the youngest pair, are by elimination the Brookes. The Brooke girl is not Claudine (clue 1) or Antoinette (clue 5), nor is she Gabriella, who is related to another twin (clue 6); she is Martina. She is not the 5-year-old twin (clue 4); by clue 2, the 5-year-old twin is Holcomb and Martina Brooke is younger than 5. Two of the twins are 4 years apart in age (clue 5); since Slater, Petrillo, and Holcomb are each a generation apart, the 4-year difference is between the Holcomb and Brooke twins. Martina Brooke is 1. By clue 5, her brother is Daniel, so her middle name is Danielle, and the Holcomb twin is Antoinette. By clue 1, then, Claudine is Slater and Gabriella is Petrillo. Gabriella's uncle is Oliver (clue 6), so Oliver is Claudine's brother and Claudine's middle is name is Olivia. By clue 3, then, Christopher is Gabriella's brother and Ronald is Antoinette's brother, and Christopher and Gabriella are 25; Gabriella's middle name is Christine and Antoinette's is Ronalda. Claudine Olivia is 50 (clue 1). In sum, the four women are:

> Claudine Olivia Slater, age 50
> Gabriella Christine Petrillo, age 25
> Antoinette Ronalda Holcomb, age 5
> Martina Danielle Brooke, age 1

41. THE HALLOWEEN BALL

The woman dressed as a skunk is not Mrs. Coleman (clue 2), Kelso (clue 4), or Yemen or Quinn (clue 5); she is either Mrs. Moore or Wilkins. Angela is neither Moore nor Wilkins (clue 3), so Angela was not the skunk; nor was she the cat (clue 3) clown (clue 6), or witch or monkey (clue 9). Angela was the ghost. She is not Mrs. Coleman (clue 6), or Yemen or Quinn (clue 11); she is Mrs. Kelso. Della is not Mrs. Moore or Wilkins (clue 3), Coleman (clue 6), or Yemen (clue 11); she is Mrs. Quinn. Beverly is not Mrs. Coleman (clue 2), Yemen (clue 12), or Moore (clue 13); she is Mrs. Wilkins. Della Quinn is not married to Michael (clue 1), Willard (clue 3), Leonard (clue 8), or Danny or Marcus (clue 10); she is married to Howard. Angela Kelso is not married to Michael (clue 1), Leonard (clue 8), or Danny or Marcus (clue 10); she is married to Willard. The woman dressed as a cat is not Mrs. Coleman (clue 2), Della Quinn (clue 3), or Mrs. Moore (clue 13); she is either Beverly Wilkins or Mrs. Yemen. Linda is not Mrs. Yemen (clue 12), so she was not the cat; nor was Yvonne (clue 2) or Margie (clue 3). Beverly Wilkins was the cat. By elimination, the woman dressed as a skunk is Mrs. Moore. Howard's wife Della Quinn was not the clown (clue 6) or monkey (clue 9); she was the witch. Linda was neither the clown nor the monkey (also clue 9), so she dressed as the skunk and is Mrs. Moore. Michael's wife is not Beverly Wilkins in the cat costume or Linda Moore in the skunk costume (clue 1), or in the clown costume (clue 7); Michael's wife was dressed as a monkey. She is not Margie (clue 1); she is Yvonne, and Margie, by elimination, was the clown. By clue 8, Leonard's wife is neither Linda the skunk nor Beverly the cat; Leonard is married to Margie the clown. Linda's husband is not Marcus (clue 5); she is married to Danny while Beverly is married to Marcus. Danny Moore was not the elephant (clue 2), monster (clue 3), lion or robot (clue 5), or dinosaur (clue 10); he was the vampire. Willard Kelso was not the dinosaur or elephant (clue 4), robot (clue 6), or monster (clue 7); he was the lion. Margie's husband Leonard was not the elephant (clue 1), monster (clue 7), or robot (clue 8); he was the dinosaur. Leonard and Margie, then, are not the Colemans (clue 4); they are the Yemens and Michael and Yvonne, by elimination, are the Colemans. Howard Quinn was not the elephant (clue 6) or monster (clue 7); he was the robot. Marcus Wilkins was not the elephant (clue 10); he was the monster while Michael Coleman, by elimination, was the elephant. In summary:

Coleman	Michael (elephant)	Yvonne (monkey)
Kelso	Willard (lion)	Angela (ghost)
Moore	Danny (vampire)	Linda (skunk)
Quinn	Howard (robot)	Della (witch)
Wilkins	Marcus (monster)	Beverly (cat)
Yemen	Leonard (dinosaur)	Margie (clown)

42. MOVIE RATINGS

No film was rated above 7 (clue 5). The Adelphi film was rated twice the spy film, which was not the lowest (clue 3). The romance was rated twice the horror (clue 6). Since all five films received different ratings, and four different films are mentioned in these two clues, either the spy film was rated 2 and the Adelphi film 4; or the spy film was rated 3 and the Adelphi film 6 (clue 5). If the spy film had been rated 2 and the Adelphi film 4, the horror would have been rated 3 and the romance 6 (clue 6). The Adelphi film would have been either the comedy or the science fiction. By clue 1, then, either the science fiction would have been 3 and the comedy at the Adelphi 4 or the science fiction at the Adelphi would have been 4 and the comedy 5. In either case, there would be no film rated lower than the spy film, which contradicts clue 3. Therefore, the spy film was not rated 2 and the Adelphi film 4; the spy film was rated 3 and the Adelphi film was rated 6. The film at the Rialto was one point higher than the one at the Plaza (clue 4), while the film at the Tower was one point higher than the one at the Bijou (clue 7). The theater not mentioned in these two clues is the Adelphi. The film at the Adelphi was rated one point higher or lower than the science fiction or comedy (clue 1). The only possibility, then, is that all five film ratings were no more than one point apart; the horror film was rated 2, the romance 4, and one film was rated 5. By clue 1, then, the comedy at the Adelphi was rated 6 and the science fiction was rated 5. The two pairs of films mentioned in clues 4 and 7 are, in some order, the romance and the science fiction and the horror and the spy film. The romance was not at the Plaza (clue 2), so the romance and the science fiction are mentioned in clue 7; the romance was at the Bijou and the science fiction was at the Tower. By clue 4, the horror was at the Plaza and the spy film at the Rialto. In summary:

Adelphi, comedy, 6
Tower, science fiction, 5
Bijou, romance, 4
Rialto, spy, 3
Plaza, horror, 2

43. TRIVIAL RISK

Monday's champion was not Jones or Foster (clue 2) or Han (clue 5); that champion was either Mr. Gonzalez (clue 1) or Ives. Monday's question was not about African history (clue 1), TV commercials (clue 2), or the American Revolution (clue 5); it was either chemistry or opera. If Mr. Gonzalez had won Monday, the question would not have been on opera (clue 4); it would have

151

been on chemistry. Althea would have won Tuesday (clue 1). Ives would have won more than Gonzalez (clue 3), who would have won $2,000 more than Brian, who won $2,000 more than the one who answered the question about commercials (clue 2). By clue 2, however, this would leave no place for Jones and Foster. Therefore, Gonzalez did not win Monday, so Ives did. Ives' question was not on chemistry (clue 3); it was on opera. Ives is a woman (clue 4). She is not Althea (clue 1), so she is Cathy. Friday's champion was not Althea (clue 1) or David (clue 4); he was either Brian or Eric. If he had been Eric, his last name would not be Gonzalez (clue 1), Jones (clue 4), or Han (clue 7); he would be Foster. His question would not have been on commercials (clue 2), chemistry (clue 3), or the Revolution (clue 5); it would have been on African history. Thursday's question would not have been on chemistry (clue 3) or the Revolution (clue 5); it would have been on commercials. Thursday's winner would not have been Mr. Gonzalez (clue 1) or Jones (clue 2); it would have been Han. This, however, contradicts clue 7. Therefore, Eric was not Friday's champion, so Brian was. Brian is not Gonzalez (clue 1), Jones or Foster (clue 2); he is Han. The one who answered the question about commercials was not Brian Han, Jones, or Foster (clue 2); Mr. Gonzalez answered that question. Althea is not Foster (clue 6); she is Jones. Brian Han's question was not on the Revolution (clue 5) or African history (clue 7); it was on chemistry. By clue 1, then, Mr. Gonzalez won Tuesday, Althea Jones won Wednesday, and the question on African history was Thursday. By elimination, Althea's question was on the Revolution, and Foster won Thursday. Foster is not Eric (clue 3); he is David, while Eric is Gonzalez. By clue 4, Eric Gonzalez won $11,000. By clue 2, then, Brian won $13,000 and Cathy won $15,000. By clue 3, David won $10,000, so Althea won $12,000 (clue 2). In summary:

> M.: Cathy Ives, opera, $15,000
> T: Eric Gonzalez, commercials, $11,000
> W: Althea Jones, Revolution, $12,000
> TH: David Foster, African history, $10,000
> F: Brian Han, chemistry, $13,000

44. PAPER NICKEL WEST

Lee was fourth (clue 7). The first in line was a woman (clue 8). The side dish she ordered was not the baked potato (clue 1), onion rings (clue 4), chili (clue 6), or fries (clue 10); it was corn on the cob. The side dish ordered last was not the baked potato (clue 1), chili (clue 6), or fries (clue 10); it was onion rings. The fifth in line, then, was a man (clue 4). The side dish ordered fourth then was not the baked potato (clue 1). A woman had root beer (clue 3), so the fourth side dish was not fries (clue 10); it was chili. By clue 6, the fifth person had fruit punch. Root beer was not ordered first or second (clue 10), so it was ordered either third or fourth. If it had been ordered third, the first and third in line (clue 3) would have been women. Fries would have been ordered second (clue 10), so the baked potato would have been ordered third. The second and fourth in line would also have been women (clue 1). This, however, would yield four women and one man, contradicting clue 4. Therefore, the root beer was not ordered third, so it was ordered fourth. The fourth in line was a woman (clue 3). Since women were first and fourth, by clue 1, there were three women and two men in the group, and a man ordered the baked potato. Since one of the men was fifth, by clue 2, the woman fourth in line ordered the patty melt, and the man who ordered the potato was third. By elimination, the third woman was second, and she ordered the fries. By clue 10, Sal was first. Lee is not Zabel (clue 2), Chase (clue 4), Whyte (clue 5), or Miles (clue 6); she is Glass. The man fifth in line was not Chase (clue 4), Whyte (clue 5), or Miles (clue 6); he was Zabel. By clue 4, the man third in line was Chase. Mr. Chase did not have lemonade (clue 1) or chocolate milk (clue 9); he had cola. Since the first two in line were both women, by clue 9, the woman second in line had chocolate milk and Mr. Chase had the tuna melt. By elimination, Sal had lemonade. The cheeseburger was not ordered first or second (clue 5); it was ordered fifth by Zabel. Sal did not order the hamburger (clue 10); she ordered the BLT while, by elimination, the second woman in line ordered the hamburger. Miles is not Sal (clue 6); Miles was second in line. By elimination, Sal is Whyte. The three remaining people are the woman second in line and the two men, so Ann was second in line. Viv was not fifth (clue 5); he was third while, by elimination, Pat was fifth. In summary:

> 1: Ms. Sal Whyte, BLT, corn, lemonade
> 2: Ms. Ann Miles, hamburger, fries, choc. milk
> 3: Mr. Viv Chase, tuna melt, baked, cola
> 4: Ms. Lee Glass, patty melt, chili, root beer
> 5: Mr. Pat Zabel, cheeseburger, onion rings, fruit punch

45. THE MOBILE GROCER

Clue 1 mentions three of the farms in order from first to last: the Perkinses', Melanie's, and the dairy farm. Clue 6 also mentions three of the farms in order from first to last: the Durhams', Tangie's, and the cherry orchard. The Perkinses do not own the cherry orchard (clue 1), nor does Melanie (clue 6), so Tangie is not Mrs. Perkins, and the cherry orchard is not mentioned in both clues. The dairy farm is not Tangie's nor the Durhams', (clue 7), so all six farms are mentioned in these two clues. There are then two possibilities: either the six in order from first to last are the Perkinses', Melanie's, the dairy, the Durhams', Tangie's, and the cherry orchard; or the six from first to last are the Durhams', Tangie's, the cherry orchard, the Perkinses', Melanie's, and the dairy. By clue 10, three of the stops in order from first to last are the Atkinses', Candice's, and the peach orchard. Tangie is not Mrs. Atkins (clue 6), and Melanie does not grow peaches (clue 1), so the only possibility is that the six in order from first to last are the Perkinses', Melanie's, the dairy, the Durhams', Tangie's, and the cherry orchard. The Durhams do not grow peaches (clue 6), so Melanie is not Mrs. Atkins (clue 10). By elimination, the Atkinses own the dairy, Candice is Mrs. Durham, and Tangie grows peaches. The man who grows cherries is not Bert (clue 2), Dirk (clue 3), Walter or Claude (clue 9); he is either Lucas or Hugh. The woman who grows cherries is not, then, Mitzie (clue 4), or Carrie (clue 5); she is Laurie. Her husband is not Lucas (clue 4), so he is Hugh. Mr. Perkins is not Bert (clue 2), Walter or Claude (clue 9); he is either Dirk or Lucas. Mitzie is married to neither Dirk (clue 3) nor Lucas (clue 4), so she is not Mrs. Perkins; by elimination, Carrie is, while Mitzie is Mrs. Atkins. Carrie does not raise either corn or wheat (clue 5); she grows apples. Her husband is not, then, Lucas (clue 4); he is Dirk. Bert's stop is fourth or fifth (clue 2). The Durhams raise either corn or wheat. Bert raises neither corn (clue 2) nor wheat (clue 8), so he is not Mr. Durham; he is Tangie's husband. The Putnams are the sixth stop (clue 2). Bert is not Mr. Rutgers (clue 8); he is Mr. Crocker, while Melanie is Mrs. Rutgers. Melanie's husband is neither Walter (clue 8) nor Claude (clue 9); he is Lucas. By clue 9, then, Walter is the third stop and Claude is the fourth. Claude does not grow corn (clue 9); he grows wheat, while Lucas grows corn. In summary:

1: Dirk & Carrie Perkins, apples
2: Lucas & Melanie Rutgers, corn
3: Walter & Mitzie Atkins, dairy
4: Claude & Candice Durham, wheat
5: Bert & Tangie Crocker, peaches
6: Hugh & Laurie Putnam, cherries

46. GLITCH-FREE VACATIONS

Four consecutive departures in order are: the one to Finland, Ms. Zimmer's, the one with orange luggage, and Robin's (clue 1). The person with red luggage left the day after the Portugal departure (clue 3), so Ms. Zimmer's luggage was not red. Nor was it a man's yellow luggage (clue 5), white (clue 7) or green, since the person with green luggage left two days before George (clue 11). Ms. Zimmer's luggage was blue. By clue 9, then, the female FLP went to Finland and Valdez left the day before the FLP—Valdez left Monday or Tuesday, FLP Tuesday or Wednesday, Ms. Zimmer Wednesday or Thursday, the one with orange luggage Thursday or Friday, and Robin Friday or Saturday. Wong left three days before the man with yellow luggage (clue 5); Wong is the FLP and Robin is the man with the yellow luggage. Since George is not Ms. Zimmer or Ms. Wong, by clue 11, Ms. Wong had green luggage and George is the man with orange luggage. The person with red luggage, then, left either Tuesday or Saturday (clue 3). If the person with the red luggage had left Tuesday, he or she would be Valdez, the person going to Portugal would have left Monday, Ms. Wong would have left for Finland Wednesday, Ms. Zimmer Thursday, George Friday, and Robin Saturday. Chris would have left no later than Thursday, and the one going to Romania no earlier than Tuesday, contradicting clue 8. So the person with red luggage didn't leave Tuesday. He or she left Saturday, Robin went to Portugal Friday, George Thursday, Ms. Zimmer Wednesday, FLP Wong Tuesday, and Valdez Monday. By elimination, Valdez had white luggage; the OPD, then, left Saturday with red luggage (clue 7). By clue 2, therefore, the VSC is Ms. Zimmer and Valdez went to Ireland, and both are women; the OPD is male (clue 7). By clue 8, Ms. Zimmer went to Romania and Chris is the OPD. Frankie and Aames left on consecutive days (clue 10); Frankie is Ms. Zimmer and George is Aames. By elimination, Ms. Wong is Mary. SPA Pat is Valdez (clue 6). The CCR and Hartke did not leave on consecutive days (clue 4), so George Aames is the CCR and Chris is Hartke. By elimination, Robin is Quinn and is the CMP. CCR George Aames didn't go to Sweden (clue 4); he went to Greece and Chris Hartke went to Sweden. In summary:

Monday: Ms. Pat Valdez, SPA to Ireland with white luggage
Tuesday: Ms. Mary Wong, FLP to Finland with green luggage
Wednesday: Ms. Frankie Zimmer, VSC to Romania with blue luggage
Thursday: Mr. George Aames, CCR to Greece with orange luggage
Friday: Mr. Robin Quinn, CMP to Portugal with yellow luggage
Saturday: Mr. Chris Hartke, OPD to Sweden with red luggage

47. HOUSE AND GARDEN SHOW

Two of the five men were sellers (clue 1) and three were buyers (clue 2), so two women bought and three sold. Willard was the only man who sold to a man (also clue 2), and Mr. Taylor was the only man who bought from a man (clue 1), so Willard sold something to Mr. Taylor. Fred was the second man who sold (clue 5), so he sold to Norma (clue 1). Two items were sold in the morning and one in the evening (clue 3); the four people who were there only in the afternoon (clue 4), therefore, bought and sold the other two items amongst themselves. Ms. Hanson was the evening buyer (clue 7) and Carolyn was the evening seller (clue 3), so Carolyn sold to Ms. Hanson. Doris (clue 7) and Mr. King (clue 8) were the morning sellers. Richard was a morning buyer, but didn't buy from Mr. King (clue 8); he bought from Doris. Since the only man who bought from another man was Mr. Taylor (clue 1), by clue 3 morning buyer Mr. Bishop is Richard, while Mr. King sold the porch swing. Norma bought from Fred, so is not Ms. Hanson. Nor is Pamela, who attended in the afternoon (clue 4); Marsha is Ms. Hanson. One person in clue 5 and one is clue 6 attended during the evening. By clue 6, then, Carolyn sold the mop. Carolyn is Ms. Smith (clue 5). Ms. Levy attended in the afternoon and isn't Pamela (clue 4) or Doris (clue 7); Norma is Levy. The item she bought from Fred was not the hoe (clue 2) or the blender (clue 5); she bought the door. The other male seller Willard, then, is Mr. King, and sold the swing to Mr. Taylor. Eric and Jack, by elimination, were both buyers; Eric bought in the afternoon (clue 4), so Jack, by elimination, is Mr. Taylor. Pamela, then, was the second afternoon seller (also clue 4). Mr. Young attended in the afternoon and isn't Eric (clue 4); Fred is Young. Eric, then, is Mr. Vogel (clue 6). Fred and Pamela both attended in the afternoon (clue 4), so Pamela didn't sell the blender (clue 5). Doris sold the blender, and Pamela sold the hoe to Eric. Pamela isn't Gavin (clue 2), so Doris is Gavin, and Pamela is Rodeno. In summary:

morning: Jack Taylor bought porch swing from Willard King
           Richard Bishop bought blender from Doris Gavin
afternoon: Norma Levy bought screen door from Fred Young
           Eric Vogel bought hoe from Pamela Rodeno
evening: Marsha Hanson bought mop from Carolyn Smith

48. SANDY BAY FAMILIES
Part I: SANDY BAY CHILDREN

The seven families are the Emersons, Dodges, McKays (introduction), Simpsons (clue 1), Robinsons (clue 8), and two sets of Montgomerys (clue 3). Matt is a Dodge (clue 2), Joey is a Montgomery (clue 3), Greg is the only Robinson (clue 8) and Geoff is the only Emerson (introduction and clue 8). There are four McKays, including Hannah (clue 5), another girl and two boys (clue 4). There are five Montgomerys, including Joey and four girls, two of whom must be in each family (clue 3). All six girls are now placed, so the Dodges and the Simpsons have boys only. The only possible combination of the same first and last initial (clue 9) is S—Sherry or Spencer, one of whom is a Simpson—and that must be Spencer as he is a boy. Joey and Sherry are siblings (clue 10), as are Kate and Alan, who are McKays. The other McKay boy cannot be Brett, who is Hannah's age; or Josh, who is Alan's age (clue 6); he is Cameron. Cindy and Christine are cousins, not sisters (clue 9), so that one is Sherry's sister and the other is Nicole's. Since Nicole and Cindy are the same age (clue 6), Nicole and Christine are sisters and Cindy is Sherry's sister. Brett has an older brother (clue 7), who can only be Matt, Josh or, Spencer. He isn't Spencer, who is the youngest (clue 2). Brett is the same age as Hannah (clue 6), who is older than Alan (clue 5), who is the same age as Josh (clue 6); so Brett's brother is Matt, and Brett is a Dodge. Josh, then, is a Simpson.

In summary, the children are:
Greg Robinson; Geoff Emerson; Matt and Brett Dodge; Hannah, Kate, Alan, and Cameron McKay; Joey, Sherry, and Cindy Montgomery; Nicole and Christine Montgomery; Spencer and Josh Simpson.

Matt is the oldest at 15 and Spencer is the youngest at 3 (clue 2). Geoff is 12 (introduction). Brett and Hannah are the same age (clue 6), which is thus 13 (clue 1). Joey is at least 5, since he is older than Christine (clue 12) who is older than Spencer. Nicole and Cindy are the same age, which is at least 7 (clue 1). Kate is at least 8, her older brother Alan (clue 10) is at least 10. Hannah is 13, so Josh and Alan (clue 6) are at most 11 (clue 1). Greg is midway between Spencer and Josh (clue 11); Josh and Alan are, therefore, 11, and Greg is 7. Greg cannot be the same age as Cindy and Nicole (clue 6), so they are 8. Kate is 9 (clue 12). Sherry is a year younger than Alan (clue 10) and is 10. Christine is 5 (clue 13). Cameron and Joey are 6 (clue 12).

In summary:
   Matt is 15, Brett and Hannah are 13, Geoff is 12, Alan and Josh are 11, Sherry is 10, Kate is 9, Cindy and Nicole are 8, Greg is 7, Cameron and Joey are 6, Christine is 5, and Spencer is 3.

Part II: SANDY BAY PARENTS

From the introduction to part 1, we know Geoff's mother is Gwen Emerson. Helen, Debbie, and Lynn all have daughters (clue 2), so they are Mrs. McKay and the two Mrs. Montgomerys, in some order (solution of part 1). Andy, Al, Dave, and Rick have only sons (clue 3) so they are Mr. Dodge, Mr. Simpson, Mr. Emerson, and Mr. Robinson, in some order. Jim, Norm, and one of the Ricks, then, are married to Helen, Debbie, and Lynn. One mother has the same initial as her daughter (clue 4): the only possibility is that Helen is Hannah McKay's mother. Three of the mothers have the same initials as their sons (clue 4); we know Gwen is Geoff's mother. Marlene is not Matt's mother (clue 5), so Sheila is Spencer Simpson's mother and Brenda is Brett Dodge's mother. By elimination, Marlene is Mrs. Robinson. Debbie is Joey Montgomery's mom (clue 5), so she is not married to Jim (clue 4); nor is she married to Rick (clue 1), so her husband is Norm. Helen is not related to either Rick (clue 6), so she must be married to Jim (McKay), and Lynn is married to Rick (Montgomery). Dave has only one child (clue 7), but it is not Geoff (clue 6), so it must be Greg Robinson. The other Rick, then, is Mr. Emerson (clue 7). Sheila is not married to Andy (clue 8), so Brenda Dodge is. Sheila's husband, by elimination, is Al.

In summary the couples are:
   Andy and Brenda Dodge, Rick and Gwen Emerson, Al and Sheila Simpson, Dave and Marlene Robinson, Jim and Helen McKay, Norm and Debbie Montgomery (parents of Joey, Cindy, and Sherry) and Rick and Lynn Montgomery (parents of Nicole and Christine).

49. MIS-MATCHMAKER, MIS-MATCHMAKER

By clue 1, the woman tattoo artist was mismatched with the man who enjoys quiet country walks. By clue 7, Ms. Eastman and the man who enjoys professional wrestling are a second mismatch. Neither the tattoo artist (clue 8) nor Miss Eastman (clue 17) is the heavy-metal concerts enthusiast so, by clue 13, Mr. Lopez and the woman who enjoys heavy-metal concerts are a third couple. Ms. Dove isn't the tattoo artist (clue 21). Therefore, since she enjoys romance novels (clue 10), she and patent attorney Huey form a fourth pairing. By clue 19, Ian Nicks was mismatched with the pediatrician. Since she isn't Ms. Eastman (clue 2), she and Ian are the fifth couple. By clue 4, Ula was paired with the plumbing contractor. Ula isn't Ms. Eastman (clue 17), and the plumbing contractor isn't Mr. Lopez (clue 18) or the man who enjoys quiet walks (clue 22); Ula is the pediatrician and Ian Nicks the plumbing contractor. By clue 16, Sally Adams was mismatched with the man who enjoys watching "Casablanca"; Sally is the heavy-metal devotee and Mr. Lopez enjoys the Bogart classic. Ms. Berger has no wedding plans (clue 20), so she is not Ula (clue 4); Ms. Berger is the tattoo artist. By elimination, Ula is Ms. Chan. Her beau Ian Nicks isn't the man who enjoys racing motorcycles (clue 5); Huey is. Plumbing contractor Ian doesn't enjoy Las Vegas or playing in a string quartet (clue 3), or a lonely beach at sunset (clue 14); Ian thrives on an all-night party. By clue 11, Ula Chan doesn't enjoy weekends in Las Vegas or playing in a string quartet; Ula enjoys a lonely beach at sunset. By elimination, Ms. Berger or Ms. Eastman, in some order, enjoy Vegas and string quartets. Neither, then, was matched with the chimney sweep (clue 3); the sweep is Mr. Lopez. The choir director wasn't matched with Ms. Berger (clue 9); he was matched with Ms. Eastman. He is not Frank or Greg (clue 15); he is Julio. Julio wasn't paired with Teresa (clue 24) or Ricki (clue 25); Ms. Eastman is Val. By clue 26, then, Val Eastman enjoys playing in a string quartet, while Ms. Berger loves weekends in Las Vegas. Val Eastman isn't the history professor (clue 2) nor the woman golf pro or television producer (clue 6); she is a used-car dealer. The history professor, by elimination, is the man who enjoys quiet walks. He isn't Greg (clue 12), so he is Frank, and Greg is Lopez. Greg's mate Sally Adams is not the television producer (clue 12); Sally is the golf pro and Ms. Dove the producer. By clue 23, Mr. King is not Frank or wrestling fan Julio, he is Huey. By clue 24, Teresa was mismatched with Huey and Ricki with Frank. Frank is not O'Hara (clue 26); he is Mr. Marinovich and Julio O'Hara. In sum, the mismatches are:

Sally Adams, golf pro, enjoys heavy-metal concerts; with Greg Lopez, chimney sweep, enjoys watching "Casablanca"

Ricki Berger, tattoo artist, enjoys weekends in Las Vegas; with Frank Marinovich, history professor, enjoys quiet country walks

Ula Chan, pediatrician, enjoys a lonely beach at sunset; with Ian Nicks, plumbing contractor, enjoys an all-night party

Teresa Dove, television producer, enjoys romance novels; with Huey King, patent attorney, enjoys racing motorcycles

Val Eastman, used-car dealer, enjoys playing in a string quartet; with Julio O'Hara, choir director, enjoys professional wrestling

50. HOUSE PAINTING

Of the six trim colors, white was used on three houses, cream was used on two, and green was used on two (clue 1), so the other three trim colors were each used only once. The Grays' house color is the same as a trim color that was used at least twice, on the white house and on the brown house (clue 4). White trim was not used on the white house and cream was not used as a main color, so green is the main color of the Grays' house and a trim color on the white and brown houses. The Grays' green house has no more than one color in common with any other house (clue 9), so it doesn't have either brown or white trim. Since neither the white nor the green house has white trim, the three houses with white trim (clue 1) are blue, brown and gray. The green house, then, is the one with neither white nor gray (clue 6). The green house also doesn't have blue trim (clue 5); by elimination, it has black and cream trim. By clue 9, then, neither the white house with green trim nor the blue house has cream trim; the second house with cream trim (clue 1) is the gray house. No two houses have more than two colors in common (clue 2); since the white and brown houses share white and green, the white house doesn't have brown trim, nor does it have blue trim (clue 5). Black was used only on the green house (clue 1) so, by elimination, the white house has gray trim. The sixth trim color was used on the blue house; it was not blue so was brown. Black and blue were the only two colors used only once; since the Grays chose black, by clue 7 the Blacks have the blue house with brown and white trim. The Whites' house color is the same as a trim color on the Browns' house (clue 3); since the Whites don't have the white house (clue 8) and the Blacks are the only family with brown trim, the Whites have the gray house and the Browns have the white house with gray and green trim. The Greens, by elimination, have the brown house. In summary:

Blacks have blue house with brown & white trim
Browns have white house with gray & green trim
Grays have green house with black & cream trim
Greens have brown house with green & white trim
Whites have gray house with cream & white trim

51. GUESS WHO'S COMING TO DINNER

The guests on the 4th were not the neighbors (clue 4), roommate (clue 5), or in-laws (clue 9); they were either the grandparents or boss. The silver used on the 4th was not Toccata (clue 1) or Grande Plume (clue 9). The silver used on the 4th cost $245, $285, or $440 (clue 3). Satin Frost cost at least $650 (clue 7), so it was not used on the 4th; either Vivace or Rose Gold was. The silver used for the boss was neither Vivace (clue 2) nor Rose Gold (clue 8), so the boss was not the guest on the 4th. Therefore, the grandparents were the guests on the 4th. The silver used on the 4th did not cost $245 (clue 1), but cost less than $440 (clue 3); it cost $285. Cara's silver cost either $650 or $830 (clue 3). The Toccata silver cost $245 (clue 1). It was not Edith's (clue 1), Gwen's (clue 4), or Amelia's (clue 6); it was Inez's. By clue 9, Inez's party was not on either the 25th or 27th; it was on either the 10th or the 16th. If it had been on the 10th, Edith would have had the party on the 4th (clue 1). By clue 7, the silver used for the neighbors would have cost at least $440, so Satin Frost would have cost $830. Inez's guests would not have been neighbors (clue 4), boss (clue 7), or in-laws (clue 9); they would have been the roommate and spouse. The silver on the 4th would

156

have been Vivace (clue 5). The silver on the 16th would not have been the $830 Satin Frost (clue 6) or Grande Plume (clue 9); it would have been Rose Gold. The Rose Gold would not have cost $440 (clue 8), so it would have cost $650. The guests on the 16th would not have been the neighbors (clue 4) or boss (clue 8) so, by elimination, the guests on the 16th would have been the in-laws. The silver used on the 25th and 27th would have been, in some order, the $830 Satin Frost and the Grande Plume. The guests on the 25th and 27th would have been, in some order, the neighbors and the boss. Satin Frost was not used at the party for the neighbors (clue 7), so it would have been used for the boss, while Grande Plume would have been used for the neighbors. Cara's silver would not have cost $650 (clue 3); it would have cost $830 and been the Satin Frost. Amelia would not have owned the Rose Gold (clue 6); she would have owned the Grande Plume. This, however, contradicts clue 9. Therefore, Inez's party was not on the 10th, it was on the 16th. By clue 9, the in-laws were guests on the 25th and Grande Plume was used the 27th. The hostess on the 27th was not Edith (clue 1), Gwen (clue 4), or Amelia (clue 9); she was Cara. Inez's guests were not her boss or her neighbors (clue 7); they were her roommate and spouse. The silver used for the neighbors cost at least $440 so, by clue 7, Satin Frost cost more than $685; it cost $830. Cara's Grande Plume, then, cost $650 (clue 3). Cara's guests were not her neighbors (clue 7); her guest was her boss, while by elimination, the neighbors were guests on the 10th. By clue 4, Gwen was hostess on the 4th. By clue 1, then, Edith was hostess on the 10th. By elimination, Amelia was hostess on the 25th. Edith did not own the $830 Satin Frost (clue 7), so Amelia did. By elimination, Edith's silver was $440. Edith's silver was not Rose Gold (clue 4); her silver was Vivace, while Gwen had Rose Gold. In summary:

> 4th: Gwen, Rose Gold, $285, grandparents
> 10th: Edith, Vivace, $440, neighbors
> 16th: Inez, Toccata, $245, roommate
> 25th: Amelia, Satin Frost, $830, in-laws
> 27th: Cara, Grande Plume, $650, boss

52. THE CONFUSING QUADRUPLETS

Since no one wore the same color for skirt and blouse (clue 1), there are twelve possible skirt/blouse combinations, and each combination was worn once. Tina wore a blue blouse Monday (clue 2), and Betty wore a tan skirt Tuesday (clue 3). Rose never wore red, Greta never wore green, Tina never wore tan, and Betty never wore blue (clue 1). Each girl, then, wore a skirt and a blouse in each of the other three colors one day (clue 1). Greta did not wear a tan blouse Monday (clue 2), so she wore a red one. Rose did not wear a blue skirt Tuesday (clue 3), so she wore a green one. On Tuesday, Betty wore either the red or green blouse with her tan skirt (clue 1). If she had worn the green, Tina would have worn the red blouse that day (clue 1), her Wednesday blouse would have been green, and her Tuesday skirt would have been blue. Tina's Wednesday skirt would not have been green, so it would have been red, and her Monday skirt would have been green. By elimination, the one who wore the red skirt Tuesday would have been Greta. Rose wore the green skirt Tuesday, so the one who wore it Wednesday would have been Betty. By elimination, Betty's Monday skirt would have been red. Greta would not have worn the blue skirt Wednesday (clue 4); she would have worn the tan one and, by elimination, Rose would have worn the blue that day. Since Tina would have worn the green blouse that day, Rose's blouse would have been tan. Betty's would not have been blue, so it would have been red while, by elimination, Greta's would have been blue. Betty's Monday blouse would not have been green (her Tuesday blouse color) or red (her Wednesday blouse color), so it would have been tan. Greta's Tuesday blouse color would not have been blue (her Wednesday color) or red (her Monday color), so it would have been tan. However, Betty would have worn a red skirt and tan blouse on Monday and Greta would have worn the same combination Tuesday, which contradicts clue 1. Therefore, Betty did not wear the green blouse Tuesday, so she wore the red one. The tan skirt/green blouse combination was worn, then, by Rose (clue 1). By elimination, the tan skirt/blue blouse combination was worn by Greta. She did not wear that combination either Monday (when she wore a red blouse) or Tuesday (when Betty wore the tan skirt); she wore it Wednesday. Rose, then, wore the tan skirt with the green blouse Monday (clue 1). The skirt Greta wore Monday with the red blouse was, by elimination, blue. The day she wore the red skirt, then, was Tuesday, and she wore a tan blouse with it. By elimination, the girl who wore the blue skirt Tuesday was Tina. She did not wear the blue blouse with it (clue 1), so she wore the green while, by elimination, Rose wore the blue blouse Tuesday. Tina wore a blue blouse Monday; the only color skirt remaining to go with a blue blouse is red, so she wore a red skirt that day. By elimination, Betty wore the green skirt and tan blouse Monday. By clue 1, then, on Wednesday, Rose's outfit was a blue skirt and tan blouse, Tina's was a green skirt and red blouse, and Betty wore a red skirt and green blouse. In summary, with skirt color listed first:

Rose, tan/green, green/blue, blue/tan
Greta, blue/red, red/tan, tan/blue
Tina, red/blue, blue/green, green/red
Betty, green/tan, tan/red, red/green

53. "SWAP MEET"

Friday's winner was not Elaine (clue 2), Chris (clue 4), or Allan (clue 5). Friday's costume was not the doll (clue 2), clown (clue 4), or alien (clue 5); it was either the man dressed as a butterfly (clue 1) or the mummy. Betty was neither the man dressed as a butterfly nor the mummy (clue 3); she did not win Friday. By elimination, Dan won Friday. By clue 8, Ms. Jinn won Thursday and the boat was won Wednesday. Dan was dressed as either the butterfly or the mummy. If he was the butterfly, he would not have won the car (clue 1). The car would not have been won Monday or Tuesday (clue 4), so it would have been won Thursday by Ms. Jinn. Ms. Jinn would not be Elaine (clue 2) or Chris (clue 4); she would be Betty. Wednesday's costume would not have been the doll (clue 2), mummy (clue 3), or clown (clue 4); it would have been the alien. However, this leaves no place in clue 5 for Ms. Betty Jinn, Thursday's car winner. Therefore, Dan was not dressed as the butterfly; he was the mummy. By clue 1, then, the man in the butterfly costume won Tuesday. Dan's prize was not the furniture (clue 3) or vacation (clue 5); it was either the car or the appliances. If he had won the appliances, his last name would not be Hobson (clue 2), Guyarre (clue 5), or Indy (clue 6); he would be Fox. By clue 2, Hobson would have won Wednesday and Elaine Monday, while Ms. Jinn would have been the rag doll. Hobson would not be Betty (clue 3) or Chris (clue 7); he would be Allan. Allan would not be the alien (clue 5); he would be the clown. This, however, contradicts clue 4. Therefore, Dan did not win the appliances, he won the car. Ms. Jinn's costume was not the doll (clue 2) or the clown (clue 4); she was the alien. The clown did not appear Wednesday (clue 9); it appeared Monday and, by elimination, the doll appeared Wednesday. By clue 2, then, Ms. Jinn won appliances, Dan is Hobson, and Elaine won Monday. Clown Elaine didn't win the furniture (clue 9); she won the vacation while, by elimination, the man dressed as a butterfly won the furniture. By clue 3, Betty did not win Tuesday or Wednesday; she won Thursday. By clue 6, Mr. Indy is neither Elaine nor Tuesday's winner; he won the boat Wednesday. By clue 5, then, Guyarre won Tuesday and Allan Wednesday. By elimination, Elaine is Fox and Chris is Guyarre. In summary:

Mon.: Elaine Fox, clown, vacation
Tues.: Chris Guyarre, butterfly, furniture
Wed.: Allan Indy, doll, boat
Thurs.: Betty Jinn, alien, appliances
Fri.: Dan Hobson, mummy, car

54. THE ELKS' FLEA MARKET

Four couples, in order, are mentioned in clue 5: the couple who won the grinder, the Yaklitzes, the Wootens, and Forrest and his wife. Three couples, in order, are mentioned in clue 2: Antonio and his wife, Tonyia and her husband, and the Dudeks. Since there are six couples in all, at least one couple is mentioned in both clues. Tonyia is not Mrs. Wooten (clue 8), so Antonio is not Mr. Yaklitz and Forrest is not Mr. Dudek. The Dudeks did not win the grinder (clue 1). The only possibility, then, is that the grinder was won the day before the Yaklitzes won, which was the day before Antonio Wooten won, which was the day before Tonyia and Forrest won, which was the day before the Dudeks won. Clue 7 also mentions three couples in order, so at least two must be mentioned in the order already determined. Connie is not Mrs. Yaklitz (clue 11). The only possibility, then, is that Maxine won the grinder, Rollo is Mr. Yaklitz, and Connie is Mrs. Wooten. By clue 10, then, Sylvia and her husband won Monday, the Neidays won the grinder Tuesday, and the Yaklitzes won the jackets Wednesday, while the Wootens won Thursday, Tonyia and Forrest Friday, and the Dudeks Saturday. Mrs. Dudek is not Carla (clue 4); she is Glenda, while Carla is Mrs. Yaklitz. Malcolm, then, attended Saturday, and is Mr. Dudek (clue 4). Monday's prize was not the weeder or rug (clue 3) or the lamps (clue 6); it was the mixer. Vincent, then, is not Sylvia's husband (clue 3); Harvey is, while Vincent is married to Maxine. Harvey and Sylvia are not the Saddlers (clue 9); they are the Luddens, while Forrest and Tonyia are the Saddlers. By clue 3, the rug was won by the Dudeks. The Wootens did not win the lamps (clue 6); they won the weeder while, by elimination, the Saddlers won the lamps. In summary:

158

Monday: Harvey & Sylvia Ludden, mixer
Tuesday: Vincent & Maxine Neiday, grinder
Wednesday: Rollo & Carla Yaklitz, jackets
Thursday: Antonio & Connie Wooten, weeder
Friday: Forrest & Tonyia Saddler, lamps
Saturday: Malcolm & Glenda Dudek, rug

55. CLYDE'S BIRTHDAY POTLUCK

The person whose gift was cologne has red hair and walked to the party (clue 2). Mr. Rudman has blond hair (clue 1). Ms. Kelly gave a CD (clue 6). Harris biked to the party (clue 3). There were two blondes (clue 1) and two brunettes (clue 7), so the one who gave cologne was the only redhead. The one who gave cologne, then, was not deSilva (clue 10); he or she was North. There were three modes of transportation: biking by two people (clue 3), bus by two people (clue 5), and walking by only North (clue 2). North is not the dentist (clue 3), engineer (clue 7), the lawyer (clue 8), or the accountant (clue 11); he or she is the tailor. Ms. Kelly did not take the bus (clue 5), so she biked. She is, then, the dentist (clue 3). By elimination, Mr. Rudman and deSilva took the bus. The lawyer biked (clue 8), so is Harris. Blond Mr. Rudman is not the engineer (clue 7); he is the accountant while, by elimination, deSilva is the engineer. DeSilva has brown hair (clue 7). Sandra also has brown hair (clue 10); she is either Harris or Kelly. She brought the bread (clue 7). DeSilva brought the pasta (clue 11). The one who brought soup biked (clue 9); that person is also either Kelly or Harris. That person is, by elimination, a blond; she is a woman (clue 1). Both Kelly and Harris, then, are women. By clue 9, Margo did not bring soup, so she is neither Kelly nor Harris, nor is she North; she is deSilva. Fred, then, is Rudman, while Margo gave the video (clue 5). By elimination, Phil is North and Tina brought the soup. The salad was brought by either Phil or Fred, so the slippers were given by the other man (clue 4); Phil brought the salad and Fred gave the slippers. By elimination, Fred brought the cheese, while Harris gave the board game. Harris, then, is not Sandra (clue 10); she is blond Tina who brought soup. By elimination, Kelly is brunette Sandra who brought bread. In summary:

Fred Rudman, blond, accountant, bus, cheese, slippers
Phil North, redhead, tailor, walked, salad, cologne
Sandra Kelly, brunette, dentist, bike, bread, CD
Tina Harris, blond, lawyer, bike, soup, game
Margo deSilva, brunette, engineer, bus, pasta, video

56. MIDNIGHT SNACKERS

The person who lives on 5th didn't eat the cupcake (clue 8), the pie (clue 4), or the sandwich (clue 6). The person on 5th isn't Faye (clue 4), Mae (clue 6), or Ray (clue 5); this person is either Kaye or Jay. If it were Kaye, then her last name wouldn't be Flood (clue 5), Jackson (clue 4), Koji (clue 2), or Martin (clue 3); she would be Ruiz. Kaye Ruiz wouldn't have eaten ice cream (clue 1); she'd have eaten cheese and crackers. By clue 8, the person who ate the cupcake would live on 3rd and the woman with the crying baby would live on 4th. The person who ate ice cream wouldn't live on 1st or 2nd (clue 5); that person would live on 4th. By clue 5, Flood would live on 3rd and have eaten the cupcake. Koji wouldn't live on 1st or 2nd (clue 6); Koji would live on 4th and be the woman with the baby; Koji therefore isn't the man named Jay (clue 1); nor could Koji be Mae (clue 6); Faye would be Koji. Mae wouldn't live on 3rd St. (clue 6); either Jay or Ray would live on 3rd. Neither Jay nor Ray would then live on 2nd (clue 3), so Mae would. By clue 6, Flood would have had to have been awakened by the truck. But Flood, who must be one of the two men, wouldn't have been mentioned in clue 3. Therefore, Kay is not the person who lives on 5th. Jay lives on 5th. Jay didn't eat ice cream (clue 1); he ate cheese and crackers. By clue 6, Ray is the man who ate the sandwich. Jay's last name isn't Flood (clue 5), Jackson (clue 2), or Ruiz (clue 1); it is either Koji or Martin. If Jay is Koji, then by clue 3, he would have been awakened by a phone call and Ray would be Mr. Martin. The person who lives on 4th isn't Kaye (clue 7), Mae (clue 6), or Ray Martin (clue 3); Faye would live on 4th. Faye isn't Flood (clue 2), or Jackson (clue 4); she'd would be Ruiz. By clue 8, the person who ate the cupcake would live on 2nd and the woman with the crying baby on 3rd. Ray Martin would then live on 1st. Mae wouldn't live on 2nd (clue 6); she'd have to live on 3rd and Faye Ruiz would have been awakened by a truck. Faye Ruiz couldn't eat ice cream (clue 1); she'd have eaten pie, but then Faye would then be mentioned twice in clue 4. Therefore, Jay is not Koji; he is Mr. Martin. Ray was awakened by the phone call (clue 3). Ray isn't Koji (clue 6), Flood (clue 5), or Ruiz (clue 2); he is Jackson. Neither Kaye (clue 2) nor Mae (clue 6) is Koji; Faye is Koji. The person who lives on 1st isn't Flood (clue 5), Faye Koji (clue 6), or Ruiz (clue 8); it is Ray Jackson. The person who ate the cupcake doesn't live on 3rd or 4th (clue 8); this person lives on 2nd, the woman with the baby lives on 3rd, and Ruiz lives on 4th. Faye Koji doesn't live on 2nd (clue 6); she lives on 3rd and, by elimination, Flood lives on 2nd. By clue 5, Faye Koji ate ice cream. By elimination, Ruiz on 4th ate pie. The person awakened by the dog lives on 2nd and is Flood (clue 4). Mae doesn't live on 2nd, she lives on 4th and by clue 6, Jay Martin was awakened by the truck. By elimination, Kaye lives on 2nd. Also by elimination, Mae Ruiz was awakened by the bad dream. In summary:

1st: Ray Jackson, sandwich, phone
2nd: Kaye Flood, cupcake, dog
3rd: Faye Koji, ice cream, baby
4th: Mae Ruiz, pie, dream
5th: Jay Martin, cheese and crackers, truck

57. GREEN THUMBS

The seven children are all two years apart (clue 1) and one child is 7 (clue 4), so the 19-year-old girl who worked the same day as Mom (clue 2) is the oldest child, who planted carrots in plot #6 (clue 1). They are not the two who worked corner plots Tuesday (clue 4), so Ramona and Dad worked Tuesday and all the others worked alone (clue 2). Mom is not Anita (clue 1), or Gabriela or Carmen (clue 3); she is Rosita. Carmen worked a corner plot opposite Dad (clue 3), so she is not the 19-year-old of plot #6. Nor is Anita (clue 1); Gabriela is the 19-year-old. By clue 3, then, the cauliflower plot and the plot worked Wednesday are plots #3 and #9 in some order, the peas in plot #4, and Carmen and Dad worked plots #1 and #7 in some order; Ramona's corner plot contains cauliflower. Gabriela and Rosita did not work Friday or Saturday (clue 1), Wednesday (clue 3), or Sunday or Thursday (clue 5); they worked Monday. Anita, then, planted her turnips on Wednesday (clue 1) in a corner plot; by clue 4, she is the 7-year-old. By clue 7, Julio planted Friday and Tuesday-planter Ramona is 11. A girl planted Thursday (clue 5); by elimination, she is Carmen, whose corner plot grows radishes (clue 4). Raphael, the asparagus planter, and Jose planted on consecutive days in order (clue 6); Raphael planted Sunday, Rosita planted asparagus Monday, and Jose is Dad who planted Tuesday. By elimination, Juan planted Saturday; he is 13 (clue 5). Raphael is two years older than Carmen (also clue 5), so Raphael is 17 and Carmen 15; by elimination, Julio is 9. Julio planted squash (clue 8). Children planted beans and peas and the bean planter is younger than the pea planter (clue 9), so 13-year-old Juan planted beans and 17-year-old Raphael planted peas in plot #4; by elimination, Dad Jose planted eggplant. By clue 3, Ramona's cauliflower plot and Anita's turnip plot are #3 and #9 in some order while Carmen's radish plot and Dad Jose's eggplant plot are #1 and #7 in some order. Mom Rosita's plot is adjacent to both Julio's squash plot and Juan's bean plot (clue 8), so Rosita's plot is #5 and Julio's and Juan's plots are #2 and #8 in some order. Both plots #2 and #8 are higher in number than Dad's eggplant plot (also clue 8), so Dad's plot is #1 and Carmen's plot is #7. Julio's plot is adjacent to Dad's (clue 7), so Julio has plot #2 and Juan's plot is #8. Juan's beans are not adjacent to Ramona's cauliflower (clue 8), so Ramona's plot is #3 while Anita's plot is #9. In summary:

#1: Dad Jose, eggplant, Tuesday
#2: Julio, 9, squash, Friday
#3: Ramona, 11, cauliflower, Tuesday
#4: Raphael, 17, peas, Sunday
#5: Mom Rosita, asparagus, Monday
#6: Gabriela, 19, carrots, Monday
#7: Carmen, 15, radishes, Thursday
#8: Juan, 13, beans, Saturday
#9: Anita, 7, turnips, Wednesday

58. THE ROMANTIC LINE

Two of the couples are the Chedworths and Cary and his wife (clue 1). A third couple is Ted Valdez and his wife, who were married on the Alaskan cruise (clue 9). Bob and Dixie are not the Chedworths (clue 14), so they are a fourth couple. Allison's first cruise was Dixie and Bob's second (clue 3) so, by clue 1, Allison is not married to Cary. By clue 3, Allison is not married to Ted, who went to Alaska. Dixie and Bob did not go on either of the Chedworths' cruises (clue 14), so Allison is not Mrs. Chedworth. Allison and her husband are, then, the fifth couple. Tara is Ted's wife (clue 11). Cary and his wife did not wed on the Rio cruise (clue 4), so the Chedworths did not second-honeymoon on the Rio cruise (clue 1). By clue 13, then, Cary's wife is the former Wanda South, and they second-honeymooned on the cruise to Rio. By elimination, Mrs. Chedworth is Bridget. Judd is not Mr. Chedworth (clue 2); he is Allison's husband while, by elimination, Rick is Mr. Chedworth. By clue 3, Dixie second-honeymooned on Allison's honeymoon cruise and by clue 1, Bridget second-honeymooned on Wanda's honeymoon cruise; by clue 7, then, the former Miss Goldman is not Dixie, Bridget, or Tara; she is Allison, who second-honeymooned to Alaska. By clue 15, Wanda second-honeymooned on Dixie's honeymoon cruise; Bob and Dixie then honeymooned in Rio. Neither of the Chedworths' cruises were on the *Venus* to Hawaii (clue 5); they went, in some order, to the Mediterranean and the Yucatan. Bob and Dixie went to neither the Yucatan nor the Mediterranean on their second honeymoon (clue 14); they went to Hawaii on the *Venus*. Cary and Wanda's honeymoon was to either the Mediterranean or Yucatan (clue 1); Judd and Allison went to Hawaii on the *Venus* for their honeymoon. The former Miss Jeffcoat is neither Tara (clue 9) nor Bridget (clue 16); she is Dixie. Mr. North is neither Cary nor Bob (clue 6); he is Judd. Cary is not Mr. Butkus (clue 13); he is Mr. Mullins, while Bob is Mr. Butkus. The Mullinses did not honeymoon on the cruise to the Mediterranean (clue 8); they were married on the way to the Yucatan, and the Chedworths second-honeymooned on that cruise. By elimination, the Chedworths honeymooned on the way to the Mediterranean, and the Valdezes second-honeymooned on that cruise. Bridget is not the former Miss Powell (clue 10); she is the former Miss Beaulieu, while Tara is the former Miss Powell. Bob and Dixie Butkus did not honeymoon on the *Juliet* (clue 17). Neither the ship to the Yucatan nor the one to the Mediterranean is the *Juliet* (clue 12); the ship to Alaska is the *Juliet*. The ship to Rio is neither the *Cleopatra* (clue 16) nor the *Cupid* (clue 18); it is the *Guinevere*. The ship to the Yucatan is not the *Cupid* (clue 8); it is the *Cleopatra,* while the ship to the Mediterranean is the *Cupid*. In summary:

Allison Goldman & Judd North, married on the Hawaii cruise aboard the *S. S. Venus,* second-honeymooned aboard the *S. S. Juliet* to Alaska

Bridget Beaulieu & Rick Chedworth, married aboard the *S. S. Cupid* cruising the Mediterranean, spent second honeymoon aboard the *S. S. Cleopatra* to the Yucatan

Dixie Jeffcoat & Bob Butkus, married aboard the *S. S. Guinevere* to Rio de Janeiro, second-honeymooned aboard the *S. S. Venus* to Hawaii

Tara Powell & Ted Valdez, married aboard the *S. S. Juliet* to Alaska, took second honeymoon aboard the *S. S. Cupid* in the Mediterranean

Wanda South & Cary Mullins, married aboard the Yucatan-bound *S. S. Cleopatra,* second-honeymooned on the *S. S. Guinevere* to Rio de Janeiro

59. COIN BRACELET

The castle was #4 (clue 4). The oldest coin from 1897 was #4, #5, or #6 (clue 4). It was not #6 (clue 8); so it was either #4 and the castle, or #5. The castle was not from Cameria (clue 4), Repona (clue 6), Kleinland (clue 7), or Zomoly (clue 10); it was from either Marita or Joraco. The oldest coin was from neither Marita (clue 9) or Joraco (clue 11), so it was not #4; it was #5. The newest coin from 1974 was not #4 (clue 5), #2 (clue 6), or #1 or #6 (clue 8); it was #3. Since the castle was from either 1910 or 1921 (clue 4), by clue 6, the coin from Repona, which was newer than coin #2, was #3 and the 1952 coin was #6. Since the castle was older than coins #1, #2, and #3 (clue 4), the castle was from 1910 and the #1 and #2 coins were, in some order, from 1921 and 1944. The Repona coin #3 was not the knight (clue 2), pine cone (clue 3), dolphin (clue 9), or obelisk (clue 11); it was the wolf. By clue 11, either the coin from Joraco was #1 and the obelisk #2, or the coin from Joraco was #4 and the obelisk #5. If the coin from Joraco had been #4 and the obelisk #5, coin #1 would not have been from Zomoly (clue 1), Cameria (clue 2), or Kleinland (clue 7); it would have been from Marita. It would not have been the pine (clue 3) or dolphin (clue 9); it would have been the knight. By clue 2, the #5 coin would have been from Cameria. The coin from Zomoly would have been #2 (clue 1). It would have been either the dolphin or the pine cone. This, however, contradicts clue 10. Therefore, the coin from Joraco was not #4; it was #1 and the obelisk was #2. By elimination, the castle was from Marita. The dolphin was from 1897 (clue 9). The Zomoly coin was not #1, #5, or #6 (clue 1); it was #2. By clue 2, then, the knight was #1 and the Cameria coin was #5. By elimination, the Kleinland coin was #6 and was the pine cone. The #1 Joraco coin was not from 1921 (clue 11); it was from 1944, and the #2 coin was from 1921. In summary:

1: Joraco, knight, 1944
2: Zomoly, obelisk, 1921
3: Repona, wolf, 1974
4: Marita, castle, 1910
5: Cameria, dolphin, 1897
6: Kleinland, pine cone, 1952

60. FLATBUSH FLYERS

Steps 1 and 15 are the captain's (clue 1). Dora never receives the ball from either Paula (clue 3) or Bobbi (clue 5), so she receives it from both Joni and Rona. She only receives it twice, then; to do three stunts, she starts with the ball and is the captain. She has the ball in steps 1 and 15, and either Joni or Rona has it in step 14. One person has the ball in steps 3, 7, and 11, while another has it in steps 4, 10, and 13 (clue 6). All five have the ball in steps 11 through 15, but at least one person has it twice in steps 1 through 5 (clue 4). The only step 1 through 5 that could be a player's second turn, then, is step 5; either Dora or the one who has step 2 also has step 5. To have three turns, then, the one who has it twice in steps 1 through 5 does not have it in steps 6 through 10. Since the same player does not have the ball twice, the possible sequences are 1 or 2, 5, and 12, 14, or 15; 1 or 2, 8 or 9, and 12, 14, or 15, and 6, 8 or 9, and 12 or 14. The one who has it step 6 would pass it to step 7, who would not return it (clue 2); the one who has step 6 does not have step 8, so she has step 9. The possible sequences, then, are 1/2, 5, and 12/14/15; 1/2, 8, and 12/14/15, and 6, 9, and 12/14. Dora has step 5 or 8; in either case, she passes it once to the one with the 6 and 9 steps. The one with the 6 and 9 steps, then, is not Paula (clue 3). Paula does not have step 2 (clue 3), so she is one of the women mentioned in clue 6. Dora has the ball either 5 or 8, so she is passed the ball by one of the women mentioned in clue 6; either Joni or Rona is mentioned in clue 6. Of the last five steps, then, Paula and either Joni or Rona have steps 11 and 13 in some order (clue 6), while either Joni or Rona has step 14, and Dora has step 15. By elimination, then, Bobbi has step 12. Bobbi, then, is not mentioned in clue 6 and has none of those steps. In step 12, Bobbi is passed the ball by the woman with steps 3, 7, and 11 and passes the ball to the one with steps 4, 10, and 13. By clue 2, then, Bobbi does not have steps 8 or 9. Since she does not have step 9, she does not have step 6. She never has a turn, then, during steps 6 through 10. To have three turns, she has two during steps 1 through 5, and has steps 2 and 5. Dora, then, has steps 1, 8, and 15. The woman who has step 7 and passes the ball to Dora (either Joni or Rona) also has step 11 and passes the ball to Bobbi; Joni never passes to Bobbi (clue 5), so Rona has steps 3, 7, and 11 while, by elimination, Paula has steps 4, 10, and 13 (clue 6). By elimination, Joni has steps 6, 9, and 14. In summary:

1:	Dora	6:	Joni	11:	Rona
2:	Bobbi	7:	Rona	12	Bobbi
3:	Rona	8:	Dora	13:	Paula
4:	Paula	9:	Joni	14:	Joni
5:	Bobbi	10:	Paula	15:	Dora

61. MARJORIE MOVIESTAR

The star of the last movie was not Lionel (clue 1), Richard (clue 2), or Simon (clue 3); he was either Brad or Greg. If he had been Brad, the genre would not have been mystery (clue 2), musical (clue 3), comedy (clue 4), or western (clue 5); it would have been science fiction. The film would not have been Candy (clue 1), Donna (clue 3), Elda (clue 5), or Amber (clue 6); it would have been Barb. Her hair would not have been black (clue 1), blonde (clue 2), red (clue 3), or dark brown (clue 4); it would have been light brown. The fourth movie would have been the mystery (clue 2). The fifth movie, then, would not be mentioned in clue 4, so the other four in order from first to last would have been the one in which she had dark brown hair, the comedy, Amber, and the one in which Greg starred. The musical was not first (clue 3), so it would have been third and the western first. By clue 9, Simon would have been in the third and Richard in the first. However, Simon would then have been in the musical, contradicting clue 3. Therefore, Brad was not in the fifth movie, so Greg was. Its genre was not mystery (clue 2), musical (clue 3), or comedy (clue 4); it was either western or science fiction. That movie was not Candy (clue 1), Donna (clue 3), or Amber (clue 4); it was either Barb or Elda. The western was neither Elda (clue 5) nor Barb (clue 9), so the fifth movie was not the western; it was science fiction. Simon was not in the musical or comedy (clue 3), or western (clue 7); he was in the mystery. Her hair in the fifth movie was not black (clue 1), red (clue 3), or dark brown (clue 4); it was either light brown or blonde. If it had been blonde, by clue 2, the fifth movie would not have been Barb, so it would have been Elda. The fourth movie would not have been the mystery (clue 2), comedy (clue 4), or western (clue 5); it would have been the musical. Its star would not have been Lionel (clue 1), Simon (clue 3), or Brad (clue 5); he would have been Richard. Brad would not have been in the western (clue 5); he would have been in the comedy while, by elimination, Lionel would have been in the western. The musical with Richard would not have been Candy (clue 1), Barb (clue 2), or Donna (clue 3); it would have been Amber. Brad's comedy would have been third (clue 4). By clue 1, Candy would have been first, Lionel's western second, and she would have had black hair in the comedy. By elimination, Simon's mystery would have been first. By clue 2, Barb would have been second while, by elimination, Donna would have been third. By clue 3, her hair would have been red in the second movie. By clue 4, her hair would have been dark brown in first movie Candy. However, this contradicts clue 8. Therefore, her hair was not blonde in the fifth movie; it was light brown. That movie was either Barb or Elda. If it had been Elda, the fourth movie would not have been the mystery (clue 2), comedy (clue 4), or western (clue 5); it would have been the musical. Its star would not have been Lionel (clue 1), Richard (clue 2), or Simon (clue 3); he would have been Brad. This, however, contradicts clue 5. Therefore, the fifth movie was not Elda, so it was Barb. By clue 2, Simon's mystery was fourth. Her hair in the fourth movie was not blonde (clue 2), red (clue 3), or dark brown (clue 4); it was black. By clue 1, then, Lionel starred third and Candy was second. The fourth movie was not Donna (clue 3) or Elda (clue 5); it was Amber. By clue 4, the comedy was third. Her hair was dark brown either first or second (clue 4); it was not dark brown second (clue 8), so it was dark brown first. The musical was not first (clue 3); it was second while, by elimination, the western was first. By clue 3, her hair was red in the third movie, and Donna was first. By elimination, Elda was third and her hair was blonde in the second. By clue 2, Richard was first, while Brad was second. In summary:

1: Donna, Richard, western, dark brown
2: Candy, Brad, musical, blonde
3: Elda, Lionel, comedy, red
4: Amber, Simon, mystery, black
5: Barb, Greg, SF, light brown

62. MIXED DOUBLES TENNIS

Since only winners went on to later rounds, Mr. Wright and his partner and Mrs. Minelli and her partner won in the quarter-finals (clue 4). By clue 9, Mrs. Clay and her partner and Mr. Brophy and his were also quarter-final winners. Mrs. Clay was not Mr. Wright's partner (clue 7), so she and her partner were a third winning pair. Mr. Brophy was not Mrs. Minelli's partner (clue 12), so he and his partner were the fourth winning pair in that round. Les Miller won at least the quarter-final (clue 8). He was not Mrs. Clay's partner (clue 2); he was Mrs. Minelli's. Tom and his partner played Carol and hers in a late-round match (clue 16), so both Tom and Carol won their quarter-final matches. Carol, then, defeated Hank in the quarter-finals (clue 3). Hank, then, did not go on to the semi-finals, so the match in which Hank Finn was defeated by Les Miller (clue 8) was the quarter-finals; Carol is Mrs. Minelli, her partner is Les Miller, and they defeated Hank Finn and his partner in the quarter-finals. The match in which Carol and Les beat Jay and his partner and Mr. Wright and his partner defeated Alice and hers (clue 4), then, was the semi-finals. Alice and Jay, then, both won their quarter-final matches. Alice was not Mr. Wright's partner, nor was she Mr. Brophy's (clue 12); she is Mrs. Clay. The match mentioned in clue 9, then, was the quarter-finals; Alice Clay defeated Mr. Lieber and Mr. Brophy defeated Mrs. Finn in that match. Tom lost to Carol Minelli in one match (clue 16); since Carol defeated Hank in the first match and Jay in the second, she defeated Tom in the finals. Tom, then, won the semi-finals; he is Mr. Wright. Mr. Brophy was in the semi-finals, but not Alice Clay's partner; he was defeated by Carol and Les, and is Jay. Ron won at least the quarter-finals (clue 10), so he was Alice's partner. They were defeated in the semi-finals, so they defeated Betsy and her partner in the quarter-finals (clue 10). By clue 1, since Les Miller played Hank Finn in the quarter-finals and Jay Brophy in the semi-finals, and Tom Wright in the finals, Tanya Miller (clue 11) was neither Jay's nor Hank's nor Tom's partner; she was defeated by Tom Wright in the quarter-finals. Mrs. Wright was not Tom's partner (clue 1), Mr. Lieber's (clue 6), or Hank's (clue 13); she was Jay Brophy's. Ron is neither Mr. Clay (clue 1) nor Mr. Minelli (clue 14); he is Mr. Plummer. He played against Betsy in the first match and was not in the third; by clue 15, then, he played Susan in the second match, and Susan was Tom Wright's partner. Mark did not win the quarter-finals, so that was the match he played Debbie (clue 5); Debbie then won that match and is Mrs. Wright, while Mark was Mrs. Finn's partner. Mrs. Finn is not Penny (clue 18); she is Lisa while, by elimination, Penny was Hank Finn's partner. Steve was not Betsy's partner (clue 17); he was Tanya's while, by elimination, Ben was Betsy's partner. Mark is not Clay (clue 5); he is Minelli while, by elimination, Steve is Clay. Betsy is neither Lieber nor Plummer (clue 1); she is Brophy. Since Susan played Ron Plummer in the second match, she is not Mrs. Plummer (clue 1); she is Mrs. Lieber while, by elimination, Penny is Mrs. Plummer. In summary, with the winners of each match listed first:

Susan Lieber/Tom Wright: Tanya Miller/Steve Clay
Carol Minelli/ Les Miller: Penny Plummer/Hank Finn
Alice Clay/Ron Plummer: Betsy Brophy/Ben Lieber
Debbie Wright/Jay Brophy: Lisa Finn/Mark Minelli

Carol Minelli/ Les Miller: Debbie Wright/Jay Brophy
Susan Lieber/Tom Wright: Alice Clay/Ron Plummer

Carol Minelli/ Les Miller: Susan Lieber/Tom Wright

63. SHARED MEALS

The five pairs are Clara and her friend and Kristine and her mother (clue 4), a husband and wife (clue 8), and two sisters and two brothers (clue 13). Ice cream was not served with peas (clue 7), beans (clue 14) or spinach (clue 16); the husband and wife had broccoli (clue 8), but not ice cream (clue 14), so ice cream and corn were part of the same dinner. Steve and Bruce did not eat together (clue 5), so one is Robert's brother and the other ate with his wife. The two brothers ate ham (clue 13); the husband and wife didn't have fish (clue 5) or meatloaf (clue 8), so had either chicken or steak. Hilda had neither chicken nor steak (clue 11), so she is not the wife, nor is she one of the sisters or Kristine's mother (clue 15); Hilda is Clara's friend. Cheesecake was served after ice cream (clue 3), which was served after at least two other meals (clue 7), so cheesecake was with the fourth or fifth meal. Two meals were served after the steak dinner (clue 1) and two meals were served after the chicken dinner (clue 6), so neither chicken nor steak was served with cheesecake; the married couple didn't have cheesecake, or jello or ice cream (clue 14). Robert and his brother didn't have cheesecake (clue 9), or jello or ice cream (clue 14). The married couple and the two brothers, therefore, had the cake and pie in some order. Linda had neither cake nor pie (clue 12), so Linda didn't dine with her husband, nor is she Kristine's mother (also clue 12); Linda shared spinach with her sister (clue 13). Susan didn't eat with a man (clue 5), so either Nancy or Rosalie did; neither ate with Bruce (clue 2), so Bruce is Robert's brother, and Steve ate with his wife. Bruce and Robert were served before Rosalie (also clue 2), who was served before green beans were served (clue 6), so the brothers didn't have beans; we know corn was served with ice cream, so the brothers didn't have corn; they had ham and peas. Peas were not served with pie (clue 10), so the brothers had cake, and Steve and his wife had pie. Rosalie didn't have pie (also clue 10), so she is not Steve's wife; Nancy is Steve's wife. Beans were not served with jello (clue 14), so beans were served with cheesecake. By elimination, the sisters had spinach and jello. Meatloaf was not served with broccoli (clue 8), or spinach or corn and ice cream (clue 16); it was served with beans and cheesecake. Since, by elimination, either Rosalie or Susan is Kristine's mother, and beans and cheesecake were not served to Susan (clue 1) or Rosalie (clue 6) Kristine did not have the meatloaf dinner. Clara and Hilda had meatloaf. Kristine and her mother, then, had corn and ice cream. Susan didn't have steak (clue 1) or fish (clue 5), so she had chicken. Nancy and Steve didn't have fish (also clue 5), so they had steak. Rosalie ate after Susan (clue 6); she had fish. Linda and her sister were served jello before Kristine and her mother were served ice cream (clue 3), so Susan is Linda's sister, and Rosalie is Kristine's mother. In summary:

> Brothers Bruce and Robert ate ham, peas, cake
> Friends Clara and Hilda ate meatloaf, beans, cheesecake
> Daughter Kristine and mother Rosalie ate fish, corn, ice cream
> Sisters Linda and Susan ate chicken, spinach, jello
> Wife Nancy and husband Steve ate steak, broccoli, pie

64. HAPPY'S BIRTHDAY PRIZES

The fifth child's book was not about astronauts (clue 3), dinosaurs (clue 5), or birds (clue 7); it was about either trolls or lizards. Neither Nick nor Jeff won the book about trolls (clue 4) or lizards (clue 6), so neither placed fifth; nor did Leo (clue 4) or Karen (clue 5), so Mary placed fifth. Mary is not Miyoshi (clue 1), Nash (clue 5), Kellogg (clue 6), or Jordan (clue 7); she is Lopez. The game Mary Lopez won was not darts (clue 4), musical chairs (clue 5), Pin the Tail (clue 6), or Drop the Clothespin (clue 7); it was Count the Pennies. Neither Nick (clue 2) nor Leo (clue 4) is Miyoshi, so either Jeff or Karen is. If Jeff were Miyoshi, Karen would be neither Kellogg (clue 1) nor Nash (clue 5); she would be Jordan. Nick would not be Nash (clue 1); he would be Kellogg and, by elimination, Leo would be Nash. The child who placed fourth would not have been Leo Nash (clue

4), Nick Kellogg (clue 6), or Karen Jordan (clue 7); Jeff Miyoshi would have placed fourth. By clue 4, then, the children would have played darts third. By clue 6, Nick Kellogg would have won the first game, Pin the Tail would have been the second game, and the third prize for darts would have been the book about lizards. Nick's game would not have been musical chairs (clue 2); by elimination, it would have been Drop the Clothespin. However, this contradicts clue 7. Therefore, Jeff is not Miyoshi, Karen is. Jeff is not Jordan (clue 1) or Kellogg (clue 6); he is Nash. By clue 4, Karen Miyoshi did not win the troll book, so Mary did. Karen's game was not darts (clue 4), musical chairs (clue 5), or Drop the Clothespin (clue 7); it was Pin the Tail. Musical chairs was won by neither Nick (clue 2) nor Jeff Nash (clue 5); Leo won that. By clue 4, Leo did not win the game just before Karen Miyoshi, so he is not Kellogg (clue 6); Nick is Kellogg while, by elimination, Leo is Jordan. Nick won just before Karen (clue 6), so his game was darts (clue 4). By elimination, Jeff's game was Drop the Clothespin. By clue 6, then, Leo won the book about lizards. By clue 5, the boy who won the book about dinosaurs was Nick. By clue 4, at least one game was played between Leo's and Mary's, and that game was won by neither Nick nor Karen; it was won by Jeff. By clue 6, then, Nick won the first game, Karen the second, Leo the third, and Jeff the fourth. By clue 7, Karen won the book about birds so, by elimination, Jeff won the book about astronauts. In summary:

1: Nick Kellogg, darts, dinosaurs
2: Karen Miyoshi, Pin the Tail, birds
3: Leo Jordan, musical chairs, lizards
4: Jeff Nash, Drop the Clothespin, astronauts
5: Mary Lopez, Count Pennies, trolls

65. HAPPY ACRES B'BALL

There are seven numbers, using ten digits, and the sum of the seven numbers is 99 (clue 7), so there are three 2-digit numbers and four 1-digit numbers; zero is not used as a first digit or 1-digit number (also clue 7). One of the 1-digit numbers is #4 (clue 10). Aspin has the highest number but its digits total less than 4 (clue 8); he has #30, and the other 2-digit numbers have 1 and 2 as their first digits. Aspin is not Stan (clue 1), Jojo (clue 2), Tyrone (clue 4), Doug (clue 5), or Buck or Craig (clue 10); he is Lew. Clue 10 lists the five starters: #4, Buck, Craig, Lew Aspin, and Tower. Either Buck or Craig is the center (clue 6), so the other four are forwards and guards. The sum of the two starting forwards' numbers equals the sum of the two starting guards' numbers (clue 3), so #4 and #30 Aspin are one pair and the other pair's numbers also total 34—that pair includes the 2-digit number with first digit 2 and a 1-digit number. Tower's number is lower than that of the substitute forward (clue 1), so he does not have the 2-digit number; either Buck or Craig does. By clue 6, Craig has the 2-digit number beginning with 2 and is Butcher while Buck is the center. Jojo's number plus Young's number equals the higher starting guard's number (clue 2); that number can't be Aspin's #30, so Craig Butcher and Tower are the guards while #4 and Aspin are forwards, and either Jojo or Young has the 2-digit number with first digit 1. Nolan's number plus Tyrone's number plus White's number (in increasing order) equals 30 (clue 4); in order to reach that sum, the 2-digit number beginning with 1 must be included, so Jojo is White and has the 2-digit number beginning with 1. Stan's number plus Tower's number equals the substitute forward's number (clue 1). The substitute forward's number is at least 9 since the 2 smallest possible 1-digit numbers are 4 and 5. If the substitute forward's number were 9, Stan would have #4 and Tower #5; but then Tower's number and Craig's number could not total 34, contradicting clue 3. So Stan's number and Tower's number have a 2-digit sum; Jojo White is the substitute forward. By clue 9, the substitute guard's number is 1 higher than the second digit of Jojo's number. There are four possible combinations for Tower's and Craig's numbers to reach 34—5 & 29, 6 & 28, 8 & 26, 9 & 25. If Tower's and Craig's numbers used the digits 6 and 8 there would be no consecutive digits left to make up Jojo's and the substitute guard's numbers, so Tower and Craig have 5 & 29 or 9 & 25. Jojo and the substitute guard, then, have either 16 & 7 or 17 & 8; Buck has 8 or 6 respectively. Since the substitute forward's number is 16 or 17, Tower's number is not 5 (clue 1); Tower has #9 and Craig #25. If Jojo's number were 16, by clue 2 Young would also have #9, an impossibility. So Jojo has #17 and the substitute guard #8; the substitute guard is Young (also clue 2). By clue 1, Young is Stan. Tyrone is not #4 (clue 4), so he is Tower; by elimination, Doug is #4. Doug is not Locke (clue 5); Buck is, and Doug is Nolan. In sum:

4 Doug Nolan, forward
6 Buck Locke, center
8 Stan Young, substitute guard

165

9   Tyrone Tower, guard
17 Jojo White, substitute forward
25 Craig Butcher, guard
30 Lew Aspin, forward

66. FINAL STANDINGS

By clue 1, the Morton's Feed team won the trophy, and two of its three scores were 4–0 and 2–2, while a second team was the Yankees, who had one score of 0–4, and a third team was coached by Axelrod, with a score of 2–2. Two of the Dodgers' scores were 1–3 and 1–3 (clue 2), so they were not the Morton's team; the Morton's team was either the Cubs or Phillies. The Morton's coach was not Grabowsky (clue 7), so that coach was either Bodine or Wallingford. If it were Wallingford, the Morton's team would not have been the Phillies (clue 6); it would have been the Cubs. The Yankees coach was not Grabowsky (clue 10), so it would have been Bodine. Morton's Cubs' third score would have been 3–1 (clue 4), for a final record of 9–3. Since Axelrod's team would have scored 2–2 against Morton's Cubs (clue 1) and the Attorneys' team would have scored 1–3 against the Cubs (clue 4), Axelrod would not have coached the Attorney's team; nor did he coach the Gas & Go team (clue 5), so he would have coached the Loyal Order's team. That team would not have been the Dodgers (clue 2); it would have been the Phillies. The Yankees scored 0–4 against the Morton's team (clue 1), while the Attorneys' team would have scored 1–3 against them (clue 4), so the Attorneys' team would have been the Dodgers and the Yankees would have been the Gas & Go team. By elimination, the Dodgers' coach would have been Grabowsky. The four teams, then, would have been: the Attorneys' Dodgers coached by Grabowsky, who scored 1–3/1–3/; Morton's Cubs coached by Wallingford, who scored 4–0/2–2/3–1; Gas & Go Yankees coached by Bodine, who scored 0–4; and Loyal Order's Phillies coached by Axelrod, who scored 2–2/3–1. The second and third placed teams would have scored 2–2 against each other (clue 3), and those scores have not yet been placed. Only the Cubs would have won more than six games (clue 1), so the Phillies' third score was not 2–2; they would have placed last. However, they won at least five games, which leaves no place for two teams with more wins. Therefore, Wallingford was not the Morton's coach, so Bodine was. The Yankees coach was not Bodine or Axelrod (clue 1) or Grabowsky (clue 10); Wallingford coached that team. By elimination, the coach not mentioned in clue 1 was Grabowsky. Two of the Dodgers' scores were 1–3/1–3 (clue 2). If they had placed second or third, their third score would have been 2–2 (clue 3), for a total of 4–8. They would not, then, be mentioned in clue 1, so they would be Grabowsky's team. The Loyal Order's coach would not have been Grabowsky (clue 2) or Wallingford (clue 8); it would have been Axelrod. Axelrod's team would then have scored 3–1 against the Dodgers (clue 2), so two of Axelrod's team's scores would have been 2–2/3–1, for at least five wins. Axelrod's team would, then, have come in second, and their third score would have been 2–2 (clue 3). However, their total wins would then have been 7, contradicting clue 1. Therefore, the Dodgers did not place second or third; they placed fourth. By clue 2, the Loyal Order's team placed second or third, with one score of 3–1. They had a second score of 2–2 (clue 3). Wallingford's Yankees placed second or third, with one score of 0–4 (clue 1) and a second of 2–2 (clue 3). Axelrod did not coach the Loyal Order's team, or they would have a total of 7 wins, contradicting clue 1. Wallingford did not coach the Loyal Order's team (clue 8), so Grabowsky did. The Dodgers' coach, then, was Axelrod. The Dodgers' three scores, then, were 1–3/1–3/2–2, for a total of 4–8, so the third place team scored 5–7 and the second place team scored 6–6 (clue 1). The Yankees scored 0–4 against Bodine's team and 2–2 against Grabowsky's (clue 3). Their third score was against Axelrod's Dodgers so, by clue 2, they scored 3–1 in that series and Wallingford is Cindy. The Yankees' total score was then 5–7, so they placed third. Grabowsky's team, by elimination, placed second for a total of 6–6. Since they scored 2–2 against the Yankees and 3–1 against the Dodgers, they scored 1–3 against Bodine's team. Bodine's team then scored 4–0/2–2/3–1, for a total of 9–3. The Cubs scored 3–1 against the Attorneys' team (clue 4). Since the 3–1 scored by Bodine's team was against the Loyal Order's team, Bodine did not coach the Cubs; Grabowsky did, while Bodine coached the Phillies. Since Grabowsky's Cubs scored 3–1 against Axelrod's Dodgers, the Dodgers are the Attorneys' team (clue 4). By elimination, the Yankees are the Gas & Go team. Mike is neither Axelrod (clue 4) nor Bodine (clue 6); he is Grabowsky. Walt is not Bodine (clue 9); he is Axelrod, while Bodine is Ben. In summary:

1st: Morton's Feed Store Phillies, Ben Bodine, 9–3
2nd: Loyal Order of Beavers Cubs, Mike Grabowsky, 6–6
3rd: Jeff's Gas & Go Yankees, Cindy Wallingford, 5–7
4th: Readem and Weep Attorneys Dodgers, Walt Axelrod, 4–8

67. SUSSEX COUNTY FOOTBALL

By clue 1, the nine W/L records are 8/0, 7/1, 6/2, 5/3, 4/4, 3/5, 2/6, 1/7, and 0/8. The Inkberry team's record was not 0/8, 1/7, 7/1, or 8/0 (clue 3). The Rattlers' record was not 6/2, 4/4, or 2/6 (clue 2), nor was it 8/0, 7/1, or 5/3 (clue 7). By clue 9, then, Inkberry's record was 6/2 and the Rattlers' was 3/5. By clue 7, then, Dahlia Glen's was 5/3 and Five Forks' was 7/1. The Five Forks coach was not Osborn (clue 3), Shultz (clue 5), Queen (clue 6), Nolan, Rather, or King (clue 7), Parker or Logan (clue 9); he was Marx. By clue 3, Carbona's record was 8/0. Coach Rather's record was not 6/2, 4/4, 3/5, or 2/6 (clue 2), 0/8, 1/7, or 5/3 (clue 7); it was 8/0. By clue 7, Coach Nolan's was 6/2 and King's was 4/4. By clue 6, since Coach Queen's team did not lose 4, 2, 1, or 0 games, the Hawks' record was not 0/8, 1/7, 2/6, or 4/4. By clue 9, since Parker's record was not 4/4, the Hawk's was not 5/3, so it was 8/0 and Parker's was 1/7. By clue 4, the Panthers' was 0/8. By clue 9, then, Bakersville and Coach Logan's records were, in some order, 4/4 and 5/3; Bakersville's was 4/4 and Logan coached for Dahlia Glen with a 5/3 record. By clue 6, since the Hawks won 8 games, Queen's team lost 8. Gardenia's record was not 3/5, 6/2, or 2/6 (clue 2), nor was it 1/7 (clue 9); it was 0/8. Alton's was 1/7 and the Tigers' was 7/1 (clue 2). Parker's Alton team with the 1/7 record was not the Badgers or Bulldogs (clue 4), Eagles (clue 5), or the Bears (clue 6); they were the Lions. The team with the 2/6 record was not the Badgers (clue 4) or Eagles (clue 5). Since Evanstown did not lose 2 games, the Bears did not win 2 games (clue 6). By elimination, the Bulldogs' record was 2/6. Bakersville's team was not the Eagles (clue 5). Neither Evanstown nor the Bears were the 4/4 team (clue 6); the Badgers' record was 4/4. By clue 4, then, Hogan's Hill's record was 3/5. By elimination, Evanstown's was 2/6. By clue 6, then, the Bears won 6 games. By elimination, the Eagles' record was 5/3. By clue 5, Coach Shultz's record was 3/5. By elimination, Coach Osborn had the 2/6 record. In summary:

0/8: Gardenia, Panthers, Queen
1/7: Alton, Lions, Parker
2/6: Evanstown, Bulldogs, Osborn
3/5: Hogan's Hill, Rattlers, Shultz
4/4: Bakersville, Badgers, King
5/3: Dahlia Glen, Eagles, Logan
6/2: Inkberry, Bears, Nolan
7/1: Five Forks, Tigers, Marx
8/0: Carbona, Hawks, Rather

68. PUBLIC TELEVISION PLEDGES

Saturday's caller was not Art (clue 1), Dorothy (clue 3), Loretta (clue 5), or Ted (clue 7); either Helen or Walter called Saturday. If Helen had called Saturday, Kato would have called Thursday (clue 8). Helen would not be from Lakeview (clue 1), Bigg City or Farmville (clue 2), Woodlawn (clue 3), or Smallburg (clue 5); she would be from Megalopolis. Her show would not have been the opera (clue 2), animation special (clue 3), ballet (clue 4), "Whodunit?" (clue 5), or play (clue 8); it would have been the documentary. By clue 1, the smallest pledge of $5 would not have been made on Saturday, Friday, or Thursday. It would not have been made on Tuesday (clue 6); it would have been made either Monday or Wednesday. The Monday pledger would not have been from Woodlawn (clue 4), Smallburg (clue 5), or Bigg City (clue 7); that pledger would have been from either Farmville or Lakeview. The one who pledged the least was from neither Lakeview (clue 1) nor Farmville (clue 6), so the one who pledged the least would not have called Monday; he or she would have called Wednesday. By clue 1, then, Art would have called Thursday and been Kato and Ms. Bacon would have called Friday. The one who pledged the least would not have been Loretta (clue 5), Walter (clue 6), or Ted, since Zander didn't call Saturday (clue 7); she would have been Dorothy. Ms. Bacon, then, would have been Loretta. By clue 5, then, Helen would have been Moore, while the largest pledge would have been made Monday or Tuesday. It would not have been made Monday (clue 4), so it would have been Tuesday. However, Tuesday's pledger would have been either Walter or Ted, and neither Walter (clue 6) nor Ted (clue 9) made the largest pledge. Therefore, Helen was not Saturday's pledger, so Walter was. His last name is not Bacon (clue 1), Stone (clue 3), Flores (clue 6), Zander (clue 7), or Kato (clue 8); it is Moore. By clue 5, then, Loretta pledged Friday. Since the one who pledged the most did not call Monday (clue 4), by clue 5, the one who pledged the most called Tuesday, the Smallburg resident called Wednesday, and the man who liked "Whodunit?" called Thursday. That man is not Ted (clue 7), so he is Art. By clue 1, then, the $5 pledge was made Wednesday and Loretta is Ms. Bacon. By clue 8, Helen called Wednesday and Kato called Monday. Ted did not pledge the most on Tuesday (clue 9), so he called Monday while, by elimination, Dorothy pledged the most on Tuesday. Mr. Stone (clue 3) is Art. Flores did not pledge the most (clue 6), so she is not Dorothy; she is Helen, while Zander is Dorothy. The caller from Woodlawn is not Dorothy, Art, or Walter (clue 3) or Ted (clue 4); Loretta is from Woodlawn. Since Helen Flores pledged $5, by clue 3 she liked the animation special, while Ted pledged $15. The one who liked the ballet pledged $25 (clue 4). By clue 6, Walter pledged $10 and the one from Farmville pledged $20. Dorothy Zander is not, then, from Farmville, nor is she from Lakeview or Bigg City (clue 7); she is from Megalopolis. Ted Kato is not from Bigg City (clue 7) or Farmville (clue 9); he is from Lakeview. Walter's pledge was smaller than Ted's, so he is not from Farmville (clue 9); he is from Bigg City while, by elimination, Art Stone is from Farmville and pledged $20. Ted did not like the documentary (clue 1), ballet (clue 4), or play (clue 8); Ted liked the opera. Dorothy, then, pledged $30 (clue 6). By elimination, the one who liked the ballet and pledged $25 is Loretta. Dorothy did not like the play (clue 5); she liked the documentary while, by elimination, Walter liked the play. In summary:

> Mon.: Ted Kato, Lakeview, opera, $15
> Tues.: Dorothy Zander, Megalopolis, documentary, $30
> Wed.: Helen Flores, Smallburg, animation, $5
> Thurs.: Art Stone, Farmville, "Whodunit?", $20
> Fri.: Loretta Bacon, Woodlawn, ballet, $25
> Sat.: Walter Moore, Bigg City, play, $10

69. AUNT LORRAINE AND THE BRIDES

Clue 2 lists 20 positions in the bridal parties. Janine had three (clue 5), Ellen had two and Serena three (clue 11), Pam had one as bride (clue 2) and another as matron of honor (clue 13), while Michelle and Lorraine had five between them (clue 17); the remaining five women, then, had one position each. The five brides were Serena, Serena's only sister, Serena's fiancee's only sister, Serena's aunt, and Serena's cousin. The five bride's last names were Ripley (clue 2), two Knights, and two Hamiltons (clue 12). Serena's fiancee's only sister is not one of the three mentioned in clue 4. One bride, Aunt Lorraine's only sister, was a mother and a mother of the bride (clue 1); that bride was Serena's aunt, who was Serena's cousin's mother. The bride who was an only child (clue 18) was, then, Serena's cousin, who is also not mentioned in clue 4. By clue 4, then, Serena, Serena's sister, and Serena's aunt all asked their only sisters to be matron or maid of honor; Lorraine was the aunt's matron of honor. By clue 2, then, Serena had a matron of honor, so her sister was married first and had Serena as a maid of honor; Serena's sister is Pamela or Janine. Pamela, who was in two weddings, is not Serena's sister, who was in three (clue 11); Janine is Serena's sister. Since Serena's wedding was after Janine's (clue 2), Janine wore pink as Serena's matron of honor (clue 5). By clue 12, Janine and Serena are the Knights, while their aunt and cousin are the Hamiltons (clue 1); Serena's fiancee's sister is Ripley. By clue 2, then, Pamela with a maid of honor is not Ripley or the aunt who had Lorraine as matron of honor; she is the cousin. Pamela and Janine had three bridesmaids, Serena and Ripley had two, and aunt Hamilton had none (clue 2). The wedding at which Pamela was matron of honor in pink (clue 13) was Ripley's. One bride wore yellow as bridesmaid in another wedding, and was not Serena (clue 16); nor was she Janine (clue 5), or Pamela, since both of her positions have been determined. Ellen was a bridesmaid twice (clue 11); the only remaining person in more than one wedding is Michelle, who is then either Aunt Hamilton or Ripley. Michelle and Lorraine were not in the same weddings (clue 17); Michelle is Ripley. The fifth bride was in only one wedding (her own) and wore champagne (clue 19) while the others wore white. Serena and Lorraine both wore green in one wedding (clue 14); they were, then, both bridesmaids in that wedding (clue 15). Lorraine was not in Michelle's wedding (clue 17), so Serena and Lorraine wore green at bridesmaids in Pamela's wedding. The three women mentioned in clue 7 were all bridesmaids in that wedding (clue 15). Only two weddings had three bridesmaids, so Blythe, Michelle Ripley, and Ms. Cole were bridesmaids in Janine's wedding. By clue 10, since no wedding had four bridesmaids, the wedding described is Serena's; Ms. Goodhue was one bridesmaid, and they wore rose. There was no green worn in Serena's wedding, so green was worn in the other four weddings (clue 14). Michelle's bridesmaids wore green, as did Lorraine as Aunt Hamilton's matron of honor. The wedding in which Michelle wore yellow as bridesmaid (clue 16), then, was Janine's, while Serena wore green as her maid of honor. By clue 6, then, Ms. Taylor wore rose as Pamela's maid of honor, and Pamela was married Friday evening. The other time the rose gown was worn was at Serena's wedding, so her wedding was Saturday evening (clue 6). By clue 5, then, Janine's wedding was Saturday afternoon, and she was the third bridesmaid in green at Pamela's wedding Friday night. Lorraine was in the fourth wedding (clue 3); she was not in Michelle's wedding (clue 17), so Michelle's was not fourth; Aunt Hamilton's was, and was Sunday

168

afternoon while, by elimination, Michelle's was Sunday evening. By clue 8, then, since only aunt Hamilton and Lorraine were in the Sunday afternoon wedding, Cheryl is aunt Hamilton, and Ms. Fitzgerald and Diane were in the Saturday afternoon wedding; Blythe is Fitzgerald and Diane is Cole. Ellen was bridesmaid in two weddings (clue 11), so those weddings were Michelle's and Serena's. Valerie wore green (clue 5); she was, then, Michelle's second bridesmaid. Michelle was not Pamela's maid of honor, since Lorraine was a bridesmaid (clue 17); Ann was, and is Ms. Taylor. Ms. Palmer was in two evening weddings (clue 9), so she is not Valerie or Lorraine; she is Ellen. Either Michelle or Lorraine was in Serena's wedding (clue 17); Ms. Goodhue, then, is Lorraine. By elimination, Valerie is Winchell. In summary:

Fri. eve.: bride Pamela Hamilton, cousin, maid Ann Taylor in rose, bridesmaids Lorraine Goodhue, Serena Knight, and Janine Knight in green

Sat. aft.: bride Janine Knight, sister, maid Serena Knight in green, bridesmaids Blythe Fitzgerald, Michelle Ripley, and Diane Cole in yellow

Sat. eve.: bride Serena Knight, matron Janine Knight in pink, bridesmaids Lorraine Goodhue and Ellen Palmer in rose

Sun. aft.: bride Cheryl Hamilton in champagne, matron Lorraine Goodhue in green

Sun. eve.: bride Michelle Ripley, fiancee's sister, matron Pamela Hamilton in pink, bridesmaids Ellen Palmer and Valerie Winchell in green

70. LOST AND FOUND KIDS

Saturday's child was not found at the pet store (clue 4), toyshop (clue 5), furniture store (clue 7), or in line (clue 8); that child was at either the bookstore or video store. The guard who found Saturday's child was not Clay (clue 2), Burns (clue 4), Endo (clue 5), or Anderson (clue 7); that guard was either Diaz or Foster. Neither Diaz nor Foster found the child at the video store (clue 6), so Saturday's child was not found at the video store; he or she was found at the bookstore. Saturday's child was not Eric (clue 2), Donna (clue 5), Craig (clue 7), or Andy (clue 10); it was either Francine or Betsy, and was a girl. The guard who found her was not, then, Foster (clue 9); Diaz found her. Her jacket was not blue (clue 2), purple (clue 5), green (clue 7), red (clue 8), or yellow (clue 9); it was orange. By clue 4, then guard Burns found Thursday's child. Saturdays' child was not Dodge (clue 1), Fuentes (clue 2), Akimoto (clue 4), Collins (clue 5), or Easton (clue 8); she was Birdsong. She was not, then, Betsy (clue 1); she was Francine. Thursday's child was a boy (clue 9). Friday's child was not at the pet store (clue 4), furniture store (clue 7), or in line (clue 8); he or she was at either the video or toy store. By clue 3, then, Thursday's boy was at neither the video or toy store, nor was he at the pet store (clue 4) or in line (clue 8); he was at the furniture store. By clue 7, then, Craig was Friday's child. By clue 8, if Andy had been found Wednesday, the child in line would have been found Monday and the child in red Tuesday. Eric would have been the boy found Thursday. He would not be Easton (clue 1) so, by clue 8, Craig would be Easton. Andy is not Akimoto (clue 1). This, however, leaves no place for the Akimoto child (clue 4). Therefore, Andy was not Wednesday's child. By clue 8, then, Andy was found Thursday by Burns, Wednesday's child wore red, and Tuesday's child was found in line. The Easton child was found either Monday or Friday (clue 8). Monday's child was not found by Clay (clue 2) or Anderson (clue 7); that child was found by either Endo or Foster. Endo did not find the Easton child (clue 1). Eric is not Easton (clue 1) so, if the Easton child had been found Monday, she would have been a girl. She would not, then, have been found by Foster (clue 9). This, however, would leave no guard for Monday. Therefore, Easton was not found Monday; he was found Friday and is Craig. Craig Easton was not found by Clay or Endo (clue 1), or by Anderson (clue 7); he was found by Foster. Eric, then, wore a yellow jacket (clue 9). Craig was not found at either the video store (clue 3) or pet shop (clue 4); he was found at the toy store. His jacket was not purple (clue 5) or green (clue 7); it was blue. By clue 2, then, guard Clay found Wednesday's child and Andy is Fuentes. By clue 7, Monday's child was a girl in a green jacket, while guard Anderson found Tuesday's child. By elimination, Endo found Monday's child, while Eric in yellow was found Tuesday. By elimination, Andy wore purple. By clue 5, Donna was Wednesday's child and Eric is Collins. By elimination, Betsy was Monday's child. By clue 4, Betsy was found at the pet store and Donna is Akimoto. By elimination, Donna was at the video store, and Betsy is Dodge. In summary:

M: Betsy Dodge, green, Endo, pet
T: Eric Collins, yellow, Anderson, in line
W: Donna Akimoto, red, Clay, video

Th: Andy Fuentes, purple, Burns, furniture
F: Craig Easton, blue, Foster, toy
S: Francine Birdsong, orange, Diaz, bookstore

71. DECK THE CAKE WITH SPRIGS OF HOLLY

Two children found 3 decorations (clue 9), and two found 5 (clue 10). Since all six children found at least 2 each (clue 11), there were 24 decorations in all, and the Goren boy found a unique number of decorations (clue 12), the Goren boy found 4 decorations and the remaining two children found 2 each. There were 12 candy canes in all, and each child found at least 1 (clue 11). Three children found at least 2 each (clue 6), and one child found more than any other child (clue 13). If the highest number found were 4, three children would have found at least 2, leaving only 2 canes for the remaining three children. Therefore, the highest number of canes any one child found was 3, three children found 2 each, and three children found 1 each. A girl found 3 decorations consisting of 2 red, 1 green, and 0 silver (clue 9). By clue 6, then, she also found 2 canes, while Beth and the English child found 2 canes each, and one found 5 decorations while the other found 2. Gene found 1 cane (clue 6). The Goren boy found 4 decorations and is not Gene (clue 1). The girl that found 2 canes and 3 decorations is not Forrey (clue 2), Dawson (clue 3), Birch (clue 4), English (clue 6), or Carson (clue 8); she is Anderson. One of the children who found 2 decorations was either Beth or the English child, both of whom found 2 canes. The second child who found 2 decorations found 3 canes (clue 13). By elimination, the Goren boy found 1 cane. Gene and the last child, in some order, found 3 and 5 decorations, and found 4 and 6 total candies. By clue 4, the Birch boy did not find 1 cane, nor did he find 2 (clue 1); he found 3. Andy, then, also found 5 total candies, and more than 2 decorations (clue 4). Andy is not Anderson (clue 1), so he is the Goren boy. The Anderson girl is not Evan (clue 2), Dirk (clue 5), or Beth (clue 6). Since the Dawson boy did not find 5 total candies, the Anderson girl is not Colleen (clue 3); she is Fran. The total numbers of candies found were 4, 5, 6, and 7. By clue 5, then, Dirk found 6 candies and the only child who found 3 silver decorations is the one who found a total of 7 candies. The only child who could have found 6 total candies is the third who found 1 cane; Dirk found 1 cane and 5 decorations, while Gene found 3 decorations. By clue 8, the Carson boy found 1 cane and more than 5 total candies; he is Dirk. Beth and Colleen are not the Birch boy, so Evan is. Only one child found 7 candies, so that child was not Colleen (clue 3); she was Beth, while Colleen is the English child and found 4 candies. The Dawson boy found 4 candies (clue 3), so he is Gene, while Beth is the Forrey child. By clue 2, Dirk found 3 green decorations, while Colleen found 2 of one color. Evan found 2 decorations of different colors (clue 2), so he found 1 red one, as did Andy (clue 7). By clue 7, Gene found at least one silver, so Colleen found no silver (clue 3). Colleen did not find 2 red (clue 6), so she found 2 green decorations, while Gene found red and silver and no green (clue 3). That accounts for 6 of the eight green, so by clue 7, Andy and Beth found 1 green each, and Evan found no green. By subtraction, Beth found 1 red, Andy found 2 silver, and Evan found 1 silver. By clue 7, Gene also found 2 silver, so he found 1 red. Since there were 8 of each color, Dirk found 2 red and 0 silver. In summary:

Fran Anderson, 2 canes, 2 red, 1 green, 0 silver
Beth Forrey, 2 canes, 1 red, 1 green, 3 silver
Colleen English, 2 canes, 0 red, 2 green, 0 silver
Gene Dawson, 1 cane, 1 red, 0 green, 2 silver
Andy Goren, 1 cane, 1 red, 1 green, 2 silver
Evan Birch, 3 canes, 1 red, 0 green, 1 silver
Dirk Carson, 1 cane, 2 red, 3 green 0 silver

72. FIGURING WITH FIGURINES

By the prices given and clue 1, either the laundry figurine is $60 and Hallie $30, or the laundry figurine is $300 and Hallie $150. The laundry figure is not $300 (clue 13), so it is $60 and Hallie is $30. The $300 figure is not Bertina (clue 2), Isadore (clue 3), Gwyneth (clue 9), Evangeline (clue 10), Clementine (clue 12), or Dominique (clue 13); it is either Felicia or Arabella. If Arabella were $300, the $275 figure would not be Bertina (clue 2), Felicia (clue 8), Evangeline (clue 10), or Dominique (clue 13). Arabella was not playing the piano (clue 5), so Clementine would not be $275 (clue 12). The $275 figure would be in the same column as Arabella (clue 6), so Gwyneth would not be $275 (clue 9). The figure kissing a doll is not worth the most (clue 10), so Isadore is not $275 (clue 3). However, this leaves no doll worth $275. Therefore, Arabella is not $300, so Felicia is. Felicia was not chasing a butterfly (clue 4), eating blackberries (clue 7), mailing letters or holding a puppy (clue 8), or kissing a doll (clue 10). Bertina was in the middle row (clue 2), so the figure feeding

170

ducks was also in the middle row (clue 11); that figure was not Felicia (clue 4). No three of the prices add up to $300, so Felicia was not picking wildflowers (clue 10). By elimination, Felicia was playing the piano. Felicia was in #1, #3, #7, or #9 (clue 4). She was not in #7 (clue 10) so, by clue 12, she was in #9, and the $45 figure was in #6. By clue 6, then, the $275 figure was in #3. That figure was not Bertina (clue 2), Isadore (clue 3), Arabella (cluc 5), Gwyneth (clue 9), Evangeline (clue 10), or Dominique (clue 13); it was Clementine. By clue 7, the one eating blackberries was not in #1, #2, #3, #6, or #8. By clue 13, since the one worth $110 is in the middle row (clue 11), the one in #2 is worth either $150 or $260. By clue 7, the one eating blackberries is worth at least $80, so #8 is worth at least $110. Since the one worth $110 is in the middle row (clue 11), #8 is worth either $150 or $260, while #1 and #7 are worth $30, $60, or $80. By clue 7, then, the one eating blackberries was not in #5, since there would then be no amount for #8. If the one eating blackberries were in #7, it would not be worth $30 (clue 7) or $60; it would be worth $80. #4 would be worth less than $80 (clue 7), so the $110 figure would be in #5 (clue 11). The ones in #1 and #4 would be, in some order, $30 Hallie and $60 folding laundry. Bertina would be in either #4 or #6 (clue 11). She would not be #4, $60 and folding laundry, or #1 would be worth less, contradicting clue 2; she would be #6 and worth $45. #4 would be feeding ducks (clue 11). #4 would then be Hallie at $30, while #1 would be the one folding laundry at $60. The one folding laundry would not be Isadore (clue 3), Arabella (clue 5), Gwyneth (clue 9), or Dominique (clue 13); it would be Evangeline. Isadore would be at least $80, so the one kissing would be at least $110 (clue 3). However, there would be no combination of prices for the one kissing and the one picking flowers that would satisfy clue 10. Therefore, the one eating blackberries was not in #7, so it was in #4. It is worth more than the one directly above it (clue 7), so it is not Bertina (clue 2). By clue 11, then, it is worth $110. By clue 5, the one mailing letters is worth more than $110 and is not in the bottom row; it is either #2 or #3 while Arabella is either #5 or #6. By clue 11, then, Arabella was feeding ducks, while Bertina is in either #5 or #6. If Bertina were #6, Arabella would be feeding ducks in #5 and would be worth $80. The one mailing letters would be #2 (clue 5). Dominique would be worth at least $110, so the figure in #2 would be worth more than $170 (clue 13); it would be worth $260, and the one in #8 would be worth $150. The one doing laundry would not be Isadore (clue 3), Gwyneth (clue 9), or Dominique (clue 13); it would be Evangeline. She would not be in #7 (clue 10), so she would be in #1, while Hallie would be in #7. However, there would again be no combination of prices that would satisfy clue 10. Therefore, Bertina was not in #6; she was in #5, while Arabella feeding the ducks was in #6. The one mailing letters was in #3 (clue 5). The one doing laundry was not Isadore (clue 3) or Dominique (clue 13). Gwyneth was in either #2 or #8 (clue 9), so she is either $150 or $260, and was not doing laundry. By elimination, either Bertina or Evangeline was doing laundry. If Evangeline had been doing laundry, she would not be in #7 (clue 10), so she would be in #1. By elimination, Hallie at $30 would be in #7, and Bertina would be $80. However, this leaves no combination of values that satisfies clue 10. Therefore, Evangeline was not doing laundry; Bertina was. The three smallest amounts: the one kissing, Evangeline, and the one in #7 are $30, $80, and $110, so the one picking wildflowers is at least $220; it is, then, $260. The only combination for Evangeline, the one kissing, and #7 is, then, $30, $80, and $150. The one kissing is not Hallie at $30 (clue 3), so Hallie is #7. #1, then, is $80. Isadore is worth at least $80, so the one kissing is worth at least $110 (clue 3); it is worth $150, and is either #2 or #8. Evangeline is, then, worth $80 and is #1. By clue 10, Evangeline was not chasing a butterfly, so she was holding a puppy. Isadore is worth $110 (clue 3), and is #4. Dominique is not #2 (clue 13); Gwyneth is, while Dominique is #8. By elimination, Hallie was chasing a butterfly. Dominique is worth less than Gwyneth (clue 13), so Dominique is $150 and is kissing, while Gwyneth is worth $260 and is picking wildflowers. In summary:

#1: Evangeline, puppy, $80
#2: Gwyneth, wildflowers, $260
#3: Clementine, letters, $275
#4: Isadore, blackberries, $110
#5: Bertina, laundry, $60
#6: Arabella, ducks, $45
#7: Hallie, butterfly, $30
#8: Dominique, kissing, $150
#9: Felicia, piano, $300

73. PIZZA, ANYONE?

There are sixteen names mentioned in all, with eight female last names and eight male last names indicated by Ms. or Mr. These 16 shared three tables (called here tables A, B, and C). Each person spent at least $3.50 for a minimum total of $56 (clue 2). All three tables spent the same total amount (clue 1). Since at least $56 was spent, each table spent at least $18.66; since each person spent at least $3.50, there were at least 5 people at each table. There were, then, six people at one table and five at the other two. Jolene, Ms. Armani, and Mr. Harrigan sat together at one table (here called table A) and shared a pizza with at least ground beef and green peppers (clue 10). Jolene spent $3.50 (clue 16), so Ms. Armani and Mr. Harrigan also spent $3.50 (clue 2). These three spent $1.00 for drinks each (clue 1), so each spent $2.50 on their pizza (clue 2) for a total of $7.50. Three people shared no smaller than the $8 medium pizza (clue 2). With two toppings, the $8 medium would cost $9. Therefore, at least one other person shared in that pizza. Four people shared no smaller than the large $10 pizza; with two toppings, a large pizza would cost $11.00. The four sharing at $2.50 each would have spent $10, not enough for the required large pizza. Therefore, at least five people shared in this pizza, which was an extra large (clue 2). A $12 extra large with two toppings would cost $13. Five people at $2.50 each would spend $12.50, so six people shared the extra large pizza, including Jolene, Ms. Armani, and Mr. Harrigan, and each spent a total of $3.50 (clue 2). The six then paid $15 for the extra large pizza; by the listed prices, it had six toppings. This table then was the one with six people, so the remaining two tables had five people at each. Anthony spent $1 more than anyone else at his table (clue 4); he was not, then, at the first table; he was at a table we will call Table B. By clue 2, he did not share his pizza with anyone, so he had a mini. Since everyone spent at least $3.50, Anthony spent either $4.50 or $5.00. He bought a $1.00 drink (clue 1), so he spent either $3.50 or $4.00 on his pizza; his mini had either one or two toppings. Since six people at table A spent $3.50 each, each table spent $21 total, with $16 spent on pizza at tables B and C (clue 1). To equal a total of $21, then, Anthony spent $5.00 and the other four at his table spent $4.00 each. Anthony, then, is not Mr. Leffler (clue 4), Kingery (clue 5), Tillet (clue 6), Watkins (clue 8), Olson (clue 11), or Serrano (clue 15); he is Mr. Marshall. By clue 11, then, Mr. Olson spent $4.50, and Rosa and Ms. Fetters each spent $4.00. Mr. Olson then sat at neither Table A or Table B; he sat at Table C. Mr. Leffler did not sit at Table B (clue 4); by clue 14, he spent more than $3.50 so he did not sit at Table A; he sat at Table C. By clue 14, then, Nathan and Donald sat, in some order, at Table A and B, and Donald spent less than Nathan. Donald, then, sat at Table A and spent $3.50, while Nathan sat at Table B. By clue 14, then, two more of the toppings on the extra-large at Table A were olives and pepperoni, while Nathan's pizza had olives and Mr. Leffler's had pepperoni. Only one small pizza was served, shared by two people (clue 15). The four at table B who all spent $4 were not, then, two pairs sharing two small pizzas; the small pizza was shared by two people at table C. One of each size pizza was bought (clue 1); the remaining sizes are medium and large. The remaining people are four people at Table B and three at Table C. Nathan shared a pizza with at least one topping and spent $4; if he shared with two others, they would have spent $12, or $9 on pizza (clue 1), and would have bought the medium with two toppings. The large, then, would have been shared by the three people at Table C. Since each table spent $21 total, Mr. Olson would not have shared in the large, or the other pair could not have afforded the small pizza. He would then have shared the small, while the remaining three people would have spent a total of $12. However, by clue 1, they would have spent only $9 on the large pizza. Therefore, Nathan shared with three people at his table. Four people bought either a large or an extra-large, so by clue 1, the large was bought at Table B by four people and the medium was bought at Table C and was shared by three people (clue 2). Four people spent $4 each and bought a large pizza; that pizza then had four toppings. Since each table spent $21 total, Mr. Olson did not share in the medium, or the other pair could not have afforded the small pizza; he shared in the small. Since he spent $4.50, the small had two toppings. The other three at Table C spent $12, so each spent $4. Since each then spent $3 on pizza and shared a medium, the medium had two toppings. By clue 12, then, Peter and Ms. Price shared, in some order, the small and the medium, so both were at Table C, and Peter shared in the small at $4.50 while Ms. Price shared in the medium at $4.00. By clue 15, Lynette spent $4 and Mr. Serrano spent $3.50, so Mr. Serrano was at Table A. By clue 7, the ham and pineapple was on either the medium or the large pizza. If the ham and pineapple had been on the medium pizza, that would have been the only two toppings on that pizza. Mr. Leffler's pizza with pepperoni, then, would have been the small shared with Mr. Olson. However, this would leave no pizza for Kimberly (clue 7). Therefore, the ham and pineapple was on the large pizza, Ms. Vincent shared the extra large at Table A, and Kimberly was at Table C. By clue 13, since 3 of the 4 toppings on the large have been identified, Ms. Croft, Tyler, and Olivia shared in the extra large, which had sausage as another of its toppings. Ms. Croft sat between Tyler and Olivia (clue 13), so she is not Yolanda (clue 8), Sylvia or Ginger (clue 9); she is Jolene. Ms. Vincent is, then, a fifth person at that table. Jolene sat between Ms. Armani and Mr. Harrigan (clue 10), so Tyler is Mr. Harrigan and Olivia is Ms. Armani (clue 13). Five of the six people at Table are Jolene Croft, Olivia Armani, Tyler Harrigan, Mr. Serrano, and Ms. Vincent. By clue 9, then, Sylvia, Ginger, and Ms. Bradshaw did not sit at Table A. Three of the five people at Table C are Mr. Olson, Mr. Leffler,

172

and Ms. Price. If Sylvia, Ginger, and Ms. Bradshaw had been at Table C, Ms. Price would be either Ginger or Sylvia, Ginger or Sylvia (whichever was not Ms. Price) would have been a fourth person, and Ms. Bradshaw would have been the fifth. However, since Kim sat at Table C, she would be Ms. Bradshaw, contradicting clue 17. Therefore, Sylvia, Ginger, and Ms. Bradshaw did not sit at Table C, so they sat at Table B and are the remaining three people at that table. The remaining topping on the large pizza was bacon (clue 9). Since Lynette and Rosa both spent $4 and Kimberly was at Table C, Ms. Vincent is Yolanda. By clue 8, then, Mr. Watkins was the sixth person at that table, while Rick is Mr. Serrano. Donald, who sat at Table A, is then Mr. Watkins. Since there were eight men and eight women, Table C consisted of three men and two women. By clue 5, Nathan is Kingery, while Johann shared in the medium pizza at Table C. Mark and Mr. Tillet were at table C (clue 6). Since both pizzas at that table had exactly two toppings, Mark is not Mr. Leffler, who had pepperoni; he is Mr. Olson, and he and Mr. Tillet shared the small with bacon and green peppers for $4.50 each. The remaining three, then, spent $4 each; since Peter spent $4.50, he is Mr. Tillet. By elimination, Johann is Mr. Leffler. Neither Rosa nor Ms. Fetters was at Table A. Since all four toppings have been identified for the large at Table B and do not include sausage, neither Rosa nor Ms. Fetters sat there (clue 11). Rosa and Ms. Fetters, then, sat at Table C; so Kimberly is Ms. Fetters, Rosa is Ms. Price, and the medium pizza had sausage as well as pepperoni. By elimination, Ms. Bradshaw is Lynette. Ginger is not Ms. Juarez (clue 17); she is Ms. Edelman, while Sylvia is Juarez. By clue 3, the third pizza with sausage was Anthony's mini, and the two with mushrooms were the Table A extra large and Anthony's mini. In summary:

Table A: Extra large topped with beef, peppers, olives, pepperoni, sausage, and mushrooms, shared by Jolene Croft, Olivia Armani, Tyler Harrigan, Rick Serrano, Yolanda Vincent, and Donald Watkins at $3.50 each

Table B: Mini with sausage and mushrooms by Anthony Marshall at $5

Large with olives, ham, pineapple, and bacon, shared by Nathan Kingery, Sylvia Juarez, Ginger Edelman, and Lynette Bradshaw at $4 each

Table C: small with bacon and peppers shared by Mark Olson and Peter Tillet for $4.50 each

medium with pepperoni and sausage shared by Johann Leffler, Rosa Price, and Kimberly Fetters at $4 each

74. FRIDAY NIGHT SPECIAL

Clyde Dash had pork, fries, peas, and pie (clue 7). Mrs. Dash had none of those items (clue 2). Adam had carrots (clue 10) and pudding (clue 12). No two people had more than one item in common (clue 2), so Beth is not Mrs. Dash (clue 8). Beth had carrots (clue 10). Mr. Aspen is not Adam (clue 1), and he had carrots (clue 10). Anna is not Mrs. Aspen (clue 1) or Mrs. Dash (clue 8), and she had fish while her husband Don had chicken (clue 11). Adam and Beth both had carrots, so they are not married (clue 2). Adam's wife is then the eighth diner, and she had cake (clue 12). Earl is not Mr. Aspen or Beth's husband (clue 8), so he is the ninth diner. Since Mr. Aspen and Beth both had carrots, Beth is not Mrs. Aspen (clue 2), and Mrs. Aspen is the tenth diner. Beth's husband is the eleventh diner, and Earl's wife is the twelfth. Bob and Frank are, in some order, Mr. Aspen and Beth's husband. Bob is not Beth's husband (clue 1), so Frank is, while Bob is Mr. Aspen. Both Bob and Frank had mashed (clue 13). Beth and Frank are not the Bakers or Farmers (clue 1), or the Clouds (clue 8); they are the Engels. Don and Anna are not the Bakers (clue 6) or Clouds (clue 8); they are the Farmers. Earl and his wife are not the Clouds (clue 8); they are the Bakers while, by elimination, Adam and his wife are the Clouds. Clyde Dash's wife is not Cheryl or Dixie (clue 1). Earl Baker had the same dessert as Mrs. Dash (clue 8), but a different one than Edna (clue 6); Edna is not Mrs. Dash, so Flo is. Edna is not married to Earl Baker (clue 1) or Bob Aspen (clue 6); she is married to Adam Cloud. Dixie is not Mrs. Baker (clue 4), so she is Mrs. Aspen while, by elimination, Cheryl is Mrs. Baker. By clue 9, one type of each item was chosen by three wives, while the other three types of each item were chosen by two men and one woman. No two people had more than one item in common, and each item was chosen by three people (clue 2). Either Beth Engel or Cheryl was one of the three women who selected the same entree (clue 3); Beth was not (clue 8), so Cheryl was. Since men had pork and chicken, that entree was either beef or fish. Dixie Aspen and Cheryl Baker did not choose any of the same items (clue 8), so Dixie chose a entree also selected by two men. Either Flo or Edna Cloud was one of the three women who selected the same vegetable (clue 5); Edna Cloud was not (clue 8), so Flo was. We already know Beth Engel and two men had carrots, and Dixie and Cheryl did not both have the same vegetable; by elimination, Anna chose the vegetable selected by three women, and either Dixie or Cheryl also selected that vegetable. Since Clyde Dash had fries, only one woman had fries (clue 9); that woman also had beef, beans, and cake (clue 14). Anna, then, did not have fries, so Earl did not have fries either (clue 8). Since the Aspens and the Bakers had no items in common (clues 2 and 8), one of these four had fries. Neither husband had them, so either Dixie or Cheryl had fries, with beef, beans, and cake. Earl and Beth had the same entree (clue 8), which was not, then, beef (clue 2) or chicken (clue 3). Earl had the same potato as Anna (clue 8), so he and Beth did not have fish (clue 2). Earl and Beth, then, had pork. Edna Cloud had cake (clue 12), so she did not also have beef (clue 2), leaving fewer than three women who could have had beef. The entree item chosen by three women was, then, fish; Cheryl had that. The woman who had beef, fries, beans, and cake was, then, Dixie. Bob Aspen did not have beef, pork, or fish (clue 8); he had chicken. By clue 3, then, Adam Cloud had beef. By elimination, the second man to have beef was Frank. Flo had the vegetable chosen by three women, as did Anna, so they did not have the same entree (clue 2); Flo then did not have fish, so she had chicken, while Edna had fish. By clue 4, Adam Cloud had a baked potato and Cheryl Baker had au gratin. Earl Baker had a baked potato, as did Anna (clue 8). That accounts for all the baked potatoes. Two men got fries (clue 9), so Don had those. By clue 2 and by examining those who got the same entrees, Flo and Beth both had au gratin, and Edna had mashed. All the carrots are accounted for. Don had neither peas nor beans (clue 2); he had broccoli. The vegetable chosen by three women was, then, beans; both Flo and Anna had those. Edna and Dixie both had cake, so both didn't have beans (clue 2); Edna had broccoli, as did Earl (clue 8). By elimination, Frank and Cheryl had peas. By clues 2 and 9, the third person to have cake was not Bob, Earl, Don, Anna, Flo, or Frank. By clue 8, Cheryl did not have cake. By elimination, Beth had cake. Earl and Flo had the same dessert (clue 8), so that was not the pie Clyde had (clue 2). Adam and Earl both had baked potatoes, so both did not have pudding (clue 2); Earl and Flo had ice cream. Clyde and Don both had fries, so Don did not have pie (clue 2) so, by clue 6, Don had pudding and Anna had pie. Since the cake was chosen by three women, the other three desserts were chosen by two men and one woman (clue 9). The woman who chose pudding, then, was Cheryl. Bob Aspen did not have ice cream (clue 8); he had pie, while Frank had ice cream. In summary:

Anna Farmer, fish, baked, beans, pie
Beth Engel, pork, au gratin, carrots, cake
Cheryl Baker, fish, au gratin, peas, pudding
Dixie Aspen, beef, fries, beans, cake
Edna Cloud, fish, mashed, broccoli, cake
Flo Dash, chicken, au gratin, beans, ice cream
Adam Cloud, beef, baked, carrots, pudding
Bob Aspen, chicken, mashed, carrots, pie
Clyde Dash, pork, fries, peas, pie
Don Farmer, chicken, fries, broccoli, pudding
Earl Baker, pork, baked, broccoli, ice cream
Frank Engel, beef, mashed, peas, ice cream

75. THE BIRDLAND MAZE

No two couples have the same street number, and only two of the couples live on the same street (clue 1). Barbara's street number is 16 times Lester's (clue 2), so Lester's is 2, 4, or 5, and Barbara's is 32, 64, or 80, so Barbara lives on Goldfinch. Michael enters Birdland on Blackhawk or Bluebird, then turns onto Goldfinch where he passes Patricia's house (clue 6), so Patricia and her husband are the second family on Goldfinch. The other families each live alone on their street or court (clue 1). Since only those on Bluebird or Blackhawk can enter the subdivision without making a turn, the Kirbys and Isabelle live on those two streets (clue 5), as do David and the Hopkins couple (clue 7); Isabelle is Hopkins and David is Kirby. Patricia isn't Patterson (clue 15); since the Pattersons' number is five times that of Brian's (clue 12), Barbara (at #32, 64, or 80) is not Patterson, so the Pattersons live at #5 and Brian lives at #1. Steven and his wife make one turn before reaching home (clue 5), so Steven lives on Goldfinch and is married to Patricia or Barbara. Of the three families in clue 8 who can visit each other without crossing a street or passing the end of a court, one lives on inner Goldfinch, another on a through street, and the third on a court, so either Barbara or Patricia has a street number divisible by 10 and is either John's wife or Mrs. Anderson (clue 8). One, we know, is Steven's wife, and Steven isn't Anderson (clue 16); nor is Tony (also clue 16), so neither Barbara nor Patricia is married to Tony, Brian at #1, Lester (clue 2), David Kirby (clue 5), or Michael, who turns onto Goldfinch, then onto a court (clue 6). Keith's house number is half that of the Montgomerys' (clue 3), so Barbara is not married to Keith. If Barbara were Montgomery, Keith would be Patricia's husband; Barbara would live at #80 and Keith and Patricia at #40. From the introduction, we know #10 Goldfinch is between Hummingbird and S. Bluebird, so #10 is on one side of S. Bluebird or the other; going clockwise, #40 is on one side of the northwest court or the other. Since Rosemary drives in on W. Blackhawk, turns left onto Goldfinch, then turns right onto the northwest court without passing anyone (clue 4), but Michael passes Patricia's house when he turns left (clue 6), Patricia doesn't live in the northwest quarter, so her number isn't #40. Therefore, Barbara is not Montgomery, nor is she Gallagher, who lives near Robin Park (clue 13) or Baker (clue 15); she is married to John or Steven, neither of whom is Anderson (clue 16). Barbara is Trimmer. John can visit others without crossing a street (clue 8) and Mr. Trimmer cannot (clue 14), so Barbara is married to Steven. Since only Barbara could have a house number twice Patricia's, Patricia isn't married to Keith (clue 3), so Patricia is married to John, who isn't Anderson (clue 8), Gallagher (clue 13), or Baker (clue 16); John and Patricia are Montgomery. Keith's house number is 6 or smaller, so by clue 3, Keith lives at #5 and is Patterson while the Montgomerys live at #10. Couples use the entrance nearest their home, so if Hummingbird were in the southeast quadrant, Michael would turn left from E. Blackhawk and reach his home court BEFORE passing Patricia's house (clue 6), so Hummingbird is just west of S. Bluebird. The two north courts are Whipporwill (clue 9) and Oriole (clue 10), so Mockingbird is in the southeast quadrant. Michael, then, lives on the east side of Hummingbird (clue 6) with either Joyce (clue 9) or Andrea (clue 10), and is Anderson in clue 8. Andrea is not Anderson (clue 15), so Joyce is Michael's wife, and Andrea lives on Mockingbird (clue 10). Lillian, the third woman in clue 8, lives on the west side of S. Bluebird; she is married to David Kirby and lives in an odd-numbered house which, by elimination, is #3. Neither Brian (clue 15) nor Tony (clue 11) is Baker; Lester is. Rosemary lives on the northwest court (clue 4) which is Whipporwill (clue 9); from West Blackhawk, she passes all of the houses with street numbers in the 30's, but doesn't pass an occupied house (clue 4). Barbara's house number, therefore, is not 32; it is 64, and Lester's is 4 (clue 2). Michael Anderson's number is higher than Lillian's (clue 8), so Michael lives at #6 Hummingbird. By elimination, Tony lives at #2. Madeline's house number is 5 or 6 (clue 13), so Madeline is Keith Patterson's wife; by elimination, they live on Oriole Court. Tony can visit the Bakers on a court without crossing a street (clue 11), so he is Isabelle Hopkins's husband and lives at #2 Blackhawk (clue 5). Even numbers are on the south side of Blackhawk, so Tony and Isabelle are on E. Blackhawk and Lester and Andrea on Mockingbird are the Bakers. By elimination, Rosemary and Brian are the Gallaghers at #1 Whipporwill Ct. In summary:

Michael & Joyce Anderson, 6 Hummingbird Ct.
Lester & Andrea Baker, 4 Mockingbird Ct.
Brian & Rosemary Gallagher, 1 Whipporwill Ct.
Tony & Isabelle Hopkins, 2 E. Blackhawk Rd.
David & Lillian Kirby, 3 S. Bluebird Dr.
John & Patricia Montgomery, 10 Goldfinch Circle
Keith & Madeline Patterson, 5 Oriole Ct.
Steven & Barbara Trimmer, 64 Goldfinch Circle